ALONGSIDE COMMUNITY

Alongside Community is a step-by-step guide that prepares social science students to be democratic citizens by examining the theory, method, and sociopolitical dynamics that impact helping those different from oneself. The first part of this book explores the more theoretical issues of helping others, including issues of social identity, values, and power. The second part of this guidebook examines action-based methods, interventions available for community-based engagement, and the sociopolitical issues that inevitably arise for those who strive to create social change including issues of race, ethnicity, social class, gender, sexual orientation, mental health, and educational and environmental justice along with suggestions on how to address these issues. The third part of *Alongside Community* critically explores how to measure the impact of community service on major stakeholders including student, faculty, college and community agency and ends with reflections and suggestions on how to be a lifelong, civically engaged citizen.

Debra A. Harkins, PhD, is an associate professor in Psychology at Suffolk University. Debra teaches Community Psychology, Psychology of Self and Identity, and Voices in Conflict. Her research and teaching interests include social justice, service learning, civic engagement, conflict resolution, and empowerment at individual, organizational, and community levels. She is currently developing and examining the efficacy of a service-learning mentoring program to support faculty, students, and community partners. She serves as editor for the *Pedagogy and Human Sciences* journal and is the founder of Leading Change Associates, providing executive coaching and consulting for nonprofit organizations. She wrote two books, *Researcher Race: Social Constructions in the Research Process* (co-authored with Lauren Mizock) and *Beyond the Campus: Building a Sustainable University–Community Partnership* (with The Community Action Project Team).

The field of service learning has exploded in the past decade but the scholarly and practice literature has not kept up with this rapid expansion with notable exceptions. *Alongside Community*, drawing upon the wisdom of numerous academics, has made an important contribution to our learning and have provided us with the "tools" and the "tool box" from which to incorporate social justice themes in service-learning. This book is destined to find its way in all of the must-read lists on the subject within classrooms and community organizations. It is highly recommended and a welcomed contribution to this field.

Melvin Delgado, *Social Work, Boston University*

The authors have created a badly needed resource in service-learning – a 'step-by-step guide' – that helps faculty and students to learn in service. It is practical as it has reflection spaces and exercises and it is intellectually solid with concepts and theories. Faculty who adopt this will wonder how they ever taught a service-learning course without it.

Dwight E. Giles, Jr., *University of Massachusetts*

As educators committed to social justice and experiential education, we often struggle to provide students with an adequate framework in service-learning courses to support their navigation in service to the community. As a white educator, I find this especially true with students who have privilege. We understand that students need to effectively see themselves in relation to others and engage in reciprocal and authentic relationships in these deep learning experiences. *Alongside Community: Learning in Service* provides us with the practical tools, paradigms and approaches to engage students in building these relationships and unearthing their identities in relation to others. This book is a ready-to-go toolkit that will support us from planning to assessment!

Suzanne M. Buglione, *Dean of Teaching and Learning,*
Bristol Community College

The triumph of civic engagement has yet to radically change the anti-democratic, neoliberal march on campuses or in communities. Authors of *Alongside Community: Learning in Service*, suggest that, if community engagement is done thoughtfully, reflexively, critically and collaboratively, engaged pedagogy can once again be a powerful tool for both learning about social problems as well as learning how to change them effectively and democratically. The authors offer a tour de force of practical methods and powerful pedagogical theory, informed by critical race studies and community organizing principles as well as community based research and service-learning literature. This book gives us a running start towards building a practice of real social change to end conditions of oppression, exploitation and inclusion in society.

Cory W. Dolgon, *Professor of Sociology, Stonehill College*

ALONGSIDE COMMUNITY

LEARNING IN SERVICE

Edited by Debra A. Harkins

Routledge
Taylor & Francis Group

NEW YORK AND LONDON

First published 2018
by Routledge
711 Third Avenue, New York, NY 10017

and by Routledge
2 Park Square, Milton Park, Abingdon, Oxon, OX14 4RN

Routledge is an imprint of the Taylor & Francis Group, an informa business

Library of Congress Cataloging-in-Publication Data
A catalog record for this book has been requested

ISBN: 978-1-138-70586-9 (hbk)
ISBN: 978-1-138-70587-6 (pbk)
ISBN: 978-1-315-20213-6 (ebk)

Typeset in Giovanni Book
by Apex CoVantage, LLC

CONTENTS

FOREWORD

Welcome to the community of human beings who recognize that the state of the world calls us to wise and compassionate service in the causes of social and environmental justice! If you are reading this book, you are most likely already deeply aware of the multitude of situations that call us to reflection and action. From my vantage point, these are some of the realities that stand out (read slowly): a billion or more people live without regular access to clean water, food, sanitation, housing, health care, and education. Meanwhile, due to colonialism, imperialism, and current capitalist economic arrangements, a dozen billionaires now own more wealth than half of humanity. This unequal distribution of wealth and resources fuels constant wars and conflict. Millions are killed, and millions more become refugees or immigrants in places far from their homes. As a result, most nations struggle to establish harmony and equity among the different cultural and "racial"/ethnic groups living within their borders. Ethnocentrism, magnified by economic insecurity, finds expression in racist practices, xenophobia, and the marginalization of non-dominant groups. Similarly, fundamentalist responses to rapid cultural change reinforce sexism and homophobia. Corporate globalization further aggravates tensions and inequities in each society as financial policies force government cuts to education, health care, and social safety nets. As a result, more and more people anxiously struggle to survive on less, on the brink of houselessness, bankruptcy, illness, and starvation. Communities and families fall apart, and rates of interpersonal violence, crime, and abuse increase. In turn, to maintain power, government leaders resort to corruption, political repression, and torture. Finally, we cannot forget the possibility of nuclear destruction and our new awareness that human economic activities are triggering climate change that threatens life on earth. Movements for peace and social justice are now intimately bound with urgent actions for environmental sanity.

Social suffering has always existed, but never has it been so unnecessary. Globally, we have the resources to meet the basic needs of everyone on the planet. Meeting those needs will require the political will to do so, and in fact, the intention has already been mapped out in various international agreements on social and economic rights.

This global scenario is overwhelming. Despair and paralysis are common reactions. It is logical to wonder where to start as just one person who hopes to make a difference. An essential first move to counter despair is to know the long history of the great struggles for human liberation over the centuries. Individuals joining together courageously have ended monarchies and dictatorships, abolished legal slavery, expanded civil rights, helped end wars, ended brutal colonial regimes, improved working conditions, and protected the environment. None of these movements achieved their goals easily or quickly. The torch of hope was passed from generation to generation, along with memories of those who dedicated their energies and often lost their lives to the cause.

It is also heartening to learn that there are literally hundreds of thousands of nongovernmental organizations and groups doing all they can to advance the cause of social and environmental justice. It is hoped you are already, or will soon be, connected to at least one of these inspiring organizations.

On the basis of my experiences in higher education and in a variety of social and environmental justice causes, I will share a few personal lessons about how to grapple with some of the core dilemmas we all face on the path of service. (And, of course, this book is full of similar counsel.)

- Stay humble and open to learning, even after you have gained a lot of experience. Learn to recognize and quell your savior mentality.

- Appreciate the power of deep dialogue, especially listening without judging and speaking from your heart.

- Keep long-term strategy in mind as your group considers specific tactics.

- Avoid acting out your own family dynamics in your social change work. Seek counseling as needed.

- Remember that group process can be as important as group action. If people are not feeling connected and enjoying the work, your group's effectiveness will be limited.

- You can't do it all. Choose one or two causes, and become an expert on them, while keeping an eye on related and overlapping causes. We need many more effective coalitions across issues in order for the "movement of movements" to succeed against the massive obstacles they face.

You are reading a book that contains wisdom not only for deep learning in service and social justice work, but also for engaged living more broadly. It is common to think of individual happiness as a goal in life. I have come to see happiness as a pleasant side effect of fuller participation in community and society along with deeper connections with others. Many forces conspire now against community and solidarity. We must all reach out with courage, love, and understanding to connect with each other and build just communities.

Tod Sloan

Tod Sloan is a leading international proponent of critical psychology, a perspective that exposes how psychological concepts and practices often maintain social systems of domination and oppression. Critical psychology also allies social justice movements to build community well-being, deep democratic practices, and environmental sanity. Sloan is the author of *Damaged Life: The Crisis of the Modern Psyche* and editor of *Critical Psychology: Voices for Change*. For several years, he was national co-coordinator of Psychologists for Social Responsibility. He has taught psychology and social theory in the United States, Venezuela, Costa Rica, Nicaragua, and Brazil. In recent years, he has focused on organizing psychosocial support for social justice activists.

ACKNOWLEDGMENTS

Alongside Community was a village project. I would like to thank my publisher Routledge/Taylor & Francis and especially my wonderful editors Samantha Barbaro and Athena Bryan for their support and help in answering questions, editing, designing, and marketing this book. Special thanks to Suffolk University and Dean Maria Toyoda for granting me a course release to work on this book.

I appreciate the chapter authors, commentators, community partners, and former students for their generous knowledge and willingness to share their experiences in this book. It has been an honor to work with such an amazing community of thinkers, educators, and practitioners.

Other community members deserve big thanks including my brother, Gary Balestrieri, for his willingness and persistence in creating just the right photos, Christina Athineos for her playful illustrations and Portia Ross for her graphic design talents, enabling me to publish this book. I would like to thank Lisa Alpers, Lauren Grenier, Shaina Hastings, Sheikh Abu Nahser, William Balint, and Katie Kozak for helping me in the process of editing and proofreading.

I would like to express my gratitude to the theorists who continue to impact my thinking including Isaac Prilleltensky, Edgar Schein, and Kenneth Gergen and the many students and community partners with whom I had the privilege to work for the past 20+ years. I continue to be amazed and thankful that you are willing to create a more socially just world.

Above all, I want to thank my husband of 24 years, Bill Balint, and the rest of my family, for their unwavering support, encouragement, and ability to keep me sane despite the time this project took me away from them.

ABOUT THE AUTHORS

Christina Athineos, MS, is a doctoral student in Suffolk University's Clinical Psychology program. She continues to pursue her interest of incorporating community psychology research and praxis into the realm of clinical psychology. Her research focuses primarily on issues of social injustice, feminism, social media, and program development.

Sharon Friedman, MEd, LMHC, has had active careers in special education, psychotherapy, and program development. Her professional interests have focused upon personal growth and the development of learning communities in nonprofit organizations. Currently, she consults with small nonprofit agencies and provides disaster mental health services throughout the United States.

Debra A. Harkins, PhD, is an associate professor in Psychology at Suffolk University. Debra teaches Community Psychology, Psychology of Self and Identity, and Voices in Conflict. Her research and teaching interests include social justice, service learning, civic engagement, conflict resolution, and empowerment at individual, organizational, and community levels. She is currently developing and examining the efficacy of a service-learning mentoring program to support faculty, students, and community partners. She serves as editor for the *Pedagogy and Human Sciences* journal and is the founder of Leading Change Associates, providing executive coaching and consulting for nonprofit organizations. She wrote two books, *Researcher Race: Social Constructions in the Research Process* (co-authored with Lauren Mizock) and *Beyond the Campus: Building a Sustainable University–Community Partnership* (with The Community Action Project Team).

Shaina Hastings, BA, University of Hartford. She currently works as an administrative assistant at Policy Analysis Inc., an HEOR consulting firm in Brookline, MA. She has a personal interest in youth education and community health.

Patricia (Pat) Hogan, PhD, is an associate professor and director of the Center for Urban and Environmental Studies at Suffolk University. She is trained as an engineer (chemical and environmental) and a chemist. Prior to coming to academia, she spent the early part of her career as a process engineer and later as a health and safety consultant. She has a lifelong interest in equity and access in the science and engineering fields for persons who are currently underrepresented so that many voices can be heard when people make technical decisions about our common future.

David J. Jefferson, JD, is a lawyer licensed in the state of California, a Fulbright Scholar, and a law and policy analyst at the Public Intellectual Property Resource for Agriculture (PIPRA), a nonprofit organization based at the University of California, Davis. At PIPRA, he conducts research and analysis surrounding the intellectual property laws and institutional IP policies of developing countries. He also provides support for PIPRA's educational and outreach programs and is a regular speaker in international events, conducting lectures in English, Spanish, and Portuguese. He is a PhD candidate at the University of Queensland in Australia, and his PhD project examines the theory, motivations, objectives, and expected impact of the new draft Ecuadorian intellectual property law specifically focused on components of the law that are relevant to Andean agricultural practices, food sovereignty, and traditional knowledge.

Kathryn Kozak, MS, is a clinical psychology doctoral student and Community Service Fellow at Suffolk University. She uses an organizational process approach to better understand how groups and social movements flourish and falter, with research focusing on service-learning programs.

She currently offers consultation and training in gender- and sexual identity-related issues for a range of audiences, including businesses and academic settings.

Abráham E. Peña-Talamantes, MS, is associate director for the McNair Scholars Program and Lecturer of Sociology and Education Studies at Suffolk University. He is also a PhD candidate at Florida State University. His research and teaching interests include issues of race/ethnicity, gender, sexuality, social inequality, and social psychology, particularly as they relate to the identity negotiation of sexual minority Latinos across social contexts. He currently serves as the co-editor of *Opportunity Matters: Journal of Access and Opportunity in Education*, a publication of the Pell Institute for the Study of Opportunity in Higher Education, and has published his own work in several high-impact journals including the *Journal of College Student Development* and *Social Forces*.

Sukanya Ray, PhD, is an associate professor in Psychology at Suffolk University. She is a native of India and trained and worked in India, Australia, and the United States. She is a community consultant, researcher, and educator for multicultural issues, minority/immigrant health issues, educational training, community outreach, and community health awareness programs. Her research interests and publication areas include Asian mental health, minority community mental health/health disparities, cultural and psychological correlates of eating problems/body image issues, trauma/resiliency, and Cyber psychology. She is an active consultant for immigrants in Massachusetts and a board member of Asian Task Force Against Domestic Violence (ATASK) in Boston. She developed an empowerment service program for women victims of violence and marginalized immigrant populations.

Carol Sharicz, EdD, is a professor, consultant and author. She is a professor in the Instructional Design Program at the University of Massachusetts Boston. She is teaching graduate courses in Communications Theory, Interpersonal Skills and Group Dynamics, and Assessment and Evaluation in the Instructional Design Process and Evidence-Based Research. Prior work experience includes being a senior training instructor and instructional designer for Motorola, Inc. To date, she has worked in the following locations: Amsterdam, Australia, Belarus, Belgium, Brazil, Canada, England, Estonia, Germany, Hong Kong, India, Japan, Moldova, and Russia.

Carmen N. Veloria, EdD (associate professor), has been an educator in the P–16 system and college access program administrator. Her scholarship focuses on systemic issues that negatively impact the educational trajectory of students of color, and issues of race, ethnicity, and language usage. She is interested in college access initiatives for underrepresented youth and equity-minded practices in higher education. She holds a doctoral degree from the University of Massachusetts at Amherst.

Felicia P. Wiltz has a PhD in Sociology and is an associate professor at Suffolk University in Boston, MA. Her current research interests include race and college persistence, diversity, and inclusiveness in organizations. She has published on diversity in the workplace.

INTRODUCTION

Alongside Community: Learning in Service is a road map for students taking a college course that requires some form of community service. We wrote this book to provide you with a social justice and culturally sensitive approach toward civic engagement. We envision giving you the tools needed to engage in empowering-focused helping while you work with urban underserved communities.

Our purpose is to provide you with a step-by step guide filled with the necessary information you need to do this work including social identity theories, action-based methods, community interventions, and sociopolitical awareness as well as the practical skills needed to engage in socially responsible helping within disempowered communities. By knowing how your social identity influences your ability to help those different from you and guiding you through the theories, methods, tools, sociopolitical issues, and practical skills of service learning, you will be better prepared to provide meaningful services to communities different from your own.

Community-based courses involve both teaching and learning through critical reflection of relevant course content and practical experiences in the community. This approach facilitates your helping role by learning in nontraditional ways as well as providing you with a framework for your practical experiences and active learning in urban communities. Community engagement involves your ongoing, continual critical reflection of your academic knowledge along with your service experience to and from the community and classroom. This book facilitates this type of learning by training you on how to plan, process, and analyze how your academic knowledge and practical experience inform one another. We incorporate information about specific contexts to provide you with the tools needed to engage in ongoing self-reflection, group exploration, and classroom discussion.

We include reflective activities, exercises, space for journaling, and approaches to help you understand your relationship as a student in the classroom and as a helper in the larger community, preparing you to connect more genuinely and thoughtfully with multicultural urban communities, addressing the sensitive and diverse issues present in our society today. The information and exercise herein allows you to have a deeper understanding of the dynamics of power differentials, challenges working with the disempowered, and how to build collaborations, creating social changes in yourself and in communities that you serve. Finally, this field book provides effective strategies for adequate meaning making of your service and evaluating your performance as a student and a civically engaged citizen through critical reflection on the process and impact of your service for yourself and the community.

This guidebook provides you with the knowledge and ideas needed to bridge the gap between academic knowledge and practical services within respective communities. Along this journey, you will be exposed to the following terms: *service learning, community service,* and *civic engagement,* and these terms are interchangeable in this book. We provide practical challenges and risks encountered for instructors, students, and community members while engaged in community service. Interspersed throughout the book, you will find the voices of former college students who have engaged in community service, giving you tips, lessons, and suggestions to consider as you engage in community service. Additionally, we hope instructors benefit from the frameworks provided herein to increase meaningful links between course content, pedagogy, and citizenship that easily integrate into your service-learning courses.

This book exposes you to a wide range of topics including education, mental health, environmental justice, poverty, race, class, gender, sexual orientation, and immigration, with the goal of expanding your knowledge about the communities with whom you will engage and the critical reflection central to this process. We structured these chapters to encourage the following:

- To support critical reflection of your social identity within a helping profession by addressing fundamental issues of social identity and social responsibility

- To expose you to contemporary social issues that impact and create the need for help by broadening your understanding of the historical, political and social factors that impact the underserved

- To train you in analyzing and creating programs that help communities by providing the skills needed to locate, gather, and use information intellectually, critically, and responsibly while helping urban communities.

Our big goal for you is to bring this knowledge together and explore how you might make a positive social change in the world.

In the first part of this field book, we discuss the complexities of helping, the importance of exploring your values and social identity when working in underserved communities, and the role of power when helping. Chapter 1 explores the challenges of helping by examining the different types of helping, the underlying assumptions that exist with various forms of helping, and how service learning can make you a better helper. In Chapter 2, we examine the role of values, power, and your social identity as you begin serving with your community partner.

The second part of this book addresses how to build your helping skills and sociopolitical awareness to empower underserved communities. We begin, in Chapter 3, on building your interpersonal skills including improving your communication, conflict resolution, leadership, and team-building competencies to facilitate healthy social change. Chapter 4 explores the intervention approaches and skills you will need to support well-being and liberation including social, organizational, community, small group, and individual interventions. Chapter 5 examines the role and responsibilities of the researcher in facilitating social change including the stance of a social change agent researcher, the types of research available to facilitate social justice, the issues of ethics in action-focused research, and how to share your research to promote social change. In Chapter 6, we help you understand the vital role of critically reflecting on your community service through the skills of authentic listening, humility, deconstructing language, and engaging in critical dialogue.

In Chapter 7, we ask you to critically reflect on how to become a more culturally sensitive helper including exploring the volatile and critical issues of race, class, ethnicity, and immigration in the United States. We address why these issues are interwoven with each other and why it is so difficult for all of us to discuss, explore, and address race, class, and ethnicity in the United States. Chapter 8 continues our reflection on cultural sensitivity by exploring issues of gender and sexual orientation identity in the United States. We explore the feminist and LGBTQ+ movements and how we can become an ally and partner in the struggle for social equality.

Navigating educational systems has its own challenges, so Chapter 9 takes a "big picture" view of how the racial and class divide impacts educational opportunities and provides three powerful practices to help you see how shifting this social dynamic can create huge benefits for many. In Chapter 10, we explore how to practice environmental justice including providing examples of successful environmental justice initiatives and provide you with tools to develop community scientific and policy literacy. Of course, there are more social *-isms* than covered in this book, but we focus on these main social issues because of our own personal expertise and experiences. We hope learning about these major social issues will encourage you to critically reflect on other *-isms* in our society.

The third part of this book addresses how to assess your civic engagement. We provide quantitative and qualitative measures in Chapter 11 to determine if you made a difference through your community service. We provide you with the tools you will need to determine the impact of community service on your own professional development, course objectives, community-university partnership building, and for the community agency itself. In Chapter 12, the final chapter, we revisit the complexity of engaging in community service and provide you with a tool kit for being a lifelong civically engaged citizen.

PART I
LEARNING TO SERVE

CHAPTER 1
UNDERSTANDING COMPLEXITIES OF HELPING AND SERVING

Debra A. Harkins

AIMS OF CHAPTER

1. Understand the role of altruism, empathy, and prosocial behavior in the practice of helping.
2. Explore the complexity and theories of helping.
3. Describe how service learning is a win-win helping approach.

REFLECTION: DO YOU HAVE ANY SPARE CHANGE?

Students often work with the local homeless community in our city. Our college is in the northeast region of the United States, with a significant number of homeless people in and around our urban campus. For many students, this is the first time they have seen so many homeless people. An often-discussed issue we have is what to do when a homeless person asks you for some spare change. Do you give money? Do you get them a coffee or a sandwich? Do you ignore them?

Some people give money and feel good with themselves for a little while. Others are fearful that this homeless person might spend the money in nefarious ways (e.g., drugs, alcohol) but feel like they need to do something, so they buy the homeless person a coffee or a sandwich and feel good with themselves for a little while. Others ignore and wish they would just get a job and get off the street.

What do you do? What do your actions toward this homeless person say about you? What assumptions do you hold about this person? What assumptions do you have about how and why we help another in our society? There is no right or wrong answer to any of these questions; rather, your answers reveal much about yourself, your values, and your assumptions about social class, poverty, and homelessness.

Helping seems like an obvious act, right? However, there are many types of helping such as helping because it makes one feel good, helping to make someone else feel good, helping based on charity, helping out of empathy, or helping out of sense of equity. What we do not often consider is how the act of helping can make the one being helped feel less than and make the helper feel—or look—more than (Schein, 2009). *Helping is an unequal act!*

So, how do we help without perpetuating the very injustices we are seeking to remove? First, we need to become aware of why we want to help. What is our own definition of helping? Are we helping because we are supposed to help the downtrodden? The sick? The infirm? Do we feel bad for the other? Do we help based on sympathy, empathy, and/or justice? Do we expect those who are helped to say "thank you" for receiving a dollar from us? What if they don't smile when we give them that dollar? What if they don't say "thank you" graciously enough? What if they don't say anything at all? Understanding our own reaction to how we help and what we expect from helping may clarify our own role in oppression and or liberation. Ironically, helping requires us to look deeply at ourselves and ask why we help. Or why we don't.

PSYCHOLOGY OF ALTRUISM, EMPATHY, AND PROSOCIAL BEHAVIOR

Do you like to help? Do you wish you were motivated to help? Psychological research may help you want to help more when you see the benefits for yourself and others. A review of the impact of altruism and prosocial behavior on cognitive, moral, and social development (Begue, 2016; Goetz, Keitner, & Simon-Thomas, 2010) reveals significant benefits of helping others for the helper, including the following:

- Improved sense of well-being, self-esteem, and self-worth
- Increased energy, mood, and strength
- Decreased aches and pains.

Do these findings motivate you to help? Unfortunately, many worry about helping for "selfish" reasons. Is it okay to help, when you are helping, because it helps you? Can you help selflessly? Well, take heart. Research confirms that most people help based on both selfish and unselfish reasons, and this combination of selfish and unselfish helping seems to create the best helpers, at least for the helper. Interestingly, there are two important reasons that explain these counterintuitive findings:

● Pure altruism can quickly lead to burnout for the helper (clearly not good for anyone).

● Receiving help can be a mixed blessing for the helpee, since the helpee can sometimes feel helpless or inferior for not being able to help themselves.

Since the helper wants to help, sometimes helping too much is not helpful at all. *Helping is complicated!*

In fact, theorists suggest and researchers (Clary, Snyder, & Stukas, 1996) find that relieving one's own distress and pain through helping others increases one's empathy and prosocial behavior in the future. Prosocial behavior (e.g., acting out of care and concern for others) serves many functions including the following:

● Allowing you to act on your values

● Increasing your self-worth

● Improving your learning and understanding of other people

● Enhancing your career development

● Improving your fit with important social groups

● Decreasing your guilt.

ROLE OF PITY, SYMPATHY, AND EMPATHY IN HELPING

Do you know the difference between pity, sympathy, and empathy? All these emotions are different empathetic responses to distress. As we describe these types of responses next, consider the type of empathetic reaction you have when you see a homeless person on the street.

In Neel Burton's (2015) recent book, *Heaven and Hell: The Psychology of the Emotions*, he describes the developmental process of empathetic reactions. For example, Burton defines pity as the lowest level of empathy, involving simple feelings of discomfort that arise from witnessing or hearing about the distress of another. Note that this level of empathy does not elicit any outward action. The next level of empathy—sympathy—involves feelings of care and concern for another and wishing that the other person felt better. Notice, there may still be no action taking place at this level of empathy, but deep evolutionary emotions are being triggered by the desire for community protection of another. There is a sense of concern for the other. The highest level of empathy—compassion—is described as "suffering with" the other and involves a strong desire to alleviate another's suffering, which often feels like your own suffering. Strong evolutionary emotions of protecting and supporting those who are considered part of one's own community trigger powerful feelings of compassion that often lead to action. Compassionate empathy often elicits helping responses focused on liberating others from suffering, including resisting oppression and improving well-being. Note that as empathy deepens, feelings of community concern and support emerge. That is, as empathy moves from pity to compassion, we often broaden our concern to include community (see Figure 1.1).

FIGURE 1.1   Empathy

REFLECTION: JOURNEY FROM CLINICAL DEVELOPMENTAL TO COMMUNITY-FOCUSED PSYCHOLOGIST

As a clinical developmental psychologist, I was trained, like most psychologists, in individually focused therapy. I learned cognitive, behavioral, and psychoanalytic approaches to help others deal with emotional issues. I provided clinical services to many children and adults, often in a standard therapy room, and some of my clients said they felt better coming to therapy and reported doing better at the end of the therapy work. However, my clinical journey took a sharp turn from many psychologists when I left the therapy room in the counseling center and began working in urban school settings.

My post-doctoral internship included providing clinical services to young children in several poorly funded urban elementary schools. As a clinical developmental psychologist, my responsibility was to provide therapy to young children who had been identified as in need of services by teachers or staff. Each week, I would meet with children one on one, in a small room within the school, for several months at a time, playing and building a rapport so they felt comfortable enough to talk with me or share their experiences through play.

On several occasions, a child would come to their weekly session with bruises and eventually she or he would tell me or show me through their play that they had been hit by someone, often an adult in their home. My training had clearly taught me what I should do in such situations; I had an ethical and legal obligation to report incidences of child abuse. My responsibility was to inform administrators that a report needed to be filed to child protective services, which I did. However, I was just as quickly told that if they, administrators, filed a report on all children who showed up with bruises, they would have no children in the school. It was in these moments, and in similar experiences, that I began to question what it truly meant to help others. I began to wonder if I could help children in the therapy room? What was the best way I could help these young children? My shift from an individual-focused helper transformed into a more community-focused helper in my struggle of trying to do individual-focused therapy in a community wrought with social disadvantage. Little did I realize how different helping would need to be to truly help these young children. My journey toward figuring out how to help was complicated, as I had been trained in a traditional form of psychology that focuses on individual mental health.

So, helping is unequal, complicated, and varies across helper identity and across cultures, genders, and communities. It is extremely difficult to help ourselves, and we often need support to do so. Imagine how challenging it is to help those different from yourself? Don't despair—there is a way to figure this out. How? Well, here comes theory to the rescue—bet you didn't think I would say that, did you?

WARNING: SOME THEORY TO NAVIGATE HOW TO HELP (DON'T DESPAIR—WE WON'T STAY HERE LONG)

Traditional Helping

If you think about how people generally get help, the following approach likely seems very natural and right to you. This is likely true for most people from Westernized countries only. For example, in the United States, when one seeks help from a traditional psychologist, they will find the psychologist asking questions to determine the client's *problem*—this approach is like what happens when one visits their medical doctor. Most psychologists are trained to ask a set of standard questions and engage in an empirically validated approach toward gathering information (e.g., motivational interviewing is one such approach). Once the psychologist identifies the issue, a diagnosis is promptly recorded in a patient's record. And, this diagnosis provides the means to determine the most appropriate (empirically validated) treatment approach to reduce or eliminate the client's problem.

Box 1.1 Are you WEIRD?

WEIRD refers to the phenomenon in social science of using individuals from primarily Western, Educated, Industrialized, Rich, and Democratic countries as research subjects (convenient participants). WEIRDs also tend to be college students.

What is particularly weird about WEIRDs is that they represent only 12% of the world population, and they vary from the remaining 88% of people on ideas of fairness, decision making, moral reasoning, and optical illusions—characteristics heavily influenced by context.

Weird!

Source: Henrich, Heine, and Norenzayan, 2010

Most psychologists work with clients on a one-to-one basis and address problems as they arise. Since traditional psychology grew out of biology and medicine, it has a long history of aligning with the social and political systems associated with medicine and proudly follows the scientific assumptions that research should be empirical and value free. This positivist scientific approach of traditional psychology typically leads to collaborations with other sciences, such as biology, medicine, and psychiatry (Fox, 2000; Freire, 1970; Martin-Baro, 1994; Sampson, 2000; Sloan, 1996). As positivist science is causally focused (i.e., tries to find support that X indeed causes Y), traditional psychologists use findings from research to deduce that clients need to comply with the treatment designed to get relief from their problem. That is, client compliance with a suggested treatment is the major goal of traditional psychology. If a client does not want to comply with the suggested treatment, she or he is viewed as resisting help—not using the time-honored empirically validated approach to reduce or eliminate their problem. This approach to helping probably feels natural and right to many of us and most often, it works very well for some of us.

Traditional psychology excels at helping mainstream American individuals. And, this is not surprising given that most psychological research is conducted by and on mainstream America, as you can see from the WEIRD research in Box 1.1. Essentially, traditional psychology is the study of middle class mainstream America, and it has high validity (truth) and reliability (repeatable findings) for the middle class in America. So, you can rest assured that if you are part of mainstream America, you will find much help and support from traditional psychologists (see Figure 1.2).

Reflect: What happens when you are not part of mainstream America? Do you think that traditional psychological approaches work with non-mainstream Americans? Why or why not? Please answer these questions before reading further.

_____

_____

_____

FIGURE 1.2 Living in America

Community-Based Helping

Many of the negative issues that impact non-mainstream America include significant disadvantages at community and systemic levels of society. This reality requires a very different approach to helping—one that examines injustices (problems) at community and social structural levels. Helpers from this perspective engage in more preventive work by focusing on the strengths of a community to overcome obstacles to well-being. Community-based helpers generally work with community members to support community empowerment and change.

This systemic approach arose in countries and communities during periods of civil and social upheaval, as social justice helpers work with communities to empower the dispossessed and underserved. Helpers from this approach generally align with social fields including law, political science, education, sociology, and economics and assumes that working with humans is always value laden and deeply subjective. Thus, this helping approach uses participatory action-based research driven by values of *well-being, liberation,* and *empowerment.* Community-based work encourages a helper to serve as a collaborator and resource to a community with the goal to empower and emancipate.

While community-based helping may feel less natural to middle class America, community-focused helping is a countervailing force that seeks to understand and work with non-mainstream communities—usually defined as the *other*—such as the underserved, the poor, the disenfranchised, the racial other, the sexual other, the gendered other, the abled other, and so forth. Community-based helpers work toward bettering a community to dismantle inequality. Check out Vanessa's thoughts on community helping.

Student Voice

Community Psychology (CP) was the first form of psychology that felt action based. I remember discussing theories in the classroom and applying them directly in our work within community programs that same week. It was also one of the first forms of psychology where the community perspective challenged traditional modes of thought—and something hard to do within psychology and society at large.

Community-focused helping pushed me to look at issues beyond the individual level—and depending on the community you serve, the issues are challenging. That perspective would go on to shape a ton of what I would go on to choose to do—working within Boston's community health centers and different areas of public health (applying to graduate school for public health alone), and traveling to over 15 countries for international community work. Even now, as I'm no longer in the health field, but currently working within tech—how I choose to think about complex problems always comes down to a societal level. How I think about empowering others and growing projects and individuals around me is largely in part to the skills I learned by helping in a community.

I love building thoughts into action. That's what makes this approach to helping so unique. You can create and evaluate programs, craft needs assessments or policies which help people control the stressful aspects of their community, and organizational environments. Everything was applied learning, which made it impossible to learn without engulfing yourself within the community you served.

—Vanessa Frontiero, Community Psychology, 2007

It's important for us to put things into a more global perspective: United States values individual expression, self-reliance, and self-actualization more highly than most, if not all, other nation states/cultures in the world. The further we move from talking about mainstream America, the more likely the communities in question are not white, not upper or middle class, not in positions of power, often immigrants, perhaps second/third generation from other cultures. Many of these communities value the group as much as or more than individuals. For these non-mainstream Americans, community-focused helping may feel more natural than the traditional US model of one-to-one therapy in a therapist's office. In addition, traditional helping often requires taking time off from work and having insurance or disposable income to afford the typical weekly therapeutic treatment, which is often out of economic and social reach for non-mainstream America.

Contemporary community helping views groups from a dynamical systems approach, meaning that what happens to your neighbors, cousins, in-laws, and so forth, can have a large impact on you. This approach may feel more comfortable to those from more group-centric backgrounds. Recognizing that attitudes in the United States are not necessarily shared, or even well understood, in many other parts of the world or parts of the United States, is a first step in helping non-mainstream citizens.

So, at this point, you may be wondering what type of helping is best: individual-focused or community-focused helping. Well—drum roll, please—it *depends* . . . on a lot of things, most especially on whom you are trying to help. We will get to that later. For now, I want to introduce you to a more holistic approach to helping that allows you to work at the individual and community level, and so much more. Let's learn about the amazing ecological approach to helping.

Ecological or Holistic Perspective of Helping

An **ecological** or holistic approach to helping others focuses on understanding the relationship between the individual and the multiple systems in which one lives (Bronfenbrenner, 1995). Ecologically oriented helpers point out that we are never separate from our context, our family, our community or our world. This ecological model of behavior was first described by psychologist Urie Bronfenbrenner, co-founder of Head Start, the most successful preschool education program for low-income children in US history. Bronfenbrenner's ecological model considers multiple levels of helping, such as the individual, micro, and macro levels of the environment (see Figure 1.3).

Bronfenbrenner's ecological approach emerged from public health initiatives that sought to prevent illness and promote health. Community-focused scientists realized that it is socially and economically sound to prevent illness and promote health than to try to treat illness. Approaches to prevention and promotion include prenatal and early infancy projects, community health programs, and competency training. Note this type of helping is critical for working with disempowered communities.

So, what does helping look like when practicing from an ecological approach with disadvantaged communities? Well, first we must acknowledge that we should help at all levels of the ecological system, from micro (individual) to macro (collective) levels. We can help at the *individual* level when we become conscious of the personal and individual struggles of those experiencing social and political inequities. We can join in solidarity between the haves and have-nots at the *relational* level, and we can engage in resistance and political and social action at the *collective* level. Ensuring well-being requires the helper to support *individual* self-esteem, competence, independence, and political rights; provide positive *relational* support and participate in social, community, and political life; and work at the *collective* level to help others acquire valued resources, including a job, income, education, health, and housing.

As you are likely beginning to realize, ecological helping is more encompassing and complex than, and quite different from, individual-focused helping. Reflective and community-based forms of helping do not shy away from the central role of *values* in research and practice, and hence community-focused helpers work within community settings. Ecologically based helping focuses on understanding how underserved and disadvantaged communities arise from past and current

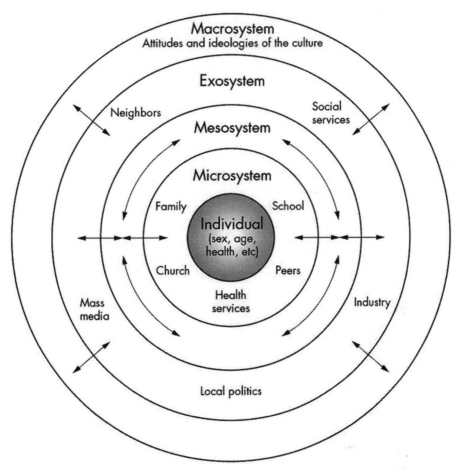

FIGURE 1.3 Bronfenbrenner Ecological Model

Source: Wikicommons

economic and social structures. Community-based helping seeks to understand, work with, and actively engage with individuals from oppressed communities as they work, struggle, and resist oppression. This type of community-based helping emerges across the world when those in the helping professions begin to focus on the oppressive conditions of individuals within their countries.

You might be thinking at this point, *yeah that's all fine and dandy, but why do I have to engage in community-based helping? I'm just looking to get my degree, and providing traditional help seems so much easier and faster.* Well, the answer is related to being an engaged and good citizen. So, let's explore what is expected of a good citizen.

LEVELS OF CIVIC ENGAGEMENT

We all help to varying degrees within different communities and organizations at various times in our lives. In some cases, you may help those who are hungry by contributing to a food drive, or you might feel more deeply about hunger and help to organize a food drive. In some cases, if the issue impacts you deeply—morally, spiritually, or personally—you may try to figure out why people are hungry in our society and seek to solve the root causes of hunger. See Table 1.1 below to understand how different types of helping impact levels of engagement.

Being a responsible citizen includes being a law-abiding good member of your community. You obey the laws, work, pay taxes, vote, recycle, and help others in crisis. Most of us are law-abiding

If you have come to help me, you are wasting our time.

But if you have come because your liberation is bound up with mine, then let us work together.
—Aboriginal native

responsible citizens, who help when needed. For example, if we hear about or notice that people are hungry, many of us would contribute money, food, or time to help in the form of volunteering for a food drive or soup kitchen. Unfortunately, many of us might be walking too quickly, thinking too deeply, or driving too fast to notice others in need. It is easy to get distracted, particularly in our fast-paced, technologically driven society, so it is far more common for us to simply not notice those in need. If you are still working toward being a responsible citizen, service-learning courses will help get you there.

The next level of citizenship involves more participatory engagement, including being a leader who works toward improving well-being for all in the community by participating in community

TABLE 1.1 Levels of Civic Helping

Type	Core Assumption	Citizen Description	Civic Knowledge	Community Experience	Sample Civic Action
Responsible Citizen	Must be a law-abiding member of a community	• Obey laws • Pay taxes • Vote • Recycle • Help in crisis	• Exercises compassion and social responsibility	Volunteerism and community service	Help with a food drive
Participatory Citizen	Must actively participate and lead to help improve well-being of a community	• Participate in community organization • Organize community effort to care for people in need, economic development	• Knows how public sectors (government, nonprofit groups) work • Knows strategies for completing tasks • Organizes and motivates others	Experiential learning (e.g., practicum, internship, field work)	Organize a food drive
Transformational Citizen	Must take responsibility to question and change unjust and ineffective systems	• Critically assess social, political, and economic structures • Educate others and develops community partnerships • Act to change injustice through policy and social innovation	• Knows how to analyze and effect system change • Knows about social movements • Willing to take stand different from others • Action oriented	Service learning	Examine why people are hungry and act to solve root causes

Source: Adapted from Duncan and Kopperud (2008)

organizations and organizing efforts to care for people in need. Some of us have found ourselves in these roles at certain times in our lives, serving as leaders and active participants for a community in need. For example, many college students have participated in Best Buddies, Jump Start, Head Start, and Upward Bound; organized a food drive; participated in clean-up of an area (painting, trash pick-up, etc.); coached a sports team; and so forth. A significant component of service-learning courses is to help students move from such responsible helpers to more participatory helpers/citizens.

Transformational citizens are those who not only are responsible and participatory helpers but also those who deeply question and try to change unjust and ineffective social systems. This requires learning about and educating others about the social, political, historical, environmental, and economic factors that contribute to the social issue of concern as well as working toward social and policy changes to enable social justice. This person must have the courage to stand in times of challenge and controversy from others and be willing to act on their convictions and understand who are the movers and shakers that can create necessary change. Service-learning courses will help you begin to understand the many areas of study needed to become a more transformational helper and engaged citizen.

Reflect: Choose a local issue you care about deeply and determine the civic actions needed for each level of helping.

Responsible citizen level of helping

low income communities, pay taxes

Participatory citizen level of helping

Participate in C. org.

Transformational citizen level of helping

You might be wondering now, *how do I become a transformational citizen?* Well, this is where service learning is going to help you.

SERVICE LEARNING

What is service learning, and how is it different from other forms of community service and experiential learning? Service learning is a form of both community service and experiential learning. Service learning is a pedagogical approach to teaching that requires critical reflection of a community service experience embedded within an academic course of study, with the goal of developing socially responsible and actively engaged citizens. As you review the goals of different types of helping in

Figures 1.4 and 1.5, notice that volunteerism (e.g., volunteering with Best Buddies, Head Start, alternative spring break) typically is the first level of civic engagement and does not require or include a critical reflective and academic study component. Experiential learning (e.g., internships, practicum) provides practical experience within an academic course, with the primary goal of providing training for the trainee but often does not include the civic component, and often represents the second level of civic engagement. Service learning includes mutual goals for the student and the community within an academic course focused on civic responsibility and critical reflection, representing the third level of civic engagement.

You may still be wondering why some colleges, universities, and faculty require students to take service-learning courses. It is important to note that the original mission of colleges and universities was to educate and prepare students to be active citizens—that is, to train individuals who could then give back to their country. To ensure this goal, colleges were formed through land grants given

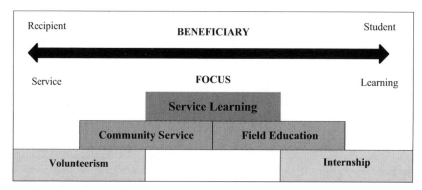

FIGURE 1.4   Service Distinctions

Source: Adapted from Andrew Furco, *Service-Learning: A Balanced Approach to Experiential Education* (1996)

Note: Experiential learning can be viewed on a continuum with internships and practicums focused on professional development and volunteering and community engagement focused primarily on civic support. Service learning resides in the middle of this continuum, focusing equally on professional development and civic engagement.

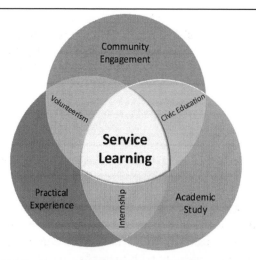

Civic Education—Students engage in activities to benefit community related to academic courses

Internship/Practica—Students engage in activities to benefit professional development

Volunteerism—Students engage in activities to benefit the community, client or partner not formally connected to an academic course

Service Learning—Students engage in activities that mutually benefit the community and the student with directed academic goals that promote reflection in their current course that promotes civic responsibility and engagement

FIGURE 1.5   Community Service Type and Goals

by the federal government to ensure that people gained knowledge and learned skills for the betterment of society. In this way, going to college was a national affair!

Many in higher education today believe that contemporary higher education lost its way when the focus moved toward educating people for personal and professional development. A clarion call to return to the original mission of higher education—to prepare future citizens—was made approximately 20 years ago by a group of college and university presidents. Campus Compact was formed as a formal commitment among these college presidents to require all their students to engage in community service as part of their college experience. As of this date, approximately 33% of colleges and universities across the United States require students to take at least one course with a strong service-learning component.

A big part of service learning involves active civic engagement with a goal to become a socially responsible and active citizen. For many people, democracy is considered a "great experiment." Democracy is often described as an attempt to bring individual experiences, beliefs, and values together with ideas of equity, security, and justice. Note how democracy is trying to *balance* individual freedom and social responsibility. In this way, democracy is the ideal of both accountability and responsibility to self and others. Forward-thinking colleges and universities are trying to combine these two *competing* ideals (individual and society) to encourage the "American Dream" by teaching students to achieve their best, with the hope that this knowledge will lead to more socially responsible citizens.

John Dewey, the father of modern American education, wrote in his seminal book *Democracy and Education* that students must not only be engaged in thought (knowledge) but also in action (skill) to develop into engaged citizens. Being a civic citizen means more than knowing, it means acting on your knowledge. When those college presidents met at the now-famous Campus Compact event, they were concerned that most colleges and universities were meeting the first goal of preparing thinkers but were failing to prepare students to act on this knowledge. Hence, service learning grew from the commitment to educate and train students to "do good" for their country by learning how to apply the knowledge they acquired through action for civic betterment.

Civic capacity occurs when we reflect on the connection between our academic learning, our social identity, and our experiences of the social and political issues within our local, state, national, and global society. Service learning provides the opportunity to make these critical connections and further your civic citizenship.

In the next chapter, we will explore your own values and how they may impact your ability to help others. We will also explore how your social identity and your values impact helping. And, we discuss how the hidden dimension of power facilitates or obstructs one's ability to help. Check out Sami's suggestion for making your community service-oriented course experience the best for you. Then, self-reflect on the ideas discussed in the chapter.

Student Voice

I—as I'm sure like most people—tend to get lost in their own thoughts often on any given day, like, planning what to do this weekend, thinking about what to eat for dinner and, how many minutes do I have before I really must get out of bed? With these thoughts encircling our minds, there comes a certain clouding and subsequent disconnect to the outside world and the people in it—especially the ones who you think are the furthest like you.

I made a friend while serving coffee at the Paulist Center on a Wednesday night. I remember him telling me how he loved watching Doctor Who, and how he disagreed with the [selection of the] actor chosen to play the Doctor for that season on his blog that he updated whenever he could. He told me about how he was kicked out of his home at the age of 16 because his parents disapproved of his homosexuality. He was homeless now and was a part of that large crowd we were serving hot meals and bottomless coffee to that night. All these things are a part of me now that wasn't before—and I think this is, at least in some essence for me, what is community and service-related learning.

Something a prospective student of this course might want to consider is to be prepared to re-evaluate and expand your moral and interpersonal spheres to include people who you think are not like you—and toward the end of the semester—hopefully arrive at the conclusion that those same people are more not unlike you than you previously thought. I think one of the most significant lessons that we were taught had to with the concept of helping. Deconstructing what helping is, what it means, how there's a science to/art in asking for it, and realizing that there are power dynamics inherent to that process that could very well impact the outcome of your practical and real-life help that's being given to the community that you're serving.

And speaking of help—learning that at the intersection of race, gender, and religion (amongst others) and helping, lies the notion of inter-ness. The idea that my struggle is your struggle is my struggle, is our struggle; the idea that oppression and suffering don't exist in a vacuum and that it's "happening to someone else." And I think this is perhaps what I meant by advising to be prepared to expand your moral spheres—it has the curious effect of not only rendering it harder to separate yourself from others, but it simultaneously becomes more difficult to view yourself as an island. It's an all at once destabilizing and stabilizing realization—a yin and yang. Besides, what is a person without people?

—Sami Bachir, Community Psychology, 2014

Reflect: After reading this chapter and Sami's reflection, answer the following questions: what does it mean to be educated? To be a citizen? To be a helper?

_____

_____

_____

Describe the ways you are ready to help those different from yourself. What life experiences have prepared you to help others?

_____

_____

_____

Describe the ways you are NOT ready to help those different from yourself. What do you still need to learn?

_____

_____

_____

COMMENTARY

Assessing Civic Engagement From a Community/School Perspective

By Dr. Catherine Constant

As a former school leader within the Boston Public Schools (BPS), the question that may be asked is, *how will community partnerships and service learning benefit the personal and professional development of all members involved?* Right now, we are just beginning to create a partnership between BPS and the university involving college students mentoring BPS students experiencing homelessness. A partnership to me is a mutual collaboration of experiences that enhance the growth of both participants by looking at perceptions and potential of others. How can they both be empowered by the experience to become leaders of change? The desire to contribute toward the growth of another or to share some of one's knowledge and experience can transform ways of thinking and how one lives in the world.

In a mentor/mentee relationship, there may be differences of backgrounds, culture, experiences, economic, and family structure. However, there is that one common denominator: *everyone needs to be valued and acknowledged as an important gift to the world.* Establishing trust in the relationship is key. Developing the confidence in the goodness that is dormant in each partner until the environment and opportunity are presented to create the possibility of serving one another through their community service. Each partner is not there to fix each other but rather to enhance the best in each other. The relationship can produce access to possibilities and solutions. Honoring the teaching moments and then encouraging one another to bring forth their best self, these values of integrity, humility, performance of excellence, and joy have a place to manifest and develop. A mutual consideration rather than a reaction to differences, an admiration for diversity and the capacity to influence others positively through humility and flexibility rather than intimidation or manipulation—these are some of the lessons that can be learned.

As the relationship finds a common ground of peace and acceptance, an exchange occurs, therefore building a community of kindness. Social-emotional currency and the capacity to communicate and relate to others increases. Cultural diversity is viewed as an asset which will enrich both the college student and the K–12 student. The college student provides a picture of what can be. Being a role model or an example of what a child can become, the student can see the future of possibilities, thus bringing hope into the situation. It becomes evident that there are long-term and short-term benefits from community service that shape the destinies of both the college student and school-age student.

RESOURCES

Bronfenbrenner, U.: www.apa.org/research/action/early.aspx
Campus Compact: http://compact.org/
Head Start: www.acf.hhs.gov/programs/ohs
Psychologists for Social Responsibility: www.psysr.org/
Teaching Tolerance: www.tolerance.org

REFERENCES

Begue, L. (2016). *The psychology of good and evil* (J. Adri, Trans.). Oxford: Oxford University Press.

Bronfenbrenner, U. (1995). Developmental ecology through space and time: A future perspective. In P. Moen, G. H. Elder, Jr., & K. Lüscher (Eds.), *Examining lives in context: Perspectives on the ecology of human development* (pp. 619–647). Washington, DC: American Psychological Association.

Burton, N. L. (2015). *Heaven and hell: The psychology of the emotions.* London: Acheron Press.

Clary, E. G., Snyder, M., & Stukas, A. A. (1996). Volunteers' motivations: Findings from a national survey. *Nonprofit and Voluntary Sector Quarterly, 25,* 485–505.

Duncan, D., & Kopperud, J. W. (2008). *Service-learning companion.* Boston, MA: Houghton Mifflin.

Fox, D. (2000). The critical psychology project: Transforming society and transforming psychology. In T. S. Sloan (Ed.), *Critical psychology: Voices for change* (pp. 21–33). New York: St. Martin's Press.

Freire, P. (1970). *Pedagogy of the oppressed.* New York: Continuum Press.

Goetz, J. L., Keitner, D., & Simon-Thomas, E. (2010). Compassion: An evolutionary analysis and empirical review. *Psychological Bulletin, 136*(3), 351–374.

Henrich, J., Heine, S. J., & Norenzayan, A. (2010). The weirdest people in the world? *Behavioral and Brain Sciences, 33*(2–3), 61–83.

Martin-Baro, I. (1994). *Writings for a liberation psychology.* Cambridge, MA: Harvard University Press.

Sampson, E. (2000). Of rainbows and differences. In T. S. Sloan (Ed.), *Critical psychology: Voices for change* (pp. 1–5). New York: St. Martin's Press.

Schein, E. H. (2009). *Helping: How to offer, give, and receive help.* San Francisco: Berrett-Koehler Publishers.

Sloan, T. S. (1996). *Damaged life: The crisis of the modern psyche.* New York: Routledge.

CHAPTER 2
EXPLORING VALUES, POWER, AND SOCIAL IDENTITY IN SERVING

Debra A. Harkins and Sukanya Ray

AIMS OF CHAPTER

1. Determine why you help.
2. Check how values and power impact helping others.
3. Determine if you are committed and ready to serve.

REFLECTION: WHY DO YOU DO SOCIAL JUSTICE WORK?

FRIEND: Why do you do social justice work?
ME: What do you mean? I asked incredulously. Why wouldn't I?
FRIEND: No, not everyone does this work. Why do you?
ME: *silence*

Almost 20 years ago, every few months, my dear friend would ask me this question, and I continued to have no answer for her beyond Why wouldn't I? I couldn't understand why she even asked me the question in the first place and why she continued to ask me.

After the first dozen times, I began to ask myself, why is she asking me this question? Thus began my journey of asking, why do I do this work? Why do I care about social justice? My answer came slowly as I continued to ask and ponder this question, and my answer deepened over these 20 years.

My very first exploration and answer led me to the most obvious reality of my life: that my mom and dad do not share the same religious background and that reality created much tension in my family, making me feel like I lived in some borderline region between two religions, never quite fitting in either. My mom is Jewish and her family suffered greatly living in Europe during WWII, while my dad was raised deeply Catholic and my sister and I were raised Catholic. As I explored why I care about social justice, I kept coming back to this reality and remembered the many Sundays that my father and sister and I went to church and how I wondered why my mom was not with us. I remember hearing the priest say that Jews were responsible for the death of Jesus. I was always shocked to hear this and felt personally wounded that the priest was implicating my mother and me in this horrible act. I felt torn and uncomfortable. It was at this point that I experienced being bi-religious, living in both religious worlds but in neither.

Reflect: So, before we go further, I am going to ask you that deceptively hard question: why do you help others?

_____

_____

_____

In this chapter, we return to our original question from Chapter 1 and ask you to explore from where came your interest in helping others as well as how your social identity impacts your helping behavior. Reflecting deeply on your own interest in helping reveals a great deal about your values, your social identity, and the role of power when helping those different from yourself. Let's begin with examining social identity and power.

Reflect: It is hoped that you noticed from the opening focused reflection that my social identity of being bi-religious impacted me in my passion for social justice. How do you think your social identity impacts you? By social identity, I mean those unspoken social categories that exist in our society like race, class, religion, ethnicity, gender, sexual orientation, and many others. For each social identity we hold, we may be on the more privileged side of the socially identified issue or the oppressed side of the socially identified issue. For example, I am a white, middle class, cis, woman, and from these four parts of my social identity, I am privileged (advantaged) in three identities and oppressed (disadvantaged) in one identity. *Choose four or five social identities you hold and identify whether you are privileged or oppressed for each aspect of your social identity.*

_____

_____

_____

We will delve more deeply into many of these social issues in later chapters, so, for now, just list the aspects of your social identity that you feel impact you the most.

_____

_____

_____

As you might have noticed, your social identity is a mixture of advantaged and disadvantaged social positions. Communities with whom you will work will likely hold not only different social positions than you but also will often be in more disadvantaged social positions than yourself. Helping those different from oneself involves understanding these differing social identities and how they relate to suffering, oppression, and challenge as well as the interpersonal and social dynamics that occur when privileged and oppressed socially identified positions attempt to work together. When we talk about privilege and oppression, we are wading into the murky waters of POWER.

We all have an intuitive understanding of which social positions have more power than other social positions. Really, no one need tell any of us who holds the most power in our culture. We would likely be unanimous in naming the gender, class, and race of who holds the most power in US society. Why we intuitively know this, yet fail to act on this information, will be explored throughout this book.

When we address power/privilege, we tend to focus on the recipients, or helpee. This is needed in terms of services offered by trained professionals. However, there is also another dimension that educators and helping professionals need to focus on. It is the "temporary status loss" of folks seeking services due to unexpected situations in their lives. Many individuals who are victims of violence (domestic, workplace, political), recent immigrant scholars/students (problems with visa extension or change of status, unemployment), and minority professionals (racial discrimination, sudden job loss, chronic experiences of micro aggressions, financial stresses) exhibit mixed feelings about their need for receiving help due to a variety of reasons including cultural shame, loss of honor, distrust, and ambivalence toward professional helpers/educators. This complex issue has not been sufficiently addressed in community service literature compared with the psychotherapy field. This issue aligns with power, privilege, socialization values, gender roles, and cultural contexts that add more complexities in terms of services and training of professionals today. Moreover, the social identity domains and implicit biases of educators/service providers could become an invisible barrier both at an individual and community levels.

REFLECTION: STATUS QUO AND STATUS LOSS

I (SR) have observed these challenges in my own personal and community service work. My child-hood exposure to class differences in my lower-class paternal and higher-class maternal family backgrounds made me more aware of "Status Quo and Status Loss" experiences that I learned to navigate through many challenges. I have personally dealt with many ambiguities and mixed emotions regarding human need, social identity, steps involved in social mobility, co-existing personal values of empathy and envy. The exposure to different worldviews and my unique experiences of parenting values anchored in spirituality allowed my personal development in a trajectory to embrace privilege and marginalization status in contextual manner. Both intellectual and experiential learning are important elements of deep insight and reflection into human condition in a community. The assumption about expert knowledge of helping or designing service could be extremely challenging without deeper understanding of specific community need. It has made me go through deep reflection on my own biases, social identity and awareness of power dynamics in reverse order toward recipients of services. As an educator, I believe that we need to incorporate these unique unconventional domains in our training to facilitate helpers/service providers' awareness and self-reflection process at individual and community levels.

Following are examples and reflective questions to address these issues.

Reflect: My personal exposure and experiences of navigating through opposite class structures shaped my own values to pursue community service and empowerment programs since my young adult years. Now, consider your own social identity (privilege or marginalization status) before you undertake your journey toward helping others.

Remember any one or two life experiences that you had which you could describe as status gain and status loss domains of your power, privilege, and social identity.

_____

_____

_____

Please describe specific values and feelings attached to each of these experiences and identify the areas that were affected (positive or negative) the most.

_____

_____

_____

Power is a complicated concept and can take many forms including the use of power to oppress, to resist, and to strive for wellness. We will return to the issue of using social identity and power to resist and increase well-being in a later chapter. The important point here is that social identity is a socially constructed category of power that is always present and functions to maintain a given social structure. Understanding social identity reveals the underlying power structures working within and across a society. It is hoped you see how power, as expressed through social identity, represents the root cause of why helping others is so challenging!

SOCIAL IDENTITY

Your social identity also intersects with your values and how and why you help others. Do you know from where arose your values? Was it family? Religion? School? Reading? It's amazing when you think about how our values impact every aspect of our lives, and yet we rarely question the validity of our values much less the origins of those values.

Many of us recognize something is clearly amiss regarding values across the globe. During the French Revolution, liberty, fraternity, and equality were considered equally important values. Although each of these values are important and ideally should be given equal importance, nations, states, and communities differ on how much weight they put on each. For example, in the United States, liberty is valued more highly than fraternity and equality. As many living in the United States witness daily, too much liberty in the absence of equality and fraternity leads to excessive greed and selfishness. Excessive self-interest creates an absence of concern for fraternity (community) and equality (fairness). We are drowning in our own self-interest. Related to excessive liberty is the strong value of individualism deeply rooted in the United States.

What values do you hold most strongly? Why are those values held at higher importance than other values? In this chapter, we ask you to critically reflect on your values and how those values may impact your ability to help those different from yourself. What if your community partner has different values than you? Do you still help them? Why? Or why not? Before going further down this rabbit hole, complete the following personal value exercise.

TABLE 2.1   Personal Values Checklist

__ Accomplishment	__ Efficiency	__ Integrity	__ Relationships
__ Achievement	__ Empathy	__ Intelligence	__ Religion
__ Adventure	__ Empowerment	__ Joy	__ Reputation
__ Arts	__ Environment	__ Judgment	__ Respect
__ Authenticity	__ Equality	__ Justice	__ Responsibility
__ Authority	__ Ethical	__ Kindness	__ Security
__ Autonomy	__ Excellence	__ Knowledge	__ Self-confidence
__ Balance	__ Expertise	__ Leadership	__ Self-determination
__ Beauty	__ Fairness	__ Learning	__ Self-esteem
__ Boldness	__ Faith	__ Love	__ Self-respect
__ Certainty	__ Fame	__ Loyalty	__ Serenity
__ Challenge	__ Family	__ Meaningful	__ Service
__ Change	__ Freedom	__ Money	__ Sincerity
__ Citizenship	__ Friendships	__ Nature	__ Social justice
__ Community	__ Fun	__ Openness	__ Spirituality
__ Compassion	__ Genuineness	__ Optimism	__ Stability
__ Competency	__ Growth	__ Order	__ Status
__ Competition	__ Happiness	__ Peace	__ Success
__ Confidence	__ Health	__ Pleasure	__ Truth
__ Contribution	__ Helping	__ Popularity	__ Trustworthiness
__ Cooperation	__ Honesty	__ Power	__ Volunteering
__ Creativity	__ Humor	__ Pride	__ Wealth
__ Curiosity	__ Independence	__ Privacy	__ Wisdom
__ Democracy	__ Influence	__ Progress	__ Work
__ Determination	__ Inner harmony	__ Public service	
__ Economic security	__ Insight	__ Recognition	

Personal Values Exercise

Using Table 2.1, list the 10 top values you hold dearly from the following value checklist. If you do not see a value, just add to the list.

1.	2.
3.	4.
5.	6.
7.	8.
9.	10.

Next, choose the five most important values from this list of 10, and prioritize them in the order of most important to least important (1 = Most Important; 5 = Least Important).

1.

2.

3.

4.

5.

Reflect on where these five values came from (e.g., parents, religion, school, peers, reading).

_____

_____

_____

Remember from Chapter 1 when we discussed how helping is good for physical, social, and emotional health? Well, helping is good for you in other ways as well. Let's examine how helping is good for us at the more sociopolitical level using the tale in Box 2.1. Questions will follow to explore more deeply.

Reflect: In what ways are others' problems our problems? In what ways do others' problems impact us socially and/or politically?

_____

_____

_____

Box 2.1 Not Our Problem: A Tale From Burma and Thailand

By Margaret Read MacDonald

The [King] sat with his Advisor eating honey and puffed rice. As they ate, they leaned over the palace window and watched the street below. They talked of this and that. The King, not paying attention to what he was doing, let a drop of honey fall onto the windowsill. "*Oh sire, let me wipe that up.*" offered the Advisor. "*Never mind,*" said the King "*It is not **our** problem. The servants will clean it later.*"

As the two continued to dine on their honey and puffed rice, a drop of honey slowly began to drip down the windowsill. At last, it fell with a plop onto the street below. Soon a fly landed on the drop of honey and begun its own meal. Immediately a gecko sprang from under the palace and with a flip of its long tongue swallowed the fly. But a cat had seen the gecko and pounced. Then a dog sprang forward and attacked the cat!

"*Sire there seems to be a cat and dog fight in the street. Should we call someone to stop it?*" "*Never mind,*" said the King. "*It's not **our** problem.*" So, the two continued to munch on their honey and puffed rice.

Meanwhile the cat's owner had arrived and was beating the dog. The dog's owner ran up and began to beat the cat's owner. Soon the two were beating each other.

"*Sire there are two persons fighting in the street now. Shouldn't we send someone to break this up?*" The King lazily looked from the window. "*Never mind. It's not **our** problem.*"

The friends of the cat's owner gathered and begun to cheer him on. The friends of the dog's owner began to cheer her on as well. Soon both groups entered the fight and attacked each other.

"*Sire, people are fighting in the street now. Perhaps we should call someone to break this up.*" The King was too lazy even to look. You can guess what he said. "*Never mind. It's not **our** problem.*"

Now soldiers arrived on the scene. At first, they tried to break up the fighting. But when they heard the cause of the fight, some sided with the cat's owner, and others sided with the dog's owner. Soon the soldiers too joined the fight.

With the soldiers involved, the fight erupted into a civil war. Houses were burned down. People were harmed. And the palace itself was set afire and burned to the ground. The King and his Adviser stop to survey the ruins. "*Perhaps,*" said the King, "*I was wrong? Perhaps the drop of honey **WAS** our problem.*"

Read the following quote from James Baldwin (1963):

If I am not what you say I am
Then you are not who you think you are.
*And that is the **crisis**.*

What have you been told about I, them, you, and us? What do you think is the message of James Baldwin? How can you use this message to help you in your work with your community partner?

_____

_____

_____

COMMUNITY VALUES

At this point, you might be asking, *well if understanding the synergy between helper and helpee social identity and values is critically important to helping, how do I figure out community's values?* The simplest way is to ask the community about their vision—*In one sentence, who or what do you want to be?* That is what would be their ideal way of being in the world. This is a deep question that many communities explore through spiritual, moral, and/or political conversations, and their answers are usually displayed or found in their sacred texts (e.g., bibles, constitutions, charters, and/or strategic plans).

Before we explore how to balance your community partner values with your values, we should examine the values underlying this vision question. Notice that to determine a community's values, we assume that you must ask the community. We must determine what community members value most and even later how community members view their current situation, what community members think they need to do to achieve their vision, and what strategies will help community members achieve their goals. Underlying this approach is a strong belief in personal, relational, and collective *well-being and liberation*.

In addition, these deep questions assessment reveal the source of our values and build on each other. For example, the first question of what is your ideal vision involves deep *philosophical* and spiritual analysis of a good life. Within the second question of what you are currently doing refers to a *contextual analysis* (e.g., physical, economic, social, and political) of what is impeding a good life or community. The third question examines the *gap* between the vision and the actual life being led (see the sidebar to understand what the Ancient Greeks defined as the Good Life). Finally, we try to determine the *strategy* or action needed to move toward the ideal good life.

Reflective moment: as you engage in community service, you will find yourself trying to balance multiple needs. You may feel overwhelmed as you realize how large the gaps that exist are. For example, balancing the philosophical views with the current realities lived will confront you as you help others. Balancing what you read with what you experience will challenge you as you attempt to make sense of a community. Balancing how and why things happen versus trying to create

> ## What Is a Good Life?
>
> Have you ever considered what makes a good life? What makes one person's life good and another's not good? The answer you provide likely lines up closely with your values. From the beginning of democracy in Athens, Aristotle, and philosophers since, have asked the question: what is the good life? What makes a good society?
>
> Philosophers generally agree a good life involves promoting values of thoughtful citizenship, practicing the good life for self, and with and in relation to others. Aristotle wrote: "*We become just by doing just actions . . . brave by doing brave actions.*" Just was defined by Aristotle as "*whatever produces and maintains happiness and its parts for a political community.*"
>
> In more contemporary language, Aristotle, and social philosophers since, define a healthy and happy life and community as one that reveres equality and social justice.

the change needed will test you when exploring helping. Finally, balancing the multiple unequal stakeholder voices will create endless questions and force you to keep reflecting on what is most important when helping others.

Yes, there is a lot to juggle when helping others. Balancing this information while reminding ourselves of our goal: *to engage in helping that increases well-being and liberation in others.* We can examine well-being and values connected with well-being at each systemic level:

● At the *individual* or *personal* level, we can increase well-being by supporting *self-determination* (e.g., control, skills, growth, and self-sufficiency with less frustration); *care and compassion* (e.g., through empathy, acceptance, love, and attention for self and other); and *health* including physical and emotional aspects for self and other.

- At the *relational* level, we can help by *respecting diversity* (e.g., dignity, acceptance, and appreciation of other identities) and *collaborating* (e.g., through participation in a mutually fair process of decision making).

- At the *social* or *collective* level, we can help by providing *community support* (e.g., a sense of bonding and community building); *social justice* (e.g., supporting economic security including food, shelter, nutrition, and health); and holding ourselves *accountable* to help.

(Prilleltensky & Nelson, 2002).

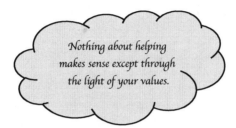

Nothing about helping makes sense except through the light of your values.

Reflect: Time for some critical reflection on these ideas. Consider the community you will be working with this semester. What kind of questions could you ask of your community to determine if needs are being met for well-being and liberation? What action can you take to help?

_____

_____

_____

To achieve the goal of well-being and liberation for disadvantaged communities, we must commit to working on our values and with their values at individual, relational, and social levels in a balanced and holistic way. Of course, you will find that some of these values will be in the foreground and others in the background in the community you serve and you will need to collaborate with community members to move the neglected values into the foreground (e.g., including community support and governmental support). Often, we want to work one-on-one with individuals to help alleviate pain and suffering. While individually focused helping provides useful and valuable ways to meet the needs of the individual served, and makes us feel good as a helper, it may provide only a short-term fix for those suffering from isolation, powerlessness, health issues, victim blaming, discrimination, and/or complacency resulting from more systemic social and political injustice. In these cases, you need to provide a broader focused helping that includes relational and community-based helping that supports long-term transformational social change such as the following:

- Critically reflecting on values that may facilitate or inhibit liberation and well-being
- Striving to ensure that personal power does not undermine the well-being of others
- Striving to enhance values across groups and communities
- Confronting people who subvert values, abuse power, or engage in self-interest that undermines others well-being
- Being accountable to self and others.

As we help others, we may find it difficult to not move into the savior mode. Once we care, we want to help, and this is when we can cause unintentional harm. We need to help by *letting the community* determine what they need and then provide the resources they need so they can help themselves. Let me say that again: We need to NOT determine what the community needs. Deciding what a community needs is just our knee-jerk response (e.g., charity model, go away). *We need to avoid paving hell with our good intentions.* This process of helping is often described as empowerment. To empower a community is to provide space and resources so that community members can create the positive change they need to make to empower themselves. I'm sure you've heard the famous saying *"Give a man a fish and feed for a day, teach a man to fish and you feed for a lifetime."* Well, that is an empowering approach to helping.

> **Go**
>
> to the People
> Live among them
> Love them
> Learn from them
> Start from where they are
> Work with them
> Build on what they have
> But of the best leaders
> When the task is accomplished
> The work completed
> The people all remark
> "We have done it ourselves"
> —Lao Tsu

Reflect: Time for critical reflection on these ideas. Read Lao Tsu's poem and relate to community-focused helping.

_____

_____

_____

Empowerment is a form of power that involves using one's power by giving it to another. Let's explore how you can use your power through empowering actions that promote positive empowering outcomes (see Table 2.2).

As you can see from Table 2.2, your empowering action can support significant positive outcomes for helpees including physical, emotional, and social support at all levels. For example, individuals who receive support from family and friends tend to live longer, recover more quickly from illness, and cope with stress better than those without support. Connection is also important outside of family and close friends such that those who belong to self-help groups live longer and provide a source of support to others in the group. And at the macro level, research reveals that communities with high cohesion experience better education, safety, and health than communities with low social cohesion. We need to remember too that community empowerment has its own challenges, as bonding to confront out-group disempowerment and conflict can undermine potential in-group conflict and inequalities as well as create more division between in and out-groups.

We need to be aware of our own power and others who have more power than they realize. Community empowerment can be inhibited by others using their power inappropriately. Examples include masking power; having too much power in the wrong hands; having too little power in the right hands; defining issues in a way so that people do not know they are losing power; and deflecting sources of oppression, inequality, and domination or excluding issues of inequality, privilege, oppression, corruption, and power from discussion. Power, like helping, is complicated. Power is neither positive nor negative; rather, it depends on how we use it. Many people in the helping professions view power warily, but we must remember power has the potential to lift people up too if used judiciously. People can use power to oppress, resist, or empower.

TABLE 2.2   Impact of Action on Outcome at Three System Levels

System Level	Action	→	Outcome
Individual	• Support critical thinking • Connect with like-minded people • Mentor • Provide value-focused activities • Participate with action groups		• Increased consciousness • More assertiveness • Better self-control • Ability to mentor others • More life options • Real social change
Relational	• Share leadership • Articulate shared vision • Co-decision maker • Team-building training		• Increased resources • Unity with other groups • More connections • Impact on public opinion
Social	• Involved in community, school, legal, government, and business organization • Understand economics and politics • Work toward liberation and democracy		• Improved health and well-being • Enhanced quality of life • Better access to services • Stronger coalitions of support for underserved through policies and initiatives • Tolerance for diversity • More government accountability • Resistance economic neoliberalism

Source: Adapted from Lord and Hutchison (1993), Zimmerman (2000), and Fox and Prilleltensky (2009)

How do I use my power to empower? Well, I have several ways including the one you're reading right now ☺. Other avenues include advising, teaching (e.g., *Community psychology*, *Social justice*, *Voices in conflict*), research, and practice (e.g., working with nonprofits that serve those with less power in our society, poor, working class, and homeless). I bet your instructors have similar avenues.

Now, read the following story and consider how this reflection connects to issues of power.

I (SR) had an interesting encounter with a middle-age professional South Asian woman from a privileged class. I was called in to provide both information and consultation relating to a domestic/ family violence situation. I felt empathy for the woman and was confident to meet her and discuss possible solutions. I had my folder with me containing lots of information on counseling, housing, legal services for women in the United States. My hope was that she would benefit from my support and resources in my role as a culturally competent community consultant and professional.

After a few minutes of friendly exchanges, she looked at me and said: how can you help me? I am a professional and I know how to navigate legal and other professional services for women experiencing domestic violence. My concern is about my loss of status and shame following my decision to leave my spouse and his family. You may not realize it, but I have many upper class, educated, and professional friends and neighbors that I care about as a professional married woman of South Asian descent. What are your experiences with someone like me? If you do not have that experience in your personal network, I doubt if you truly can understand my struggle and offer the right solutions. I know most professionals have expertise and experiences working with women who are victims of violence from underprivileged social classes, am I right? I nodded, reluctantly. She continued: my challenge is, how do I deal with losing status with my family and community?

I felt at some level the inadequacy of trying to help women in privileged positions who need a different strategy. Moreover, my confusion was about balancing both professional help sought by this woman while being pressured by the norm of privileged status. In addition, her ambivalence

about upholding the status quo, suffering in a private setting along with sensitivity to cultural norms, made the situation quite challenging. Some of my questioning related to the type of interpersonal skills needed in relationship to my teaching, consulting, and training. I wondered whether we get sufficient exposure and training to address issues across different social positions, power dynamics, and complexity involved in addressing issues both from privileged and oppressed social conditions. I had to explore strategies much more deeply and at multifaceted levels than what I feel professionals are mostly aware of through education and experience working with survivors of underprivileged class.

This gave me a great insight into cultural complexity and community work for specific groups and role conformity that impact interpersonal dynamics. This reflection led me to understand better the ripple effect of class privileges, post-colonial mentality that still exists in many cultures including South Asia. I would consider this work being challenging but very educational to address the issues of power dynamics across experts and novices.

I believe we need to more deeply explore questions such as, have I contemplated closely enough my own social identity and power when trying to engage in interpersonal relationships with members across different classes? Many professionals find their work effective with helping others due to their compassionate care and empathy toward folks with less privileged status. However, I feel strongly about reflecting and developing skills to work with folks with privilege and power which add more challenges for professionals as well as folks seeking guidance.

Reflect: How might your own social identity and power affect interpersonal relationships across different classes?

_____

_____

_____

COMMITMENT TO SERVE

We explored how your social identity and values can and will impact the help you provide, how you can ask questions to explore community values, and how power can be positively used to facilitate or negatively used to inhibit helping others. Our final area to explore in this chapter is the issue of your commitment. Presumably you are taking a course with a community service component because you want to help others (or perhaps you're here because you had to take this course—sorry), so let's explore how important commitment and accountability is for helping.

When making a commitment to help, we need to determine what and to whom we will commit. For example, our commitment often includes the following:

- Our values
- Our personal development and well-being
- Helping others close to us
- Helping communities worthy of our respect and obligation
- A profession that promotes liberation and well-being.

> *The ultimate measure of a man is not where he stands in moments of comfort and convenience, but where he stands at times of challenge and controversy.*
>
> —Martin Luther King

When we commit to working with others, we are simultaneously committing to engage in self-reflection of our values, our personal development, and our own well-being. By increasing our awareness of the sociopolitical factors that impact helping and people, we commit to promote liberation and well-being for a profession and a community.

Reflection on My Commitment to End Poverty and Homelessness

It may at first seem haphazard who you help and who you don't. At least that is what it seemed to me when I started focusing my helping on working with the homeless communities in the Boston area. However, I soon learned from my continued deep questioning of why I help that the issue of poverty and homelessness is deeply personal to me. Besides being bi-religious in my upbringing, I am also from a working class family. While growing up, like many people, I did not realize we were working class and only began to recognize this much later in life. Going to graduate school, becoming an academic, and being surrounded by middle class people in the workplace, I felt different in some way that was hard to describe, feeling like there was something I did not know, some basic unspoken skill set. This experience is common to many who grew up working class but later find themselves living in a middle class world and is described clearly in the book *Limbo: Blue-Collar Roots, White-Collar Dreams* (Lubrano, 2005). It is from this place of living between these two economic social classes that my interest in homelessness and poverty emerged.

Reflect: Who do you want to help? Why do you want to help this group of people? Look deeply within yourself to find connections with whom you want to help and your own background to find your answers to whom, what, and where is your commitment.

_____

_____

_____

Using Prilleltensky's (2008) and Bronfenbrenner's (1995) models to help us explore what commitment to help means, let's review commitment at the personal, relational, and collective levels to understand how we can help through research and action at the personal (individual), relational, and collective (social) levels to eliminate oppression and promote well-being and liberation. When addressing concerns of social justice, Prilleltensky provides us with many ways we can demonstrate our commitment—through research and action—to reduce oppression and promote well-being and liberation. Review the following and reflect on what you can do to help your local communities in need.

To Reduce Oppression, We Can Do the Following

- At an *individual* level, we can study feelings of powerlessness including learned helplessness, shame, addiction, and mental health issues. We can build awareness and prevent acts of oppressions, and we can use our own power to empower and call out those who use their power to disempower.

- At a *relational* level, we can study the role of political and psychological power, the lack of support, horizontal violence, and fragmentation within disadvantaged groups. We can build awareness of the struggle against in-groups and out-groups, the dominations, discrimination, sexism, and violence suffered. We can build awareness of our own prejudice and participation in horizontal violence.

- At a *social* level, we can oppose globalization, colonization, and exploitation of suffering nations and communities, and we can describe and resist any roles that oppress others.

To Promote Well-Being, We Can Do the Following:

- At an *individual* level, we can support well-being by studying and supporting personal growth, sociopolitical development, leadership, training, solidarity, making meaning, and through spirituality. We can contribute to personal and social responsibility and awareness of subjective disempowerment when in positions of privilege.

- At a *relational* level, we can study and support well-being by increasing egalitarian and democratic participation, trust, connection, and participation in promoting social justice. We can build awareness of the sociopolitical forces preventing solidarity.

- At a *social* level, we can study and support economic well-being and help to create institutions that support emancipation, protect the environment, and promote social justice.

To Promote Liberation, We Can Do the Following:

- At an *individual* level, we can study and support sources for strength, resiliency, solidarity, activism, and leadership. We can resist complacency and collusion with the hegemony, and we can commit to helping others recover their personal and political identity.

- At a *relational* level, we can study and support solidarity and compassion with those who suffer. We can support resistance against objectification of others, and we can help develop accountability processes that support social justice.

- At a *social* level, we can study and support networks to deconstruct social injustice and support resistance to upend structural disempowerment.

Student Voice

Before I took Community Psychology, I never thought of myself as someone who would discriminate against oppressed, financially crippled people. I did not think I added to the problem of the willing blissfulness that is attached with classism. Through my service, however, I found that I was wrong.

At the service site, I was asked to help in the office with tasks like data entry and organizing files. During my time there, I met some of the newspaper salesmen and women as well as writers for the paper. They were all homeless or had recently been housed. I spoke to some of them and listened to their stories. They had been kicked out of their homes, rejected by family, fired from every job, displaced after serving time in the army, or were battling drug/alcohol addiction with little to no help. As tragic as their stories were, they all shared one thing: the strength to keep fighting for a better life.

One man told me that when you are homeless, you are essentially invisible: no one sees you, hears you, asks about your day. I asked why. He said that homelessness makes people uncomfortable. Ashamed, I thought about the times that I had walked past someone homeless without acknowledging them. It was true. I had felt embarrassed . . . awkward?

After I spoke to that man, I left the office and observed the reactions of homelessness around me. These men and women on the street were truly invisible. I was devastated. I had, subconsciously, been part of this problem. I soon changed my approach. These men and women deserve recognition and respect.

Even to this day, if I am out and about in Boston, I will greet a street paper salesman/saleswoman with a smile. They earn 25 cents off that 1 dollar paper and to me, that is noble and honest work.

They deserve a smile and a "how's your day going?" just as much as the next guy. Compassion is so incredibly important yet, so often, taken for granted. During my service, I was forced to see the divide of rich and poor. I saw that ignorance truly is bliss, and I no longer wanted to turn a blind eye to oppression. I wasn't going to cowardly stare at the ground anymore and for this, I am grateful.
—Lorraine Tashjian, Community Psychology, 2011

Reflect: For your final reflection in this chapter, read Lorraine's reflection on community service and consider what can be done by you and others with your community partner to improve well-being, reduce oppression, and support liberation. Reflect on what you can you do at an individual level to ensure commitment and accountability. Consider how you might speak with community stakeholders on how to balance well-being at personal, relational, and collective levels and how you might address potential conflicts of interest that impede well-being and liberation. For example, you might consider how to create safe spaces for dialogue about interests, values, limitations, and ethical dilemmas Your turn: what can be addressed, through research and/or action, at the individual level with your community partner?

_____

_____

_____

Next, let's examine what could you do at a relational level to ensure commitment and accountability. Consider how you could enhance solidarity among stakeholders, creating trusting, feasible, and sustainable partnerships across communities with mechanisms in place to identify potential subversions of collaborative processes and leadership structures that include equitable representation from all stakeholders. Your turn: what can be done, through research and/or action, at the relational level with your community partner?

_____

_____

_____

Finally, let's consider what you could do at a collective level to ensure commitment and accountability. How might you address conflicts, abuses of power, self-interests, or subversion of values that inhibit the well-being of a community? For example, you could explore constructive solutions for creating opportunities for community-based conflict resolution; transparent procedures to openly address opposing views; or issues of abuses of power, the exclusion of members, and self-interest. Last one: what can be accomplished, through research and/or action, at the collective level with your community partner?

_____

_____

_____

We covered a lot in this chapter, and you did a lot of self-reflection. Kudos! Rest, then onward.

RESOURCES

Institute on Character to promote values: http://viacharacter.org/
Journal of Community Psychology: http://onlinelibrary.wiley.com/journal/10.1002/(ISSN)1520-6629
Psychologists for Social Responsibility: www.psysr.org
Society for Community Research and Action: www.scra27.org/

REFERENCES

Baldwin, J. (1963). www.npr.org/2017/02/03/513311359/i-am-not-your-negro-gives-james-baldwins-words-new-relevance

Bronfenbrenner, U. (1995). Developmental ecology through space and time: A future perspective. In P. Moen, G. H. Elder, Jr., & K. Lüscher (Eds.), *Examining lives in context: Perspectives on the ecology of human development* (pp. 619–647). Washington, DC: American Psychological Association.

Fox, D., & Prilleltensky, I. (2009). *Critical psychology: An introduction*. London: Sage.

Lord, J., & Hutchison, P. (1993). The process of empowerment: Implications for theory and practice. *Canadian Journal of Community Mental Health, 12*(1), 5–22. doi:10.7870/cjcmh-1993-0001.

Lubrano, A. (2005). *Limbo: Blue-collar roots, white-collar dreams*. Hoboken, NJ: Wiley.

Prilleltensky, I. (2008). The role of power in wellness, oppression, and liberation: The promise of psych political validity. *Journal of Community Psychology, 36*(2), 116–138.

Prilleltensky, I., & Nelson, G. (2002). *Doing psychology critically: Making a difference in diverse settings*. New York: Palgrave Macmillan.

Zimmerman, B. J. (2000). Attaining self-regulation: A social cognitive perspective. In M. Boekaerts, P. R. Pintrich, & M. Zeidner (Eds.), *Handbook of self-regulation* (pp. 13–39). San Diego, CA: Academic Press.

PART II
BUILDING HELPING SKILLS AND SOCIOPOLITICAL AWARENESS

CHAPTER 3
SERVING AS CHANGE AGENTS

Debra A. Harkins

AIMS OF CHAPTER

1. Prepare you to work with communities in need.
2. Explore interpersonal skills needed to be a social change agent.
3. Assess your leadership, emotional competency, communication, community building, and conflict resolution skills.

Are you prepared to work with communities in need? At this point in the semester, you are likely getting ready to start with your community service. One important, but often overlooked, issue to consider as you begin community service is your own safety. To help you prepare, read two former students' reflections on their community service work regarding safety.

Journal Entry From April 2013

Yesterday something happened. I haven't had the mood nor the strength to sit down and write about it. Today I don't either, I volunteer with the homeless at a soup kitchen (amongst other things). I feel a deep connection with many of these people who come for food. I even began to feel like I might want to continue working with this population. Anyway, what happened was that I started talking with a man at the dinner. "Paul" is a middle-aged, alcoholic man who lost his fiancée to alcohol abuse. He told me she had been bleeding and was rushed to the hospital where she eventually died.

After speaking with him for a while inside the church, I felt we really connected. He was crying to me and everything! The church was closing so they asked us to end our conversation and leave. I told Paul to meet me outside the church on the big steps. We talked for a long time on those steps. He told me a lot of details about his life and even took a sip of his vodka in front of me. He kept touching me . . . I thought it was in a friendly way until finally he hugged me and tried to kiss me on the lips! I was so nervous and scared. I pushed him off in a giggly manner because I did not want to hurt his feelings. Deep inside, I kept thinking I needed to get out of there immediately. Paul told me a lot of scary things about his family! They kill people! He told me he used to steal cars just for the thrill of it and then set them on fire He told me he tried to commit suicide over the weekend. He wouldn't stop crying about loving his fiancée and about losing her.

I feel so dumb, naïve, stupid, moronic, stupid . . . for putting myself in that situation. Thank God nothing horribly bad happened. I'm just worried I will get myself into unsafe situations like this again! Also, will I be able to handle the terrible things my clients will tell me in the future? Will I go through situations like this again? If I were a man, this never would have happened, and it never would have been a problem! I'm meeting with my professor tomorrow to talk about it, so we'll see.
—Laurah Shames, Community Psychology, 2013

Now, read another student's reflection on the same incident:

I always considered myself a very caring person and always reached out to my immigrant community members. There was one crucial experience that I will not forget. As women, we live in a world that may not always be safe. When sexual harassment takes place, we are programmed to sweep things under the rug and "just ignore it." My concern for a fellow classmate after I saw her being too friendly, innocently of course, with another member of the underserved community, raised lots of issues for me. As a survivor myself of various experiences, my body immediately shifted into ALERT mode. The next day I had a serious discussion with my instructor. Leading up to that discussion though, I experienced self-doubt and shame. "Maybe I'm just making too much of a big deal. I will just be told to let it go, and stuff like that just happens." Well I was SHOCKED! My instructor not only gave me time to express my concerns and check up on my fellow classmate . . . but she called a meeting with the board responsible for the outreach program! Myself, my fellow classmate, and instructor sat in a meeting with others to discuss safety protocols so that events like this don't happen again. I feel proud and more closure to know that my VOICE may be responsible for avoiding future harassment against women.
—Panayiota Bakis Mohieddin, Community Psychology, 2013

Reflect: Before reading further, reflect on how you would respond in a similar situation. Who would you seek out for help to deal with a safety concern? How can you prepare yourself to be safe?

_____

_____

_____

Read Laurah's reflections four years after the initial incident.

Journal Entry From April 2017

I remember that night so vividly. I remember how embarrassed I felt to tell my professor what had occurred. My intentions were to prove to myself that I could be a great helper and that I was ready at that moment. What I didn't know at the time was that I first needed to help myself. I had to first be sure that I was safe in the situation before I provided any kind of support. Since then, I have learned that my safety comes first and I need to be sure of that before I help others to be most effective. That night, I thought I was helping Paul. In the end, I only put myself at risk because I was too afraid of letting him down. But what about me? All throughout college I remember feeling eager to start working in the field, but I now understand that no matter how ready you think you are there is always so much more to learn about how to be a better helper and how to handle situations that may feel uncomfortable.

Once I finally spoke with my professor and told her about everything that had happened, we both realized how important it was for this message to be shared. We realized how common it is to feel invincible at that stage in our careers as students because we are so eager to get started with helping every person that comes our way. It is in our nature to want to help others, and that's why we chose this career path. For that reason, it is important for those in the helping field to learn about keeping ourselves safe. My professor and I decided to go to the department of community service to explain what had happened. It was because of my story that the university decided to create a training program that all students take before beginning community service work.

When I think back to that night I realize I thought I was really helping Paul. In the end, I put myself at risk because I was too afraid of upsetting him or letting him down. But what about me? That night when I got home I was so mad with myself. I didn't understand what had just happened. If I was trying to help this man, which is the best thing someone could do for another, then why was I feeling so horribly about it? Even though I felt embarrassed, ashamed, upset, and sad at the time, I now feel grateful because I have made it a point to share that story with as many people as possible with hopes of teaching the lesson that my professor taught me. "What do they say on the plane at the beginning of the flight?" "Secure your mask first before helping those seated next to you." Meaning, always be sure you are safe before helping those around you.

—Laurah Shames, Community Psychology, 2013

HELPING AS AGENT OF CHANGE

Let's explore the inter- and intrapersonal skill sets needed to work in community settings to impact social change. As helpers, we can work inside (e.g., working for the community or as a significant stakeholder) or outside (e.g., as a consultant or community member) of the community as experts, facilitators, directors, consultants, resource guides, or collaborators. Whatever helping role you take with a community will involve collaboration, inclusivity, and interpersonal skills. Let's explore five interpersonal skills you'll need to work as a positive and critical agent for community change:

- Leadership
- Emotional competency
- Communication
- Team or community building
- Conflict resolution.

Leadership

Being a good leader probably seems straightforward, right? Well, as in all things, leading is a deceptively complex skill. Are you a good leader? What qualities make a great leader? Take a moment to reflect on these questions.

An incredible amount of theory and research exists exploring the qualities of a great leader from the fields of psychology, sociology, management, government, and public policy (see Collins, 2001; Edinger & Sain, 2015; Fullan, 2001; Goulston & Ullmen, 2013; Wheatley, 2006). Seven common characteristics of world-class leaders emerge such that the best leaders are:

- *Communicators*. They are empathetic and powerful listeners who meet people where they are.
- *Connectors*. They are focused on winning hearts and minds with the goal of bringing people and ideas together for a common purpose.
- *Collaborators*. They are mentors and coaches who develop others and ironically avoid hoarding power.
- *Citizen exemplars*. They are trustworthy, compassionate, and inspiring activists who guard core values while challenging the status quo. They focus on doing the right thing rather than doing things right.
- *Creators*. They are visionaries who think outside the box with no fear of being a contrarian.
- *Critical thinkers*. They are curious and daring builders of new ways of being.
- *Confident*. They are strong, resilient, and competent people who consistently hold self and others accountable.

Early leadership literature focused primarily on qualities related to *competence*—strength, confidence, and agency—as critical to being a leader. More recent behavioral research demonstrates the equally important interpersonal skills of *warmth*—connection, communication, and trustworthiness—as integral to a leader's repertoire. In *Connect, Then Lead*, Cuddy, Kohut, and Neffinger (2017) draw from literature to describe how these two critical dimensions—competence and warmth—impact how others respond to a leader. For example, if a "leader" demonstrates competence without warmth, they will be simultaneously envied and judged as arrogant. If a "leader" demonstrates warmth without competence, they will be viewed with pity. Those "leaders" without competence or warmth are often viewed with contempt, whereas leaders with high competence and high warmth elicit admiration. Strength and warmth significantly outweigh other qualities in terms of how we form our opinions of others and especially leaders.

Which is more important—competence or warmth? Well, both are important. But the quality that is initially emphasized makes all the difference in whether one is accepted as a leader. Can you guess which of these qualities—competence or warmth—should come first? Most people emphasize their competency first. When you project strength first without building trust, it creates fear. People cannot be creative, problem solve or be productive when they are fearful. Begin building warmth with others—creating an atmosphere of trust and communication. Then, people who feel safe will notice your strengths and competency and hear your ideas. Think of someone who you consider a good leader, and someone who you consider a poor leader. Rate them on their warmth and competence. Does the previous theory and research on leaders align with your anecdotal experience? Are you a happy warrior—someone who exudes warmth first and then, when trust and communication is developed, you express your ideas confidently? Perhaps you need to work on your warmth. Take heart. The rest of this chapter is about assessing and building your emotional, communication, team building, and conflict-resolution skills.

Being an impactful leader requires being able to confidently communicate a powerful, persuasive message. Telling a story with a common goal, using personal pronoun language (i.e., *we* and *our*), and sharing compelling reasons can demonstrate deep connection, compassion, and citizenry. Before we move on, test your skills at detecting leadership through famous speeches by past and present leaders regarding the issue of justice. Read the following quotes from Abraham Lincoln, Bernie Sanders, and Donald Trump in Table 3.1 and reflect on how and why their words reflect (or do not reflect) great leadership.

TABLE 3.1   Quotes From Past and Present Leaders

Four score and seven years ago our fathers brought forth, on this continent, a new nation, conceived in liberty, and dedicated to the proposition that all men are created equal. —Abraham Lincoln	Finally, let us understand that when we stand together, we will always win. When men and women stand together for justice, we win. When black, white, and Hispanic people stand together for justice, we win. —Bernie Sanders	As your president, I will do everything in my power to protect our LGBTQ citizens from the violence and oppression of a hateful foreign ideology. —Donald Trump

Emotional Competency

One of the most critical skills an agent of change needs is emotional competency. Daniel Goleman's best-selling book *Emotional Intelligence* (2010) provides a useful framework for understanding emotional competency through the lens of emotional intelligence (EQ). Researchers clearly find that individuals with high EQ possess strong self-awareness, self-regulation, motivation, empathy, and social skills.

Goleman's EQ skill set is focused at the personal and relational levels of emotional intelligence. Nelson and Prilleltensky (2010) expand Goleman's framework to the collective level, describing the transformational potential of emotional competency to upend oppression and injustice. For example, those with transformational EQ potential would possess the following skill sets:

- Self-awareness of the impact of systemic oppression on self
- Self-regulation including ethics, accountability, and willingness to be challenged
- Motivation, commitment, and pursuit of liberation and ability to mobilize and work with others to create social change
- Empathy including promoting others' self-agency, respect of other's experience of oppression, and awareness of power dynamics
- Social skills to be in solidarity with oppressed, ability to motivate others to promote social justice, and engage in value-based collaborations.

Reflect: Take a moment to reflect on your current emotional competency skill set. What are your personal EQ strengths and challenges (areas you need to strengthen)?

_____

_____

_____

What are your collective transformational EQ strengths and challenges?

_____

_____

_____

Communication

Communication is another critically important skill helpers must have or acquire. Are you a good communicator? What do you think is the number one quality of good communication? Most people think it is to speak clearly and with confidence (Stone & Patton, 2010). While this is important, the number one quality for being a good communicator is LISTENING! Are you a good listener and communicator? Let's find out. Take the quiz in Table 3.2 and then check out how you did.

TABLE 3.2   Communication Quiz

On a scale of 1 (*never*) to 10 (*always*)	Score
1 How often are you preparing what you will say while you are listening?	
2 How often do you get (and stay) off-topic during a conversation?	
3 How often do you fidget or look away during a conversation especially when the speaker is talking?	
4 How often do you interrupt the speaker's story to indicate something similar happened to you?	
5 How often do you monopolize or use big, confusing words during a conversation?	
6 How often do you tell someone how to "solve their problem" when they tell you something?	
7 How often do you lecture, moralize, or command (e.g., *You should X* or *Do X now*)?	
8 How often do you analyze someone (e.g., *You're the kind of person who X*)?	
9 How often do you overgeneralize (e.g., *You always/never do X*)?	
10 How often do you make defensive statements (e.g., *You did X wrong*)?	
11 How often do you talk indirectly to someone as if to third person (e.g., *That was great*)?	
12 How often do you dwell on the past (e.g., *Last time you X*)?	

Source: Adapted from Stone and Patton (2010)

Add up your response for a total score. The lower your score on each of these questions, the better the listener you are. If you scored above a 50, consider three common "listening" pitfalls including talking while listening, interrupting the speaker, and problem solving.

1. *Talking while listening.* When most of us listen to someone speaking, we are preparing what we will say as soon as the speaker finishes their story. Unfortunately, as you engage in this internal preparation, you are not listening! We need to practice listening better by trying to shut down our internal speaker. *What will I say when they finish speaking?!* you might be thinking anxiously. No worries: Try it, practice it and you'll likely find that you have lots to say after you listen carefully. Or, you may find that the most you muster is *Thank you for sharing your story with me.* Many will be relieved and glad you listened. Going off topic is often related to the internal speaker in our heads. If you find yourself drifting from what the speaker is saying, turn the conversation back to the issue before you drifted away.

The word LISTEN has same letters as SILENT. *Coincidence?*

In addition, we sometimes engage in non-verbal gestures that make it more difficult for us to listen. Try looking at the speaker during the conversation and sitting in a relaxed, calm way, to demonstrate that you value what the speaker is saying. Check out some of former student Jerica's suggestions for listening.

Student Voice

Participating in service learning completely changed my perspective. I was ready to save the world. I made plans and executed them; I was eager and efficient. But no real growth happens from a top-down approach. Each community already knows what it needs, and the truth is that the world does not need saving! The people that make up communities need encouragement, empowerment, for their voices to be heard and their stories to be told. The best advice I can give is to keep an open mind. Leave your preconceived notions and prejudices behind. Humble yourself. And listen. Really listen. Allow yourself to be molded by this experience; surrender to change. Open your eyes and your heart and I promise that you will get more out of it than anyone you help along the way.

—Jerica Lucero, Community Psychology, 2008

2. *Interrupting the speaker.* A second common communication mistake is interrupting a speaker. Some of us find ourselves interrupting the speaker to indicate we understand, or that something similar happened to you. We want to empathize, right? But even if we're trying to empathize, this causes several problems: we may not hear their whole story, we may minimize the speaker's feelings when we say something similar happened to us, and we may take up too much space with our own story and fail to give space for the speaker to process their own story.

You may be thinking, *Wait, now I can't even empathize?* You can empathize—but only after you have heard the speaker's full story and you have had time to reflect on whether your story will benefit the other. If we interrupt the speaker, we often are trying to share our own knowledge or experience on the topic. This can lead us into monologues using big, complex words to show how much we know. Instead, once we fully hear the speaker's story, try using brief, simple, clear language as you both take turns reflecting on the issue.

3. *Problem solving.* The third communication mistake many of us make is trying to solve the problem for the other person. You want to help, right? *So, what's the problem with helping someone solve their problem*, you might be asking. Well, it is hoped, you know at this point that helping is complicated. There may be no problem with you solving the speaker's problem IF that is what the speaker asked of you. Unfortunately, much of the time, people are not telling you their story to have you solve their problem but rather to share an experience with you or to process an issue aloud.

This time, you might be thinking, *Wait, so now I can't even help people solve problems?* There are many ways to help someone solve their problems including listening to their story while they process how to solve the problem for themselves. If they don't solve it themselves, they might just ask you. If they ask you for solutions, don't preach, overgeneralize, or command them on what they should think, feel, or do. They might not trust you to be compassionate or understanding in the future. Instead, try direct, clear statements, such as *I can see how X is difficult. Could we try Y? What do you think?* You can also respond with questions that help the speaker explore and reflect on the issue more deeply. For example, you could ask, *Can you tell me a little more about what you think about X?* You can avoid making a speaker defensive by speaking from your own position (e.g., *I feel X when Y happens*), using direct speech (e.g., *I'm frustrated with how you X*), and avoiding overgeneralizations by testing your ideas and allowing the speaker to reflect on those ideas (e.g., *I wanted to check something out with you. I saw X and thought Y and I'm wondering how you see things.*) and focusing on the present and future (e.g., *What should we do now?*).

Now, it's time for you to reflect on your communication skills.

Reflect: What are your communication strengths and weaknesses?

_____

_____

_____

What can you do to improve your communication skills?

_____

_____

_____

As you think about your listening skills, consider how you can get yourself ready to listen to others. One way to prepare yourself is to read books with the voices of those different from yourself. For example, *Voices of the Poor: Crying Out for Change* (Narayan, Chambers, Shah, & Petesch, 2000) is a book that includes people's voices from 23 countries representing 300 communities. Or, listen to the stories of homeless told by the homeless on the YouTube channel *Invisible People*. Seek out videos, books, podcasts, and other media. Learn about your community partner by listening to them tell their own stories.

Community Building

FIGURE 3.1   Five Functions of a Team

Source: Adapted from Lencioni (2002)

Another important skill set to have when engaged in community service is community building. Let's explore team building to help us understand the larger issue of community building. In the book, *The Five Dysfunctions of a Team: A Leadership Fable*, Lencioni (2002) states that team building requires five important skills: honesty, the ability to constructively debate, commitment, accountability to the team, and attention to results.

The foundation of team building is honesty or trust. Unfortunately, it can be one of the most difficult tasks to accomplish, usually due to history and experiences between individuals and groups. Consider the history of race, ethnicity, gender, and class in our society—building trust will be challenging with those whose trust has been broken repeatedly in the past.

Similarly, in *The Decision to Trust: How Leaders Create High-Trust Organizations*, Hurley (2012) describes the mental calculations people use when deciding whether to trust others including personal factors such as one's own personal risk tolerance (how much risk one is willing to take in a relationship), how quickly one adjusts to change, and one's own relative power. Situational factors that impact trust include feeling a sense of security in the environment, shared values, interest alignment, compassion, competence, integrity, and an ability to communicate openly.

So, what can you do to build trust if you find yourself working in a community where there is a history of harm, violence, or distrust among community members? First and foremost, trust must be genuine and cannot be faked. To be honest with others and yourself requires some of the following skills:

- Learn as much as possible about the sociopolitical history related to community harm. When and where did harm occur? Who was involved? Who were the perpetrators, and who were the victims? Were reparations ever made? Is the conflict ongoing? If so, what is needed to repair the harm?

- Be honest and act with integrity and be consistent with all including yourself. If something is not working well, share as soon as possible so community members can address the issue and perform better.

- Share good news with community members as soon as possible. Share bad news too. Keep everyone on the team informed—good or bad.

- Find, explore, and discuss common interests, values, and identity.

- Do your share of the work the best you can. If others feel a need to pick up your slack, trust diminishes. Don't steal credit for other's work. Gain will be short lived and destroy trust with your team. Instead, build team spirit by congratulating those whose work makes for a better team.

- When you make a mistake, admit it and get help if needed. If you hide your mistakes, honesty suffers and leads to more work for others on the team. If you can't do something, be honest about your skills, abilities, and weaknesses. Admit when you are wrong in discussion or action and apologize.

Another important skill set for community building is respecting boundaries of all members. Respectful personal boundaries might include *asking* if you can help with something rather than giving help to a reluctant person. Respectful boundaries around individual possession might include asking permission to use materials rather than using them without asking. Respectful boundaries around thoughts and feelings might include accepting how the other feels without trying to change their mind rather than making fun, putting them down, or arguing with the other about their feelings. Respectful boundaries around commitments might include stating that someone should be asked what they can do, rather than promising something on another's behalf.

Now, it's time for you to reflect on your community-building skills.

Reflect: What are your strengths and weaknesses?

_____

_____

_____

What can you do to improve your community-building skills?

_____

_____

_____

Conflict Resolution

The last skill to discuss relates to community building, and that is when community building is disrupted through conflict. How can we resolve conflicts and build community trust? Before we figure out how to resolve conflict, let's define it. The first words that might come to mind for you might be *war, violence, fighting, argument, anger, misunderstanding,* or *hurt feelings.* You might also acknowledge that conflict is inevitable and a natural part of life that creates tension and leads to change—positive change, even. Although conflict is not inherently evil, how it is addressed can be positive or negative. Many of us are taught that conflict is bad and that conflicts with others are a sign of a failure in that relationship. Rarely do we learn how to constructively use conflict at home, school, work, and in society to create positive social change. Conflict can be beneficial to all involved if addressed from a place of inquiry. When conflict arises, sadly, dialogue is a rarity.

Three Ways People Deal With Conflict

- **Avoid** or **ignore** the conflict by pretending the conflict is not happening. Some of us hold our feelings in to avoid confrontation. Others may get angry with people not involved, like getting angry with your partner after frustration with co-worker. We might get angry with ourselves, thinking, *I'm such a jerk for doing that*. Unfortunately, avoiding or ignoring conflict does not make it go away. Avoidance just causes more negative feelings.

- **Fight** by attacking verbally with insults or threats, either passively or aggressively, or physically. Disputes often escalate to fights when not addressed constructively.

- **Problem-solve** conflict together by determining the root causes. This creates a reframing of the conflict, a deeper understanding, and a strengthening of a relationship.

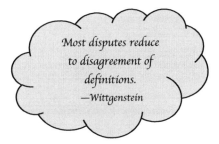

Most disputes reduce to disagreement of definitions.
—Wittgenstein

Myths About Conflict

- *More communication always creates clarity.* **False.** Quality of communication matters more than the number of words spoken.

- *There is always an answer or solution to a conflict.* **False.** Conflicts can be rooted in historical, cultural, contextual, and hierarchical systems that impede one-to-one resolution of conflicts. Many interpersonal conflicts are rooted in systemic issues like religious or racial inequality that trickle down into our personal and professional lives and relationships.

Box 3.1 The Trickster

Two longtime neighbors looked up from their fields—just as the trickster walked by on the dirt road between their farms. On the right side of the trickster's body, she was dressed in elegant red silk, but on the left side of her body she wore tattered rags.

The first neighbor observed to his neighbor, *"What a rich and important person has come by!"*

"Oh no," said the neighbor, "our visitor is a poor but pious soul."

"You blind fool," yelled the first neighbor, *"can't you see?"*

And, so the neighbors argued and argued until it looked like they might come to blows.

Upon which the trickster turned around, revealing to the neighbors her two-sided attire—and abruptly halted the dispute. *"Ah,"* said the trickster, *"so it is—that you are both right, or"* paused the trickster, *"you are both wrong."*

Source: From *Peace Tales: World Folktales to Talk About* (MacDonald, 1992)

- *Managing conflict is primarily about doing things differently.* **False**. The main way to address conflicts is through listening and understanding deeply.

- *Peace is the absence of conflict.* **False**. A lack of fighting does not imply cooperation; rather, it could simply be an avoidance or ignoring of the conflict. This can be dangerous, as avoiding conflict can often escalate into verbal or physical violence. See the trickster tale in Box 3.1.

Conflicts based on cultural and ethnic differences are some of the most challenging conflicts to resolve. Review Table 3.3 to learn how basic differences in worldviews can create huge chasms in attempting to understand each other.

TABLE 3.3   Attributes of Individualistic and Collectivist Communities

Attributes	Individualism	Collectivism
Attachment to group	Emotional detachment	Defined by group
Goals	Individual primary	In-group primary
Family	Small	Large
Behavior	Regulated by attitudes and cost-benefit analysis	Regulated by in-group norms
Conflict	Confrontation acceptable	Confrontation avoided
Countries	Western including US, UK, and many European	Eastern including India, China, and Middle East
Relation to social power	Privileged groups including white, male, straight, and wealthy	Oppressed groups including non-white, female, LGBTQ, working class, and poor

Source: Adapted from Triandis, McCusker, and Hui (1990)

Reflect: Consider your own worldview. How might it be similar to or different from the community with whom you will be working?

_____

_____

_____

Another way to examine conflicts is exploring the worldview differences that exist among various sociopolitical groups. The US and Western societies are generally considered individualistic, but each country has different communities with their own sociopolitical histories and cultures. For example, as we discuss across many chapters of this book, many social identities exist within the United States. Table 3.4 explores worldview characteristics across different sociopolitical contexts.

Consider the community that you are working with and the community that you come from. What sociopolitical context best describes these communities?

Reflect: How might these sociopolitical contexts impact potential attempts to resolve conflicts between you, your community partner, or stakeholders at your community site?

_____

_____

_____

TABLE 3.4   Characteristics of Low-Context (LCC) and High-Context Conflict (HCC)

Conflict Explanation	Low-Context Conflict	High-Context Conflict
Why	Analytical, linear, and logical	Synthetic, spiral logic, and expressive
When	Individual-oriented	Group-oriented
What	Direct, confrontational, and solution-focused	Indirect, non-confrontational, and relationship-focused
How	Open and explicit communication codes, rational rhetoric	Implicit communication codes, intuitive, and affective rhetoric

Source: Adapted from Gudykuns, Stewart, and Ting-Toomy (1985)

Now that you are sufficiently aware of the possible challenges in resolving conflict, let's discuss some constructive ways to address conflict. Following are five steps you can use to try to problem-solve your way toward positive conflict resolution (Conger, 2008; Fisher, Ury, & Patton, 2012; Stone & Patton, 2010).

1. *Listen to all sides.* Many of us are not good at resolving conflict. You know more than most at this point, so you should do the most listening.

2. *Paraphrase* to slow the conversation down and make sure you are understanding.

3. *Identify feelings,* which is extremely important. You may not agree with the other's feelings and that's okay. Acknowledge and validate these feelings. This is not the same as agreement with other feelings, and it does not invalidate your feelings no matter how different. Connecting emotionally is critical to resolving conflicts.

4. *Frame common goals* to remind all stakeholders of common beliefs, values, and interests.

5. *Brainstorm options* toward resolution.

The first step—listening—might sound familiar to what we discussed at the beginning of the chapter. Listening is the first and most important step. Little can be achieved without stopping and listening. Second, make sure you understand what was said by paraphrasing what you believe the speaker said. Be sure to ask if you understood correctly. Do this before beginning to express your feelings or ideas. Third, let everyone express their feelings. They need not agree on their feelings. They just need to hear how the other feels. Fourth, once thoughts and feelings are clearly expressed by all involved, brainstorm solutions together. Many people have challenges getting beyond the second step, so practice with your friends and families until they tell you that you listen well. Challenge yourself by trying this with family and friends whom you know you disagree with and see if you can listen without interrupting.

With whom will you practice this skill? We recommend trying someone easy at first and then working your way up to someone more challenging. Listening take lots of practice. Don't give up. Never stop practicing your listening skills.

Reflect: What conflict resolution step will be the easiest for you? What step will be the most challenging?

_____

_____

_____

In this chapter, we explored the interpersonal skills of leadership, emotional competency, communication, team building, and conflict resolution. These skills are needed to serve as an effective social change agent. Be sure you understand your interpersonal strengths and areas where you need to learn more to best help others. In the next chapter, we explore the intervention approaches available to promote individual, relational, and collective empowerment.

REFERENCES

Collins, J. (2001). *Good to great.* New York, NY: Harper Business.

Conger, J. A. (2008). *The necessary art of persuasion.* Boston, MA: Harvard Business Press.

Cuddy, A. J., Kohut, M., & Neffinger, J. (2017). *Connect, then lead.* Boston, MA: Harvard Business Press.

Edinger, S. K., & Sain, L. (2015). *The hidden leader: Discover and develop greatness within your company.* New York: AMACOM.

Fisher, R., Ury, W., & Patton, B. (2012). *Getting to yes: Negotiating an agreement without giving in.* New York, NY: Random House Business Books.

Fullan, M. (2001). *Leading in a culture of change.* San Francisco: Jossey Bass.

Goleman, D. (2010). *Emotional intelligence: Why it can matter more than IQ.* London: Bloomsbury.

Goulston, M., & Ullmen, J. (2013). *Real influence: Persuade without pushing and gain without giving in.* New York: American Management Association.

Gudykuns, W. B., Stewart, L. B., & Ting-Toomy, S. (Eds.). (1985). *Communication, culture and organizational processes.* Thousand Oaks, CA: Sage.

Hurley, R. F. (2012). *The decision to trust: How leaders create high-trust organizations.* San Francisco: Jossey-Bass.

Lencioni, P. (2002). *The five dysfunctions of a team: A leadership fable.* San Francisco: Jossey-Bass.

MacDonald, M. R. (1992). *Peace tales: World folktales to talk about.* Little Rock, AR: August House.

Narayan, D., Chambers, R., Shah, M. K., & Petesch, P. (2000). *Voices of the poor: Crying out for change.* Oxford: Oxford University Press.

Nelson, G. B., & Prilleltensky, I. (2010). *Community psychology: In pursuit of liberation and well-being.* Houndmills: Palgrave Macmillan.

Stone, D., & Patton, B. (2010). *Difficult conversations: How to discuss what matters most.* New York: Penguin.

Triandis, H. C., McCusker, C., & Hui, C. H. (1990). Multimethod probes of individualism and collectivism. *Journal of Personality and Social Psychology, 59,* 1006–1020.

Wheatley, M. J. (2006). *Leadership and the new science: Discovering order in a chaotic world.* San Francisco: Berrett-Koehler.

CHAPTER 4
INTERVENING TO CREATE SOCIAL CHANGE

Debra A. Harkins and Carmen N. Veloria

AIMS OF CHAPTER

1. Explore the types of social-focused change interventions.
2. Describe how to assess change through praxis.
3. Learn steps toward long-term sustainable change.

8 Questions

REFLECTION: WHY DON'T THEY TAKE ADVANTAGE OF WHAT'S AVAILABLE?

I (CV) am fortunate to teach in an area of the country that's rich in resources. Despite the constant threat of funding cuts for programs that service low-income, inner-city youth, some-how this geographic area offers academic and enriching after-school programs, programs that offer multiple pathways to secondary education, and programs that focus on specific needs of students.

However, offering services and making sure that the individuals who need them the most access them are two different things. A common question that students often ask is: "why don't they take advantage of what's available?" Followed, by "if I only had the opportunity," "what's the matter with them?," "why don't they appreciate what's being offered?," and so forth. This is in response to data and trends that seem to signal that youth do not always participate in activities that would greatly benefit them by connecting them to rich social networks, providing cultural capital and thus setting them on a path to success.

I often ask students to reframe the issue by asking a set of other questions: Are the programs/intervention developed in a way that considers culture (micro/macro), social context, and students' lived realities? Are they developmentally appropriate, planned with a positive youth development frame in mind, and focused on incorporating and building on youths' strengths and assets? Are they truly accessible . . . meaning taking place in their neighborhoods, at convenient times, and structured around other competing interests and responsibilities?

There's a tendency to simply focus on what's being offered rather than when, why, and how programs are being offered. I encourage students to think of program planning and developing as a reflective process that is linked to action, all of which are influenced by an understand-ing of history, culture, and local context. For example, how are the programs framed and even offered? Should programs consider distinct youths' communication styles, interactional styles with adults, peers? Do they need to get buy-in from family members or other community mem-bers (trust factor)? What else should be considered when developing programming so that it is truly accessible/attended?

Many (maybe even you!) are stressed, frustrated, and unhappy with aspects of personal, relational, and social situations. So, why is it so hard to change those things that make us stressed and unhappy? We're in charge, right? Well, sort of. You see, part of the problem is that most of us don't know how to create change for ourselves and others. Creating change is deceptively simple, yet exceedingly complex. This chapter focuses on learning about the types of change or social interventions and how to assess what is needed to change and the steps needed to create long-term sustainable change. First, let's explore the theory behind how to create change—this means understanding the concept of *system*.

What is a system? Most everything you can think of is a system—that is, an organized pattern of behavior—from an individual cell all the way up to the universe—individuals, relationships, organizations, communities, countries, and the world are all systems. So, why do systems—even though they may be ineffective or damaging—not like to change? Psychologists describe this behavior as resulting from a fear of change. Most of us would rather stay with a "damaging known" than enter a space of the unknown. Another way to say this is that systems like to maintain equilib-rium and will fight against change. One way to create change is to determine the *leverage point*—the place where change will reverberate throughout—of the system (Senge, 1990). Sometimes the

TABLE 4.1   Ameliorative Versus Transformative Helping

● Alleviate problem	● Alter system
● Treatment-focused	● Prevention- and liberation-focused
● Apolitical with values in background	● Political with values in foreground
● Immediate individual need-focused	● Sociopolitical need-focused
● Expert-driven helper	● Solidarity and partnership helper

Source: Adapted from Nelson and Prilleltensky (2010)

leverage is a small place, a moment, or a person, but is critical enough to reverberate and create significant system change. At other times, the leverage must be large to restructure the system. In this chapter, we will consider multiple levels and types of interventions available to create change in the system. Like the extensive body of research on leadership, the study of change and creating change is vast. We will limit this chapter to exploring intervention approaches with a more systemic community focus.

Ameliorative interventions seek to *alleviate* living in a socially unjust, prejudicial society. Note that this interventional approach does not seek to change the social conditions or systems of power that sustain the social injustice. This approach is often viewed as a first-level temporary intervention, necessary but not sufficient for long-term social change. Examples of this level of treatment-focused and empirically based intervention include feeding the hungry; individual counseling; group therapy; and providing funds for social services, education, and necessities to an individual or a targeted community. As this approach aligns more with the use of empirically validated approaches, helper values are more in the background. Needs are examined at the personal level primarily (e.g., helping one person, group, or community within the current *hegemony*), and helpers are likely to focus on enhancing protective factors (e.g., self-esteem, self-worth). The goal of ameliorative intervention is to enhance well-being without regard to political issues. Helpers traditionally are expert driven and work in collaboration with multiple stakeholders to intervene (e.g., support around program development and evaluation). See Table 4.1 for differences between ameliorative and transformative intervention approaches.

Transformative interventions are designed to *alter* the conditions that lead to community suffering and tend to be focused on liberation and prevention (e.g., supporting full employment, universal health insurance, promoting a culture of equality, and teaching psycho-political awareness). As this approach aligns with liberation, helper values are unabashedly in the foreground. Needs are examined in relation to power dynamics that impact individuals, groups and the community's health and well-being. Helpers are likely to focus on reducing the systemic risk factors (e.g., racism, sexism, poverty) that create social injustice. The goal of transformative interventions is to address the unequal power dynamics underlying social injustice at individual, relational, and social levels. Helpers become partners working in solidarity with oppressed groups (e.g., partnering around social and political action).

Reflect: Consider the service you have engaged in in the past. Was it ameliorative or transformative? If it was ameliorative, what type of service would make it a more transformative intervention? Think about your current service work too. Is it ameliorative or transformative service?

INTERVENING AT SOCIAL, ORGANIZATIONAL, AND INDIVIDUAL LEVELS

Another way to think about creating social change is by reviewing interventions available using Bronfenbrenner's system model. As you may remember from Chapter 1, Bronfenbrenner and Prilleltensky remind us that we need to practice at the individual, small group, community, organizational, and societal levels. We will review the goals, settings, the role of the helper, and the steps at each of these levels of intervention later in this chapter (see Table 4.2).

Societal level intervention requires change agents to work at the collective level, where our major goal is to create transformative change by challenging the status quo to achieve social justice for those suffering from oppression and scarcity. This type of intervention often happens through work within governmental (such as Department of Education, Federal Reserve Board, and Internal Revenue Service); NGO (non-governmental organizations such as YMCA, Save the Children, and Oxfam); and SMO (small movement organizations such as PETA, Peace Action, and the Congress of Racial Equality) settings. Social movements that create transformative societal change include educating those suffering, and those not suffering, from oppression caused by institutional structures that impede social justice. Consciousness raising of social injustice requires helping people become aware of the sociopolitical and historical roots of oppression that create personal suffering. Unfortunately, social change requires extreme, and usually negative, social events to seep in and change the consciousness of society. Thus, the timing of social movements is unpredictable. When people feel the arrival time of a movement and need to organize for social change, advocates, activists, and policy makers can support the movement through coalition building, media campaigns, lobbying, and protesting to ensure positive social change happens.

Organizational and community level intervention requires change agents to work at the relational level, where the major goal is to create ameliorative and transformative change for those working with organizations that serve communities in need. Organizational intervention can happen internally or externally to the organization (i.e., internal or external advisors and consultants) as well as with the community served. Organizational and community intervention includes working on organizational development issues to support an organization's mission to serve a community in need. Organizational issues might include co-creating and co-implementing a plan for vision building, strategic planning, and leadership development team building as well as communication, conflict resolution, and advocacy training. An organization's internal processes and structures must be healthy and sound to promote and serve the well-being and liberation of a disadvantaged community.

Read how one of our community partners describes the role that service-learning students play in working toward their organizational mission.

Community Partner Voice

When you're engaging in community service, it is important to know your community partner and what is the nature of their work; gathering as much info and getting to know the partner can and will make you more effective. For example, the first group of community service students that worked with our organization took time to learn what we were about and what empowerment was all about; they did this by working in our distribution office, talking with our vendors and staff, participating in our group meetings, and spending time with our editor. By doing these simple yet extremely important things, they helped us with grant writing, editing, marketing, writing appeals, and even helping us put on a successful fundraiser, developing a resource guide, and [holding] education fairs. Many of those students ended up serving on our board and becoming part of our staff. They were successful just by getting to know us.

—James Shearer, Co-founder and Board Chair
of Homeless Empowerment Project,
Spare Change News, Boston, MA

Reflect: In what ways does your community service support the organizational mission and vision? What steps could you take to help your community partner to create more organizational and community change?

_____

_____

_____

Student Voice

One of the most important lessons that I learned from community service work is that . . . it is not about you. I worked as a volunteer editor for Spare Change News. *I understood that the paper itself shed light on issues of homelessness, and the customers who bought the paper were going to be exposed to a subset of the community that didn't get enough shine. It was important for me to preserve the voice and intent of each article I edited. I wanted to ensure that the readers received the sadness, pain, humor, facts straight from the people who were living it every day. I was just the messenger, and nothing else. When I work with a client now, I spend time listening before I talk. I assess the needs of the individual and I make sure that any suggestions I make are client centered and clear of my own bias.*

—Bryant Antoine, Community Psychology, 2012

Reflect: After reading this intervention section, Bryant's reflection, and reviewing Table 4.2, reflect on what steps you could take to help your community partner create more social or transformative change.

_____

_____

_____

Individual and small group level intervention requires change agents to empower individuals and small groups, and this can occur in any setting (home, work, or community). Our role as helper includes being a great listener, meaning maker, problem solver, vision finder, assessor, and implementer. We can explore individual and group vision and mission, how they make sense of work, and help with creating a life or group plan to meet their goals. Implementation, sustainability, evaluation, and accountability are as important at an individual and small group level as they were at the organizational and community level for creating long-term change.

TABLE 4.2   Types of Interventions

	Social	Organizational and Community	Small Group and Individual
Goal	Challenge the status quo in service of social justice	Connect immediate citizen concerns with structures of inequality	Develop solutions that empower individuals and small groups
Setting	Government NGO* SMO**	Internal or external to organization and community served	Anywhere
Role of Helper	Advocate Activist Policy maker	Partner maker Change maker Knowledge maker	Listener Sense maker Solution finder Effort assessor Implementer
Steps Toward Change	Encourage and support people power and collective action to move from consciousness raising to organized action (e.g., coalition building, media campaigns, lobbying, and protesting)	Create awareness and need for change Determine goals Implement intervention Create sustainability Evaluate efficacy Become empowering community	Explore purpose Define work Create goals and plan Implement action Create sustainability Evaluate process Develop accountability procedures

Source: Adapted from Nelson and Prilleltensky (2010)

*NGO = non-governmental organizations, **SMO = small movement organizations

Consider the following community partner's suggestions on what we need to think about when we intervene and try to help empower children struggling with homelessness:

Students should understand that there are some boundaries that the students need to respect when entering these relationships and that extending beyond those boundaries may not be helpful to both the student and the child. Students should also know how the experience of homelessness is traumatic in its very nature, and that one must understand the effects of that trauma to navigate these relationships effectively. To that extent, students need to keep an open mind as to how trauma may manifest in these relationships and make sure to always be honest in dealings with homelessness, not materialistic. Last, students should understand that help is always up to the interpretation of those who are being helped, and that the smallest of favors may be of the greatest importance to those who need it.

— Mary Williams, founder of Homeless Education
Resource Network, Boston, MA

ASSESSING CHANGE THROUGH THE CYCLE OF PRAXIS

Praxis is an iterative and cyclical process, and all elements of the process are bi-directional, impacting each other. Assessing change involves understanding the gap between vision and mission and the history, context, obstacles, and opportunities for individuals, communities, and society. If you understand the gap, you can create and change an action plan. Once action is taken, *vision, context,* and *need* can be re-evaluated to determine the next *action,* and the cyclic process begins again. We will explore praxis even more in Chapter 5, using a needs assessment approach.

Let's provide an example to help clarify. We work with a local homeless nonprofit organization that has a vision to eliminate homelessness with a set of strongly stated values of empowerment and liberation. The current situation includes lacking the economic resources to get the word out, a lack of political will by politicians to get involved, and social and cultural views that view homeless negatively, so few are willing to help the organization. Their need, among many others, includes trying to educate others about the real reasons for homelessness. One action is to collaborate with others who have economic and political power and resources to educate others about homelessness.

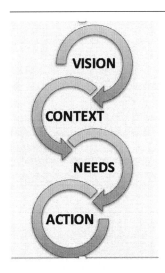

Vision means asking what is the ideal goal for that group, community, or organization and what values guide the vision. What should we be? The first goal is to determine a community's ideal way of being in the world, which often arises from community members' deep dialogue of what they consider to be profoundly and morally important. Sometimes, this is easiest to find by reviewing the "official" vision or mission statement of an organization.

Context refers to what is currently happening in terms of the cultural, social, economic, and political situation. By determining the actual state of the situation, one can get clues of how individuals and communities believe they came into their current situation and understand the social conditions that led to the current state.

Needs refers to what is missing between the vision (ideal state) and context (actual state). By determining the gap between the desired or ideal state and the actual state, one can get clues on how to solve the situation.

Action refers to what can be done to address the need. That is, one can determine a feasible, effective strategy for achieving vision by acting on the need.

FIGURE 4.1   Cycle of Praxis

Reflect: Now reflect on how to help using the process of praxis. Consider a community you are working with or perhaps one with whom you would like to work, then determine vision, context, needs, and action. Note, you likely will need to gather information from your community partner to answer these questions. How can you find this information?

What is the expressed vision for this community?

_____

_____

_____

What is their expressed actual context/situation?

_____

_____

_____

What are the social, economic, and political factors impeding their vision?

_____

_____

_____

What action is needed to realize their vision?

_____

_____

_____

STEPS TOWARD LONG-TERM SUSTAINABLE CHANGE

Change agent expert John Kotter spells out the cycle of praxis and process of change through his research and writing. In *Rules for Change*, Kotter (2012) articulates eight steps needed for positive and sustainable change to happen. Although Kotter was writing for the corporate business world, his ideas apply across any system seeking change.

1. *Establish a sense of urgency.* As mentioned earlier, people and systems fear change even when most recognize something needs to be done. Another related reason change fails to happen is because not all relevant stakeholders recognize how critically important and necessary is the change. Some of this inertia may be apathy, ignorance, frustration, anger, or fear. By examining the context and identifying and discussing crises (past, present, and future) and the potential opportunities available, one can begin to determine what issues need to be communicated and how to communicate them and who needs to be involved in the change process.

2. *Form a powerful guiding coalition.* Critical to the change process is creating a powerful group who can lead the change effort. This coalition should include leaders both formal (e.g., directors, presidents, managers) and informal (e.g., those with social influence and/or intellectual power) who must work as team to lead the change.

3. *Create a vision.* Key to successful change is clear vision and strategy that directs the change. Including people from all levels of the organization into the development of the vision provides necessary commitment for the organizational change. Using current vision and mission "formal" statements may help to guide, build, and reimagine new ideas or return to an original idea.

4. *Communicate vision.* Once the coalition is formed and a vision and strategy developed, communicating the vision and strategy becomes the major task. Using every possible venue available to spread vision and strategies is paramount. By serving as an example, the coalition can model and teach new behaviors that support and develop the vision.

5. *Empower others to act on vision.* Once the vision is communicated and understood, leaders must eliminate obstacles by changing structures that block vision and encourage ideas, activities, and actions of risk takers to help ensure the vision's success.

6. *Plan and create short-term wins.* Every performance improvement must be visible, communicated, and rewarded, creating a win-win atmosphere that encourages further creative improvements.

7. *Consolidate improvement and keep working on more change.* Share and communicate the combined improvements and use the successes as creditability to continue to make changes including systems and policies changes that do not match the vision. Hire, promote, and develop people on the basis of who supports the vision and continually refresh the process with new projects, ideas, and people willing to create change.

8. *Institutionalize new ideas.* Share and communicate how the vision relates to the goals of the organization and create a sustainable succession and leadership plan that continues the vision.

Reflect: When you consider your service site, go through each of Kotter's leading change steps to determine if each action has been implemented at your community site. If interventions have occurred in the past and failed, what step(s) are (were) missing? If intervention is ongoing, what step is needed to ensure success? Go through each step and check off if your service site is leading a successful change process.

In the next chapter, we explore research for social change. Note that in community-based work, intervention and research intermingle, supporting each other toward effective and successful change. This is an arbitrary division here but a familiar distinction to many, so we are keeping it separate for ease of reading and comprehension.

COMMENTARY

Mental Health Justice Issues

By Michelle Ronayne, PhD

Most of us, including myself, go into the field of mental health with the intention of doing good. Unfortunately, sometimes we do more harm than good as we try to help. We want to help people who are facing challenges and work with them to get better. Often, we don't stop to ask what it means to get better and whether that definition is ours or theirs. The reality is, for most of history, "experts" have determined what "well" means. Adults and families come to us attempting to bring themselves in line with what "well" ought to be according to standards set by someone else. Depending on their reasons for being there—personal, state, partner, or school—they may be making decisions out of a feeling of powerlessness.

We have an obligation to keep all of this in mind. Yet, we rarely think of mental health in terms of the disparities that exist or of the feelings of oppression that may be there for the people we treat. There are various types of disparities—racial, ethnic, gender, and class—in how we assess mental health, how we treat mental health, and then in how services are accessed. For example, psychotic disorders are disproportionally *racially diagnosed* in African American/black consumers at rates three to four times higher than European American/white consumers and Latino American/Hispanic consumers are three times higher than European American/white consumers (Schwartz & Blankenship, 2014). However, mood disorders are less likely to be diagnosed and services can be more difficult to obtain among communities of color.

Another mental health justice issue concerns *social class*. For example, children and families in affluent communities may have easy access to multiple services and to testing for their children when they suspect issues such as learning disorders or ADHD. Those services are often harder to access when families are in less affluent areas. Often, families do not have the time to come to the meetings that teachers offer when their children are on an Individualized Education Plan. These meetings occur annually, and teachers feel frustrated that parents, usually in the lower income areas, do not want to attend. However, those parents may work two jobs or lack transportation. Generally, what happens is the child's mental health suffers because the tension between the parent and the school is obvious. As a mental health professional, we can be an important bridge when we are aware of the role of these socioeconomic barriers.

Many mental health justice issues concern how *therapy, medication,* and *hospitalization* treatment connect directly to long histories of systemic oppression of certain groups. It is important to note that many people get better in therapy, with countless studies demonstrating that supportive therapy, interpersonal therapy, and many of the evidence-based therapies improve mental health and growth. An important factor in this is a willingness to be in treatment (Benkert, Hollie, Nordstrom, Wickson, & Bins-Emerick, 2009; Kohn-Wood & Hooper, 2014).

Mental health justice issues occur within *child mental health treatment.* Many families do not want their children in treatment or on medication, and many adults are reluctant to engage as well. We do not often try to engage at systems levels and work toward community-based, prevention-oriented approaches. Even after the deinstitutionalization movement of the 1960s, we still typically rely on individualized community mental health to solve problems. If people do not want it, and if there are forces that can make them get treatment, they are then forced to do so. Unfortunately, overmedicating children, particularly those in foster care, occurs far too often. For example, one governmental study looking at rates of medication in the Medicaid population found foster children being prescribed psychotropic medication at rates 2.7 to 4.5 times higher than non-foster care children. Certainly, they are exposed to more trauma, which could lead to more mental health issues, but the rates are alarming nonetheless. Parents involved with the department of children and families (DCF) or social services, who are often from underserved communities, may feel they must medicate their children because they are advised to do so. They think that they have no choice for fear of the power of systemic forces.

Traditional therapy may be more effective for middle class Americans and less useful to those addressing more basic social issues (e.g., hunger, homelessness, violence). In these cases, community-based helping may be the best way helpers can help. Trying to solve community issues through individual-focused therapy can potentially create situations where the "client/patient" sees these social issue as their individual problem rather than rooted in socio, historical, and political systems that may need to be addressed as a community or collective. It also gives rise to a psychiatric system that sees itself as most useful in "fixing" individuals rather than understanding people as part of a complex and dynamic interplay of their lived social worlds. Often, working with children, we might think 50 minutes of therapy is enough to work on the trauma they are facing, but it does not go far enough if we fail to address the systems that led to the community violence. It is time to rethink our notions of traditional therapy even as we continue to offer it in "traditional" spaces. We need to think creatively about who we involve. For example, newer "wrap around" models of care for families privilege the child and family voice, involve family partners with lived experiences and are trying to bring in peer mentors who have navigated the child mental health system. This is a good start to expanding the views on helping.

Individual therapy for such social issues would need to reframe the work from diagnosing and searching for personality or individual problems toward ways to give voice to create social change.

Often, we spend lots of time trying to figure out what is "wrong" in that effort to make a person "well." Traditionally, therapy has focused on diagnosing an individual with a specific problem, and we are in many instances forced to do so due to insurance regulations. However, it is often useful to tell clients that what is important is the relationship and finding ways to make the changes they want, rather than to focus on the problem that they have.

Traditional individualized therapy remains the mainstay, a therapy that is ahistorical, morally neutral, and politically silent, whereas empowerment models embrace values while exploring historical and social injustice. This is a key difference between traditional "deficit" models of therapy and empowerment-based models of helping. Traditional or deficit models of helping assume that people seek therapy because they have a problem that needs to be fixed. Often, clients will talk about themselves in terms of their problems as if they are their problem. Empowerment-based models of helping (e.g., feminist and narrative therapy are two forms of this therapy) is non-pathologizing and empowering. Empowering-based helping seeks to help people see how they are part of larger socio and political systems in society including the ways our society is racist, sexist, and xenophobic centered.

There are advocates working for the rights of consumers of mental health services or for people with mental health issues that either support more rights or advocate against the use of professional services. These movements have developed out of our history of neglecting the voices of the people we are trying to help. The Icarus Project (theicarusproject.net) is an organization dedicated to providing space for people with mental health issues looking to support one another. They also provide training for mental health professionals aimed at teaching how not to create further systems of oppression. They often have meetings and spaces that are for people with lived experiences only and do not allow professionals to attend so people can discuss any emotions they may be having without fear of involuntary commitment. They advocate strongly for using each other as support. They do not rule out experts when necessary but they make suggestions like have a written plan so people know what kind of treatment you will and will not accept—if there are hospitals you do not want to go to, medications you do not want to take, or a therapist you will call. They are trying to give a voice to people who are often disempowered at a time when they are their most vulnerable.

Working in the field means considering the disparities that exist, paying close attention to them, thinking about what it means to be an "expert," and how to avoid being part of the problem rather than working alongside people to help with their growth. Certainly, we can do this as mental health professionals. We just need to be mindful of our power, acknowledge we have it, not be afraid to join with our clients, provide a safe space, and know that we are not all knowing. We do not necessarily know what it means to be "well." We only know that together with our clients we should be making it better.

REFERENCES

Benkert, R., Hollie, B., Nordstrom, C. K., Wickson, B., & Bins-Emerick, L. (2009). Trust, mistrust, racial identity, and patient satisfaction in urban African American primary care patients of nurse practitioners. *Journal of Nursing Scholarship, 41*(2), 211–219.

Kohn-Wood, L., & Hooper, L. M. (2014). Cultural competency, culturally tailored care, and the primary care setting: Possible solutions to reduce racial/ethnic disparities in mental health care. *Journal of Mental Health Counseling, 36*(2), 173–188.

Kotter, J. P. (2012). *Leading Change.* MA: Harvard Business Review.

Nelson, G., & Prilleltensky, I. (2010). *Community psychology: In pursuit of liberation and well-being* (2nd ed.). New York: Palgrave Macmillan.

Schwartz, R. C., & Blankenship, D. M. (2014). Racial disparities in psychotic disorder diagnosis: A review of empirical literature. *World Journal of Psychiatry, 4*(4), 133–140.

Senge, P. M. (1990). *The fifth discipline: The art and practice of the learning organization.* New York: Doubleday.

Taylor, P. C., & Medina, M. (2011). Educational research paradigms: From positivism to pluralism. *College Research Journal, 1*(1), 1–16.

CHAPTER 5
RESEARCHING TO PROMOTE EMPOWERMENT

Sharon Friedman and Debra A. Harkins

AIMS OF CHAPTER

1. Compare community-based participatory research (CBPR) to other research paradigms.
2. Describe needs assessments, SWOTs, and SMARTER evaluation tools used in action-based research.
3. Learn about CBPR community-based action research from a community partner and student researchers' perspectives.

[handwritten: 14 questions]

IN THE BEGINNING—ONE COMMUNITY-BASED PARTICIPATORY RESEARCH PROJECT

It started when the executive director asked for help to reduce the violence happening in her low-income diverse urban preschool center. Young children (3–5 years old) were getting into verbal and physical fights with each other and teachers did not seem to know how to help the children resolve the daily, ever-increasing peer conflicts. Our first step as researchers was to determine what teachers thought were the reasons for the conflicts and why teachers felt stymied on how to resolve the conflicts.

This required us to create and distribute surveys across the entire urban center including surveys to parents and administrators. In addition, we conducted interviews with parents, teachers, and staff individually and in small groups and conducted observations of teachers and children in their classrooms. We attempted to assess the conflict situation, report back to the community, and then decide together what type of conflict resolution training might work in this setting. This needs assessment served as the first stage of a five-year action-based research project involving three rounds of assessments and trainings. Papers were written for the center, and this work was presented at academic conferences, in journals, and finally into a book (Harkins and Community Action Project Team, 2013).

Reflect: Please answer the following before reading further. Does the previous work sound like research to you? Why or why not?

_____

_____

_____

An important note to make before we move forward is to realize that community-based participatory research is directly tied with community-based interventions. Research and intervention approaches really cannot be separated even though we've done so by discussing interventions in Chapter 4 and research here in Chapter 5. As you'll read in this chapter, much of community-focused research involves assessing and evaluating past, present, or potential social change interventions. This chapter is written in three parts: one from the university partner perspective, the second from the perspective of the community partner who participated in this five-year community-based participatory action research project, and the third from two service-learning students who were involved with the project and who share how their participation impacted their professional careers.

RESEARCH PARADIGMS

Many imagine research as taking place in a lab setting with a participant blind to the real study and the researcher figuring out if their study provided statistical support for their hypotheses. We might even imagine the researcher in a lab coat poring over chemicals, formulas or numbers, trying to reveal information that will advance science. This method of study, called the *scientific method*, seeks objective truth by holding all behaviors (e.g., variables) constant while manipulating only one behavior (usually defined as the independent variable) to determine its effect on a second behavior (usually defined as the dependent variable). That is, does X (first variable or behavior) *cause* Y (second variable or behavior)? Did you know that the scientific method is only one research paradigm of many to study behavior? Let's explore some of the lesser known research paradigms.

TABLE 5.1   Differences in Research Paradigms

Research Paradigm		Method		Example*
Positivism (scientific method) Auguste Comte	Objective ↑	Experimental Seeking to confirm hypothesis with numbers and facts	Quantitative ↑	A positivist fisherman standing near a river bank describes *(without getting his or her feet wet)* the properties of a species of fish *by observing and testing* the general tendency of their behavior.
Post-positivism Karl Popper and Thomas Kuhn		Survey and interview Seeking to predict with numbers and words		A post-positivist fisherman supplements quantitative observations of properties of a species of fish by conducting structured interview of fish to *determine their reasons* for swimming the way they do.
Constructivism Jerome Bruner		Field research and interview Seeking to understand and build theory with words and numbers		The constructive fisherman enters the water, swims and establishes rapport with the fish, striving to *understand their experience* of being in water while recognizing the inability to fully commune with fish, and reflecting on his or her own experience of being fish-like in water.
Critical Michel Foucault	↓ Subjective	Historical and comparative Seeking to emancipate with discourse and experiences	↓ Qualitative	The critical fisherman enables the fish to *perceive the pollution* in their water, to find the source of pollution, and identify harmful effect on themselves. Critical fisherman empowers the fish to organize themselves as a lobby group, protest to Fisheries' Department and advocates on their behalf to have river cleaned up.

Source: Example adapted from Taylor and Medina (2013)

One such approach is action based. When a researcher is looking at social change, the major goal is to engage in an examination that is practical and valid for the immediate situation, and justice oriented. As discussed briefly in Chapter 1, community-based participatory research approaches do not shy away from the subjective aspects of field-based research. This is in stark contrast to traditional forms of research that value and use the scientific method. Banyard and Miller (1998) explain these methodological differences as reflecting deep philosophical or moral differences in the what, where, and why of truth. Methodological differences in paradigms often described in terms of *ontology* (what is considered the form and nature of truth) and *epistemology* (what is considered real knowledge or truth) that lead to differences in *axiology* (relationship of researcher to participants) and *method* of study (e.g., lab-based versus field-based). See Table 5.1 to further examine the differences for each type of research paradigm including the differences between post-positivism and constructivism. One can see how post-positivism aligns with traditional science and how constructivism aligns with more qualitative and critical approaches to understanding.

Taking a closer look at the table, *positivism*, or the standard scientific paradigm, seeks to understand knowledge and assumes this can happen only through strict empirical measurable regularities, whereas, a post-positivism paradigm assumes that a priori (not based on prior study or examination) theories and assumptions impact all observations. Taking the *post-positivism* paradigm further, a *constructivist viewpoint* assumes that all truth is socially created and hence the role of the researcher is to understand the experiences of those investigated. The newest research paradigm, the *critical method*, accepts the assumptions within the constructivist paradigm and adds that power is always implicated in all aspects of experience and investigation including the researcher's power, as well as the social and political power of those investigated.

Each of these research paradigms can be furthered viewed on a continuum of assumptions regarding the value of *objectivity* (e.g., with positivism being the most objective) and *subjectivity* (e.g., with the critical paradigm being the most subjective). Another set of assumptions can be viewed on the continuum regarding the importance of *quantitative* (e.g., with positivism being the most quantitative or number based) juxtaposed to *qualitative* (e.g., with the critical method being the most qualitative or narrative based) regarding methods of data collection. Qualitative-focused research emphasizes the how and why of behavior, whereas quantitative-focused research examines the what, where, when, and who of behavior. While both are important, each explores different facets of behavior.

Reflect: Choose an issue that you would like to study and describe how you would examine that issue using each of the methodologies just described.

Community-Based Participatory Research

When a community representative partners with a university representative(s), there is usually a common interest to explore a community need or issue. When the university and community members work together toward understanding, addressing, and researching community issues, this research process is called community-based participatory research (CBPR). When CBPR works well, partners respect and value each other for the resources and skill sets they bring to addressing the community issue, combining knowledge and action to create social change. Given the complexity of community-based social issues, researchers, funding agencies, and state and national organizations recognize the critical role social, economic, political, and historical factors play in creating transformational social change. Many of these researchers recognize that research must be more systemic and therefore must employ mixed-method research designs, methods, and analyses (including quantitative and qualitative measures). In this way, the research findings lend themselves to evidence-based practice and policy change.

CBPR is very different from traditional, positivist research—which seeks knowledge for knowledge's sake or knowledge to expand a field of study. Instead, CBPR emerged from several disciplines and has its roots in Australia and Brazil, where researchers sought to empower disadvantaged communities using the work of feminist and anti-racist activists. Social scientists incorporated the assumptions that science is politically and historically situated and that those factors consciously and unconsciously impact the research process.

CBPR has grown to become an interactive and collaborative process that involves traditionally "trained experts" working with community members as equal partners to give voice to disadvantaged populations. CBPR is an iterative process that cycles between action, research, and critical reflection. Community members work alongside the research partners to design and implement the project as well as share research finding, resources, knowledge, and skill sets (Troppe, 1994). Some of the principles of community-based participatory research include the following:

1. Using empowerment, social action, and a social justice lens to set goals that create social change

2. Establishing a collaborative and participatory process between the university research team and community members

3. Ensuring that the research includes reflexive practice

4. Valuing and validating multiple sources of knowledge, methods of discovery, and dissemination of knowledge.

Personal Account

I came to graduate school with an undergraduate background exposing me only to traditional, lab-based research. When I heard about the opportunity to do community-based action research in preschool classrooms I was sold. However, the transition into action-based research from a positivism paradigm to a critical paradigm was a challenge. I remember the first day I tried to collect data in a preschool classroom. I came back in tears feeling like "my" research was full of confounds and uncontrolled variables. With support and guidance from my research mentors, I took the risk to embark on a research journey that taught me how to join with a community rather than attempt to impose variables and controls onto individuals. What I found was that not only had I played a role in transforming a community but I had the privilege of being personally and professionally transformed as well. I continue to use this experience to inform how I engage in my role as a clinical psychologist working with children and families as well as consulting with school teams. I also use a critical framework personally in my roles as a parent, partner, and neighbor.

—Elizabeth Doppler Bourassa, Ph.D.

Needs Assessment

As you may recall from Chapter 4 in our review of the cycle of praxis, determining needs to engage in action is critical for helping. A needs assessment is praxis in motion. This assessment begins when the researchers query what needs (issue) the community has identified and what kind of help do they want. Like praxis (see Figure 5.1), a needs assessment explores the following aspects/questions:

- **Vision**—*What should we be?* The first goal is to determine a community's ideal way of being in the world, which often arises from members' deep moral, spiritual, and political thinking.

- **Context**—*What is?* To answer this question, the community members and the researchers describe the current state of affairs, giving attention to how the community got to the point that has raised the issue/need. A brief history of the social conditions will also inform the direction of the research.

- **Needs**—*What is missing?* Through open-ended interviewing, the researcher can solicit from the community members the ideas they have to obtain their desired state and to solve their current situation.

- **Action**—*What can be done?* Upon review of initial findings, the researcher works with the community members to determine feasible and effective change strategies based on the current situation.

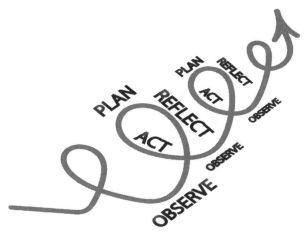

FIGURE 5.1   Praxis Cycle

The next step in this process is to gather data that can answer the questions, What are the strengths, assets, and resources that can be used to address community needs? Could the community benefit from a specific program? Thinking about these questions will provide some guidance about the kind of data to collect and how those data are gathered. Some examples of data collection include observations, surveys, interviews, focus groups, photos, archival data retrieval, and organizational documents review.

Another effective assessment tool is a SWOT analysis. Through surveys, interviews, and focus groups of community members at all levels, a SWOT analysis explores the Strengths, Weaknesses, Opportunities, and Threats in the agency or organization. To obtain a fuller picture, interviews should be conducted both within and outside of the target environment. Information from such an analysis can help an organization develop relevant mission and vision statements as well as an operational strategic plan with specific action steps. See Figure 5.2 for an example of a SWOT analysis.

> **Reflect:** With the knowledge that you have gained so far, what are some questions you would ask participants and stakeholders to get a sense of the strengths, weaknesses, opportunities, and threats of an organization or agency? Then read the next paragraph to learn more about internal and external factors.

_____

_____

_____

One other way to look at the quadrants of the SWOT analysis is to look at the positives and negatives both internally and externally. Strengths and Weaknesses refer to the *internal* factors that may contribute to success or failure. Opportunities and Threats refer to *external* factors that may contribute to success or failure. In addition, how participants perceive an operation/program is just as important as what is quantitatively happening. Oftentimes a SWOT analysis helps an organization see where they can be challenged from a positive perspective and perhaps drop something that may be holding them back.

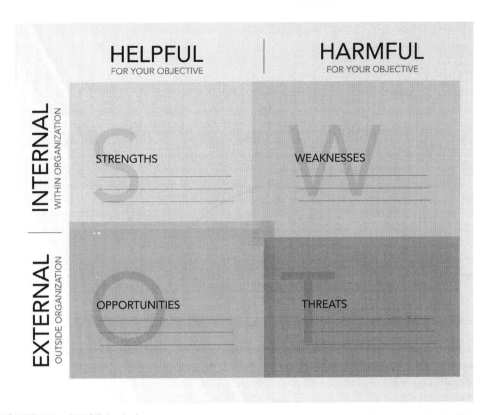

FIGURE 5.2   SWOT Analysis

Program Assessments

While a SWOT analysis looks at a program or event from four viewpoints, a program evaluation using the SMARTER framework can help the evaluator assess a program while it is in its developmental stage (Nelson & Prilleltensky, 2010). This perspective can be very useful for CBPR. Its flexibility helps to address problems or concerns of the community members as they emerge, rather than wait until the "research" period is complete. It also can be used to evaluate program goals and objectives and to test if they are understandable to all participants. These goals and objectives, along with the action plan, are common elements that one would find in a strategic plan. When you go to your field placement, ask about the agency's strategic plan and find out if they have used it to help evaluate their program. Once you see what they have done, use the SMARTER elements shown in Figure 5.3 to determine the following:

● Did the goals have action steps?

● What worked? What failed? Why?

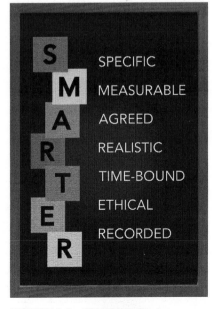

FIGURE 5.3   SMARTER Goals

- What needs to be changed to benefit the target audience/behavior?
- What is relevant to success?
- Can it be replicated?

Examining a program using this lens can let you know about the efficacy of a program. This can be further understood and examined in terms of program outcome (did the program run well—sometimes called *reliability*; did the program do what it said it would do—sometimes referred to as *validity*). In conducting CBPR, these are extremely important questions that need answers. And yet many organizations have neither the time nor the resources to conduct this kind of study. Using the CBPR approach can be extremely helpful to a community. It helps the members determine whether the programs they run are useful to those they serve.

> **Reflect:** Now, it's your turn to think about what type of assessment would be most useful with your community service site. Pick an issue or program and then create a set of questions and determine the type of data needed for one or more of the following types of research assessments. You could do this together with your community service site or share with your site representative.

_____

_____

_____

COMMUNITY PARTNER (SF)

I will discuss the CBPR from my perspective (as the community partner) and describe what you (the student) may want to consider as you get involved in such a project and the lessons learned from my perspective. Here is a bit more background regarding the genesis of this partnership. The reason for the initial request is highlighted at the beginning of this chapter. I would like to add here that the university partners, from a major institution in the Boston area, included undergraduate and graduate students as well as the lead researchers who are professors at the university. I reached out to the university because I was alarmed by the amount of fighting among the children about toys, sharing, hitting, and just plain roughness. The teachers were asking for help and were becoming increasingly frustrated by issues, including lack of resources, the high turnover rate among the aides, and lack of support from the administrative team. I had already brought in training for staff around age-appropriate early childhood development. I wondered why the training was not effective in diminishing the frequent altercations observed on the playground and in the classrooms, especially among the preschoolers. Why did the training fail? What was I missing? Why were the teachers not appreciative? Why were the students still fighting? Why was the morale still so low and the staff turnover so high?

> **Reflect:** Take a moment and ask yourself how you would answer those questions.

_____

_____

_____

MORE BACKGROUND INFORMATION

The early learning center (ELC) was very spacious, with two infant classrooms, four toddler classrooms, six preschool classrooms, and two classrooms each for kindergarten, first, and second grade. There were two cafeteria spaces, a full kitchen, and two outdoor and indoor play spaces as well as office spaces for administrators and support staff and space for teachers to have breaks and lunch. The program served about 350 children and hosted a staff of about 60 full- and part-time educators. The ELC served two primarily low-income communities with the following demographics:

> 37.7% identified as Caucasian, 23% Latin American or Hispanic descent, 13% African American or Cape Verdean, 3% Asian, and 26% undisclosed. And, 98% of the children qualified for free breakfast, lunch, and snacks.

When a community enters a partnership with a university, I believe that it is important to have a conceptual framework from which you can have the "long view." Throughout my career, I have been greatly influenced by the work of Abraham Maslow and his hierarchy of needs.

MASLOW'S HIERARCHY OF NEEDS

Generally, physiological needs (food, shelter, etc.) must be met first, then needs for safety, followed by belonging and on up to acceptance of self and others (see Figure 5.4). At the ELC, the teachers were asking for help. The teachers—all of whom came from the community—did not want to be perceived as not being able to handle their classroom. Their expectation was that the

FIGURE 5.4   Maslow's Hierarchy of Needs

administrators (all of whom also came from the community except me—and who the teachers perceived sat in their offices all day) should step in and do their jobs by fixing the problems both behaviorally and resource wise in their classrooms. The administrators and the executive director at the same time felt strongly that the teachers are responsible for handling the children in the classroom and that they respond to those issues. This conflict in expectation led to all sorts of problems that spanned the first three levels of the hierarchy of needs. Although most of the basic needs (biological and physiological) were met, the needs of safety and belongingness were essentially absent. There were numerous complaints about poor communication and substantial lack of support. The teachers felt like they were on their own. As the teachers at the center continued to ask for help, I then reached out to the university. The initial step in the partnership was to develop a needs assessment. This required participation from many areas of the organization: teachers, aides, parents, and administrators as well as support staff.

> **Reflect:** With what you have learned so far in your readings, what do you think were the factors that contributed to the unease and frustrations at the ELC? How would you begin to interact with this community partner?

_____

_____

_____

THE STUDY AND LESSONS LEARNED

For the rest of this chapter, I will share some elements of the study and reflect on the lessons learned from the point of view of the executive director and the community partner. I recognize that I am one voice in this multiyear project. The details of this study as well as other voices and perspectives can be found in *Beyond the Campus: Building a Sustainable University—Community Partnership* (Harkins & Community Action Project Team, 2013).

The project went through three main phases. Phase one had an exhaustive needs assessment, conflict resolution training, and extensive data collection and analysis. Phase two brought along a second needs assessment, analysis, and team building for the administrators. Phase three included yet another analysis and interviews with the executive director. The perspective that I present is from the administrative point of view. While not all community-university partnerships will be as extensive as the one we went through, I believe that there are important aspects of the study that can provide guidance as you enter these relationships.

REFLECTION ONE

The assessment portion took much more planning and much more time to conduct than we had anticipated. As immediate results were not present, the staff grew very impatient. For example, during this time, one of the teachers said that she needed help right away to deal with the problems she was experiencing and did not have time to wait for the "know-it-alls" to come in to fix the problem. It was then clear to me that the teachers wanted the problems to be fixed right away by the administrators. And, as the fixes could not be made fast enough for everyone, the tension mounted. This sense of urgency and the need to fix the problem is very common in a lot of organizations. So, one important aspect to know for yourself as you enter a partnership with a community is how much tension can you hold while an intervention is being crafted.

REFLECTION TWO

I want to share with you one of the set of dynamics that were present when I had the initial discussions with the university partner. It is important to understand the organizational dynamics of the place in which you are working. Using Maslow's paradigm that I outlined earlier, I understood that the conflicts in the center spanned all three of the lower levels of Maslow's hierarchy of needs. These were articulated by complaints about poor communication and lack of support as well as a high staff turnover rate. Missing was a sense of belonging and a pervasive lack of trust. As the project got underway, I felt that there was no room for trust because of the assumptions that were being made on all levels of the organization's structure and that the assumptions were different from the parents' perspective, the teachers' viewpoint, and that of the administrative team. As a result, energy was expended creating alliances that would support one's viewpoint. And when competing viewpoints met at the classroom door, chaos often ensued.

When the thought of bringing in conflict resolution training into the center was first mentioned to the staff, the initial reaction was one of skepticism and resistance. Doing something new was viewed as a threat to the status quo, especially for those who were marginally satisfied with the current system. It is a phenomenon of human response that no matter how bad things are, many times staying with something that is familiar is better than welcoming something that you do not know or understand. So, for many of the staff, bringing in an outside entity meant change, and change was inherently bad.

Reflect: Faced with such a reality, or with the understanding that change is not always appreciated, welcomed, or wanted, how would you enter this environment? Write some ideas here:

_____

_____

_____

OTHER CONSIDERATIONS

Before you go to the community site and start an intervention, you might want to consider the following elements: who are the people with the most power and privilege? What are the power dynamics? What does the diversity look like? Are people in the community aware of the many cultures around them, and how do they interact with each other? Are they able to communicate with each other, and what does that communication look like? What are the linguistic characteristics of the community? Your observations in these areas will greatly impact how change may be made, how ready the community will be to accept what kind of changes are determined to be needed, and what you will need to consider as you craft an intervention that will make sense for the community participants.

REFLECTION THREE

Whenever you initiate change, you should expect some pushback. In my case, the pushback was enormous. I had to manage resignations, behavioral dynamics from remaining staff that included skepticism, outright disregard for following established procedures, and an increase in formed alliances that created a hostile environment. These dynamics were deeply experienced by many of the children and contributed to their increased sense of insecurity, unease, and aggression.

MORE BACKGROUND

As a seasoned program administrator, I had many years of training and experience with models of change, especially those of Prochaska and Norcross (*Changing for Good*, 2007) and Lencioni (*The Five Dysfunctions of a Team*, 2002). Check out Prochaska and DiClemente's stages of change model (1983) in Table 5.2.

One thing to note is that with an understanding of change from this perspective is that lasting change goes through distinct phases and that it takes time and support. And the support shifts as change takes place. I recommend that you become familiar with these change models, as they can help you through the tough times and lend guidance for the long view. Additionally, these models give you some assistance with determining how the partners in the community may respond to the intervention.

TABLE 5.2 Prochaska and DiClemente's Stages of Change Model

Stage of Change	Characteristics	Techniques
Pre-contemplation	Not currently considering change: "*Ignorance is bliss*"	• Validate lack of readiness • Clarify decision is theirs • Encourage re-evaluation of current behavior • Encourage self-exploration • Explain and personalize the risk
Contemplation	Ambivalent about change: "*Sitting on fence*"	• Validate lack of readiness • Clarify decision is theirs • Encourage evaluation of behavior change
Preparation	Some experience with change: "*Testing waters*"	• Identify and assist in problem-solving obstacles • Identify supports • Verify they have skills needed for change • Identify areas for skill development • Encourage small, initial steps
Action	Practice new behavior or skills for 3–6 months	• Focus on restructuring and provide support • Bolster self-efficacy to deal with obstacles • Combat feelings of loss and support long-term benefits
Maintenance	Continued commitment to sustain new behavior	• Plan/provide follow-up support • Reinforce intrinsic rewards • Develop plan to address relapses
Relapse	Return to old behavior: "oops" "*Fell off wagon*"	• Evaluate triggers for relapse • Reassess motivation for change and barriers • Develop plan to reinforce desired change

Source: Adapted from Prochaska and DiClemente stages of change model, 1983

CONSIDERATION TWO

When you enter a community, it is important to have an idea of how long you will be there. It is equally important for you to have a good idea of how you will leave! This may seem counterintuitive at first, so let me explain. Unless you live in the community and plan to participate for a long time (more than two semesters), you will always be an outsider. At the same time, you will need to work on gaining trust in the community for which you will be engaging in the partnership. In my experience, it is important to be able to interact in ways that both support the larger community, support the issue for which they have requested help, and give community members something that will last beyond your stay.

> **Reflect:** As you get ready for your community service project, how do you see yourself entering the community, and how will you exit? Write your thoughts here:

_____

_____

_____

MORE BACKGROUND

The university partner completed an extensive assessment, and after the presentation of the results, the community agreed that conflict resolution training was the way to go even though everyone was a bit wary of what that would bring. As the executive director, I was very supportive of the training. I had studied a bit of the work of Peter Senge (1990, 1994) and had what I thought was a good handle on the dynamics of the organization for which I was responsible. I also knew that I wanted an intervention to be one that the community could use immediately as well as after the partnership ended. And I knew that I would not be connected to the community in another 10 years or so. This sense of community learning is inherent in Senge's model and one that I believed in deeply. One aspect of the model that is related to a partnership experience is the Ladder of Inference, which reveals the steps that occur in our thinking that often lead us to make the wrong conclusions. As we move from an individual fact to meaning, assumptions, decisions, beliefs, and finally action, we often forget that we acted based on limited data. We need to be aware of how we often jump to conclusions based on our own meanings, assumptions, and beliefs. A reflexive loop is an endless loop of selecting data that fit our beliefs.

The reflexive loop is talked about in different ways in other chapters of this book including as praxis. At the same time, it relates to beliefs that you may bring to your partnership. As you go up and down the ladder, it is important to keep in mind the assumptions that you bring to the community and the assumptions under which the community is operating. Some of the questions to ask yourself as you engage in the partnership are as follows:

- What assumptions do I have going into the community?
- What kind of beliefs do I bring?
- How are these beliefs influencing my first impressions?
- How are the beliefs going to influence the development of relationships?

Reflect: Take a moment and write some of the assumptions that you hold and what you think the impact of those assumptions could be as you enter the community in which you will partner.

_____

_____

_____

As the partnership got underway, there was a list of beliefs that were important to me:

1. If I kept my perspective on the horizon, the community and I could weather the pushback and the difficulties that change brings.

2. That the community could change, and it could be a safe and welcoming place for everyone: staff, children, and their families.

3. That the intervention would be worth the investment in time and energy.

LESSONS LEARNED

I learned many valuable lessons during the community-university partnership and I want to share with you here two of them.

1. _Trust._ To begin this sort of a project, a high level of trust is needed between the university and the community partner for the CBPR to succeed.

Before the initial needs assessment, I had a prior professional knowledge of the work and skills of the lead researcher. Having this knowledge brought a level of trust to the planning and implementation. Referring again to Maslow's hierarchy, this level of trust allowed for the movement between the levels so that the CBPR could become operationalized.

2. _Planning takes time._

Because I missed some key aspects of this "living organism" (as described in Senge's work), the changes that I was expecting did not happen. The problems and the conflicts did not go away. I did not have a good read on the intra-systemic relationships and the power of coalitions that already existed in the community before I arrived and continued to develop as I tried to initiate change. As a result, the work of the partnership took a solid five years instead of the two years that I had initially envisioned!

MORE INFORMATION

The next step in this journey was to develop and then introduce a model that would incorporate the needs as found in the assessment and then to do the work of training that would bring the community to the place that would bring, most important, safety and well-being and have a community where learning is not only valued but also a primary dynamic that enhances all relationships. Figure 5.5. is the schematic of the empowerment model used over the three-year period and the "glue" that held the community and the university partner together through the difficulties of change.

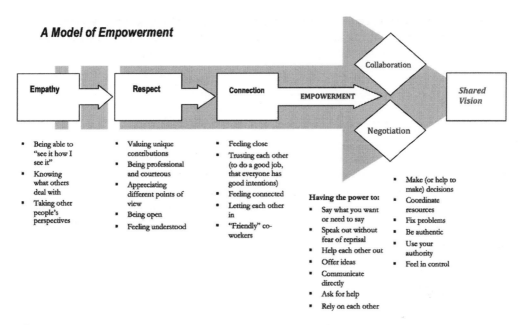

FIGURE 5.5   Empowerment Model

Source: Adapted from Harkins with Community Action Project team (2013)

It is from this model that the university partners developed training for the teachers, aides, parents, and eventually the administrative staff.

Reflect: What were some of the elements that helped create some buy-in for the skeptical staff? And what did the university partner need to know as the training was shaping up? Before we go on, what are some of your thoughts?

_____

_____

_____

REFLECTION FOUR

From my perspective, a few things needed to be in place.

First, it was paramount that the students doing the training and participating in the community had to have the following in place:

● A full working and empirical understanding of the model they were using

● An ease with the language of the model and ability to communicate that in words the community in which they were working could easily understand

● That all members of the university team whether graduate or undergraduate students shared the vision of growth and change for the community

- That the members of the team understood each other's strengths and weaknesses
- That the team had a clear understanding of their roles as trainer/support person/evaluator in the project.

The other important aspect that occurred and was important for buy-in by the community was that the university partners practiced the model in their interactions with the community members. The university partners met with staff and parents, conducted formal interviews, observed classrooms and over several months, developed an intervention that focused on conflict resolution skills that made sense for the community. This model was one that could be used not only by the teachers in their classrooms but also by parents in their homes. In this way, the children who were exposed to the conflict resolution model would also have the benefit of consistency. This training required a lot of support from the partners and time commitment from staff. Eventually, the teachers noticed shifts in behaviors. Before I list some of the changes, here is the essential conflict resolution model (Evans, 2002):

1. Approach calmly
2. Acknowledge feelings
3. Gather information
4. Restate the problem
5. Ask for solutions and choose one together
6. Follow up.

While at first blush, this may seem simple and straightforward, for the staff, parents, and administrators, it was very difficult to actualize.

Reflect: With what you have read so far, what are your ideas about why this 6-step approach to resolving conflict would be so hard?

_____

_____

_____

Let me share with you some of the dynamics that made this challenging. One aspect not to be overlooked was that with the learning that was going on, and the increased stress due to the implementation of something new, the university partner was an outsider and that in and of itself was a big hurdle. One aspect to keep in mind is that no matter how well the community partner welcomes you, it is important to maintain a perspective that you are intruding just by the mere fact that you come with something different. You are disrupting the status quo. Some members of the community will want that and welcome it and others will not. Understanding those nuances and how to address them can mean all the difference between a successful partner intervention and one that is replete with unsuccessful results.

A second aspect is that everyone needed time and space to figure this out. Figuring it out meant that staff, parents, and administrators needed to try on the model, feel its awkwardness, stumble and be supported as they learned, and have spaces where it was safe to do this hard work. The "critic" in all of us had to take a back seat while the learning took place. The teachers needed support while they learned the language, they needed space to rest and recharge, and they needed a place to meet with each other to share and learn together sometimes by themselves and sometimes with their university partner. The support of the administrative team and a restructuring of the workday was needed to do this. Again, it took about two years for all of this to happen!

A third aspect was that I, the executive director, needed the support of the university partner, as we together waded through this uncharted water of change. Even though I knew and had experience with the models that were being brought into the center community, I was not fully prepared for the disruptions and the increased tension and conflict that would arise. I was particularly struck by the tension that emerged between the teachers and the administrative staff.

Reflect: Take a moment and ask yourself what you think was the emerging problem. Why was there an increase in animus and conflict between the teachers and the administrative staff?

_____

_____   12

_____

REFLECTION FIVE

As we set out well intentioned, the training was focused on the teachers, parents, and children and the quantitative analysis data showed that the intervention produced some very good and reliable results: The classrooms were calmer, the teachers were happier being with the children, and relationships with parents were much improved. And importantly, the previous high turnover rate was substantially reduced. We now had a much better organizational system that was eager to learn together. Almost!

What the university partner and I neglected was a focus with the administrative team—an important component in the organization. I, as executive director, assumed that as the teachers learned and as the levels of conflict in the classroom and in the play yard diminished, the administrative team would pick up the model, learn the language, and support the teachers. Well, I was wrong! What really happened was that the teachers felt empowered and began to use their knowledge and power to ask for more resources and support—support from their supervisors that the supervisors did not know how to give because they did not fully understand the models, and they did not have a thorough understanding of the impact of the changes that had taken place. This disconnect resulted in additional conflict for the administrative team, including me, the executive director. We were not at a point where power could be shared. Trust between the teachers and the administrative team was not quite there either.

After two years of the project, with their new skills, understanding and power, the teachers grew to resent some of behaviors and attitudes of the administrative staff. They felt that they had been through this training and their supervisors (the administrative team) had not and therefore did not understand what they were doing and why.

Thus came another two years of training; this time for the administrative team. What ensued was another needs assessment, specific training in the models of empowerment and conflict resolution, and specific training and support in leadership development. The teaching staff closely observed the mechanics and responsiveness of the administrative staff to this training.

This process of change was just as difficult for the administrative team as it was for the teaching staff. At the same time, the specific issues were a bit different. For example, the administrative team complained that they were not getting good direction from the executive director, and they refused to put down in writing what they were frustrated about regarding their job responsibilities. Once

I, the executive director, better understood that there were similar issues that were seen in the initial part of this community/university collaboration, a plan for remediation could be developed. Some of those issues included clarifying administrative roles and responsibilities, ensuring that the administrative team knew both the model and how to operationalize the model into practice. The team also needed to learn good supervision skills. One other very important element was that the administrators did not have a good sense of their own strengths and weaknesses, and they were not able to articulate their strengths in relation to the empowerment model. This is where the university partner was crucial. One of the researchers used the Myers-Briggs assessment to help the administrative team learn what were their strengths and how the team members connected to each other.

Understanding those relationships helped to identify new ways in which the administrative team could support each other as well as the rest of the center staff. Once the relational areas were better understood, roles clarified and support provided around skill development, the team began to work with each other, rather than at each other. One of the benefits of this shift was that once the teachers saw that the administrative team was also engaged in learning and implementing what they had learned, the teachers were able to begin the process of trusting the rest of the community, and the feeling of belonging opened opportunities for better communication and problem solving. This growth was demonstrated in the last round of interviews, observations, and quantitative analyses that was completed by the university partner. In addition, throughout the entire project, it was paramount to keep front and center the overall goals for both the community and university partner.

And last, the community/university partnership would not have been successful if the university had not made a commitment to be in the community for the long haul. That commitment helped to show the community that growth can happen, and when the commitment is there, lasting change can happen.

> **Reflect:** As you think about your role in the partnership experience, what do you think is important in being effective? How do you know that what you are doing is meaningful to the community?

REFLECTION SIX

I want to conclude with some observations and anecdotes regarding the community/university partnership. Some of the changes that occurred during the partnership helped to sustain the center as it sought new opportunities for continued engagement in learning and procurement of resources that would benefit the staff, children, and their families.

1. It was a lot of very hard work from everyone who participated. Some staff left as the project got underway because they did not want to do the work and some could not see the benefits of the intervention. As new staff came on board, the university partner had to invest in additional hours and training to get the new members up to speed.

2. As conflicts became more pronounced, it was important to have the expertise of the university partner to help guide the process. It was very important to have the university partners well trained in the model that they were using. Staff and students had occasion to engage

in feedback meetings both at the university and in the community setting, and those exchanges helped to enhance the trust and build confidence in the model that was being implemented.

3. While I have not talked about it much in this chapter, supervision was key during the intervention. After the intervention, the administrative team developed a more consistent supervisory schedule, as did I. Time and space was made to meet with teachers, and both the administrators and teachers continued to learn together.

4. From the lessons learned, the center embarked on a rewriting of its vision statement. A team was formed, communication remained active among all community members, including some students from the after-school program, and the resulting vision statement relied on the empowerment model that was introduced at the beginning of the project.

5. The conflict resolution model was made available to parents during the study, and the parents who engaged in the model reported that they saw improvement in their children's behavior at home and they had better and more in-depth conversations with the teachers.

6. Some staff recognized that they were having difficulty with the resolution of a conflict and requested help from the executive director. Prior to the intervention, the problem would have gone underground, resentments would have been built, and the teaching in the classroom would have continued to suffer.

7. New learning takes time to become part of a system. With support and time, the staff and administrators found their voices. As they became more empowered, the system became more dynamic. Many appreciated that conflict was a part of daily life. Now, all members of this organic organization had the tools and support among each other to solve the problems in a consistent and reasonable way. Members of the community feel supported, and even the children have a way to resolve conflict among themselves, sometimes without the intervention of the adult in the room.

REFLECTION SEVEN

I want to discuss one last, but very important, part of any partnership: the exit. The success of the exit can be seen in what the university partners leave behind.

Reflect: Before I go further, and with the information presented in this chapter and in others throughout this book, how would you exit your project, and what would you hope to leave with the community?

_____

_____

_____

The following elements summarize what I believe are important in the community/university partnership:

● Development of a model that makes sense for the community
● Provision of support and training that is generic to the model

- Clear entrance and exit for the community
- Flexibility on the part of the university to meet challenges that emerge as intervention is implemented
- Time and dedicated space for meetings and reflection.

With this clear articulation and planning, I believe that the university (and the students) can have a successful experience with a community member. The strength and success of the partnership can also be appreciated once the university students are gone. In my case, I knew that the partnership was successful. Here are some examples.

1. The center developed a vision statement that used the strategies and communication pathways that staff learned during the partnership.

2. One parent who had, over time, enrolled four children in the center and who went through the conflict resolution training, remarked that she has used the model with other members of her family and that she has had increased confidence in talking with teachers in the public school system. She is now a better advocate for herself and her children.

3. Staff continued to use their voices to get resources in their classrooms.

4. The executive director used the success of the training to leverage participation in other projects that would support continued growth for the program. Notably, after the community partner left, the center was selected to participate in a three-year evidence-based literacy program for the preschool program.

In short, when the intervention is planned and developed, it is at the same time important to look ahead to what will happen when you leave. Organizational change takes time, commitment, endurance, trust, focus, shared values, and goals. And sometimes you, as the university partner, will not know the enduring results of your intervention. Rather, you do have the privilege of knowing that you made an impact with people who entrusted you to provide help, support, and compassion relative to some specific problem that they identified. You also learn more about your own strengths and how they intersect with the dynamics of an organic system. The lessons that you learn can provide guidance as you navigate the myriad opportunities that present themselves as you pursue your own professional and, in some cases, personal goals.

In the next chapter, we will explore how you can reflect more deeply on your research, knowledge, and community service. Before moving on, listen to two former students describe their experience with this long-term, community-based action research and its impact on their professional life.

JOHNNY'S CBPR JOURNEY BY JOHNNY NGUYEN

What started as a service-learning course in my sophomore year extended to a three-year engagement in a research project working at a preschool program south of Boston. I recalled moments when I met with families and how appreciative they were for our presence there and hearing them say thank you. A simple thank you to some, but to me that meant the world, and it was that experience that kept me going the distance and coming back to help as much as I could. Beyond that I even remember the long distances traveled to and from in between classes to help. I remember my class ending at 11:50 AM in Boston, MA, and leaving to head to Pawtucket, RI, to help and returning to campus in Boston by 6:00 PM for my 6:30 Chemistry class every Tuesday and Thursday for three years. I remember feeling overwhelmed when I first started, but as time went by I became a part of the project and the community I worked with and felt like it was natural for me to do so. In the time of traveling to and from, I reflected on the experiences of the day and processed the encounters of so many community members at the center. Some of those experiences made me laugh, some sad, and some frustrated. These were the moments that I realized that it wasn't just a project for me, it wasn't just community service, it was a part of me. These experiences affected me more than I knew.

After the experience of working with this community ended, I found myself feeling a loss of connection to something larger to help others. I was led into the path of public health working with youth around HIV/AIDS prevention, which again provided me that same feeling that I had before when I was working with the YMCA. I was making a direct contribution to helping others through community education and community outreach. Eventually this journey led me to return to school and get my master's in mental health counseling and to starting my own nonprofit working with youth to boost self-esteem. I continue to find myself seeking opportunities to help other organizations including serving on boards of local nonprofit organizations.

Next, Clare, who worked as an undergraduate on this community-based action research project, describes how this research impacted her professional life.

CLARE'S CBPR JOURNEY BY CLARE MEHTA (EMMANUEL COLLEGE)

How CBPR Impacted My Professional Life

Becoming involved in the CBPR completely changed my career trajectory. Until I [joined] this CBPR project, I didn't really know how research was conducted and what it looked like—it always seemed so abstract in my research methods classes. After my first project visit to the early learning center where the CBPR project was taking place, I remember feeling as though I had found my calling—I wanted to be a psychology researcher. I think it is important to highlight here that the key to my newfound love of research was that I was doing CBPR. I believe that if I had been engaged in less socially compelling research—watching rats press levers or counting the number of times someone said "red" when they should've said "blue"—I do not think that I would've developed the passion I have for research, and my career path would have been very different.

I graduated from college a semester early, and while I looked for a job, I dedicated my days to CBPR project activities, including giving presentations at two conferences. It was during this time that a professor I interviewed with at the BU school of dentistry put me in contact with his neighbor, who was the Dean of the Boston University School of Education, thinking that the Dean may be able to find me a full-time paid research position. Seeing my newfound passion for research, the Dean suggested that I go back to the United Kingdom (where I am originally from), get a master's degree, and return to the United States to complete a PhD at a land grant university, where my tuition would be paid. This is exactly what I did.

For my first master's degree, a Master's of Research (MRes) in Education, from the University of Bath in the UK, I used data I helped collect as part of the CBPR project as the basis of my master's thesis. This gave me a whole new perspective on the project as I connected what I had experienced doing CBPR with the wider research literature. Consequently, CBPR not only encouraged me to pursue a career in research, but also provided me with substantial research training, teaching me how to conduct a thorough literature review, analyze data, and write an academic paper.

After I completed my MRes, I returned to the United States to attend West Virginia University, where I earned a second master's degree and PhD in life-span developmental psychology. Having already worked on a significant research project, I felt confident in my research abilities as I pursued my PhD. I had already been a part of a research team, and consequently I had the confidence to contribute to research discussions in my graduate program. I also felt that I had more maturity and creativity as a researcher in comparison to my peers in the program, and this, undoubtedly, came from being a part of a CBPR team. I completed a post-doctoral fellowship at Boston Children's Hospital and Harvard Medical School, and accepted a tenure track faculty position at Emmanuel College in Boston, where I am currently a tenured associate professor. At Emmanuel College, I continue to reap benefits from being a part of a CBPR project as an undergraduate. I use examples from the CBPR project in my child development classes. I find these examples especially compelling to students as I'm able to explain to them that I was at the same career stage as them when I participated in the project. Additionally, because my experience of doing research as an undergraduate was so transformative for me, I involve students in all my research and strive to ensure that students in my lab are invested in the research projects we undertake. My lab meetings are structured similarly to the CBPR project meetings from my undergraduate years, where ideas are solicited from all team members, and all members' thoughts are carefully considered. As was modeled for me, I strive to empower my undergraduate students to work independently and take responsibility for and feel ownership of the research projects we work on. I believe that the influence of the project reaches even further when my own undergraduate students decide to pursue careers in psychology research.

Finally, I believe that my continued commitment to social justice in my professional and personal life comes from participating in CBPR. CBPR opened my eyes to issues relating to social justice and made me realize how important it is to include communities and systems in work that promotes social change. The knowledge and insight I gained from the CBPR project has helped me learn about and call out racial and gender injustice.

Looking Back, How Was the Work You Did at the Early Learning Center Different From Traditional Research?

(You may find some of the answer to this previously where I talk about how it is more interesting than watching rats press levers. ☺)

There is a saying that expertise is widespread, but opportunity is not. The work that we did at the early learning center really sought to provide all members of the community with the opportunity to share their expertise. This is not always the case with traditional models of research, where the researcher holds the power and is believed to have the expertise. Preschool teachers, researchers of all levels, including undergraduates, university faculty, center administrators, parents, and other community members shared power, expertise, and were equal partners in the research project. The commitment to equality and power sharing went beyond the day-to-day running of the research project. Community members co-authored conference presentations and research papers, and the research team strove to make sure that the research was truly inclusive.

CBPR Lessons Learned

I learned so much by participating in CBPR, about organizational politics, systems theory, how to interact with and value the expertise of people of all ages and from all walks of life. I learned all of this in addition to important research skills. As such, my advice for students engaging in community-based research is to fully engage in the process. Realize that you have been handed an important opportunity, and make the most of the experience. Work hard and make sure you listen, really listen, and learn from all members of the team. Do what is expected of you and then ask for more. Do not be discouraged if a path you are headed down in your research becomes a dead end. Listen to your mentors and the community members of the research team and go where the research takes you, even when it is not in a direction that is expected or makes sense to you. You may come up against oppressive or unjust structures and systems. Pay attention to these and observe how they affect people. Do not be discouraged by them, but rather ask questions about how and why these systems exist and how they could be changed or dismantled. Find support—I spent a lot of time talking about my experiences with graduate student mentors who could answer questions that I had and who could help me if I was feeling lost or overwhelmed. Finally, enjoy the experience! It is a privilege to be able to participate in CBPR, and participation in this type of research can change you and your worldview in positive and powerful ways.

RESOURCES

To review a case study of community-based action research see Harkins, D. A. & Associates. (2013). *Beyond the campus: Building a sustainable university-community collaboration.* Charlotte, NC: Information Age Publishing.

To engage in participatory action research and organizational change, check out: https://participaction.wordpress.com/whatpar/defining-par/

REFERENCES

Banyard, V. L., & Miller, K. E. (1998). The powerful potential of qualitative research in community psychology. *American Journal of Community Psychology, 26*(4), 485–506.

Evans, B. (2002). You can't come to my birthday party: Conflict resolution with young children. NY: High Scope.

Harkins, D. A., & Community Action Project Team. (2013). *Beyond the campus: Building a sustainable university-community partnership.* Charlotte, NC: Information Age Publishing.

Lencioni, P. (2002). *The five dysfunctions of a team: A leadership fable.* San Francisco, CA: Jossey-Bass.

Nelson, G., & Prilleltensky, I. (2010). *Community psychology: In pursuit of liberation and well-being* (2nd ed.). New York: Palgrave.

Prochaska, J. O., & DiClemente, C. C. (1983). Stages and processes of self-change of smoking: Toward an integrative model of change. *Journal of Consulting and Clinical Psychology, 51,* 390–395.

Prochaska, J. O., & Norcross, J. (2007). *Changing for good: A revolutionary six-step program for overcoming bad habits and moving your life positively forward.* New York: HarperCollins.

Senge, P. M. (1990). *The fifth discipline: The art and practice of the learning organization.* New York: Doubleday.

Senge, P. M. (1994). *The fifth discipline fieldbook: Tools for building a learning organization.* New York: Crown.

Taylor, P. C., & Medina, M.N.D. (2013). Educational paradigms: From positivism to multiparadigmatic. *Journal for Meaning-Centered Education,* 1–16.

Troppe, M. (1994). *Participatory action research: Merging community and scholarly agendas.* Providence: Campus Compact.

CHAPTER 6
REFLECTING ON HELPING

Carmen N. Veloria and
Abráham E. Peña-Talamantes

AIMS OF CHAPTER

1. Understand the importance of self-reflection before helping in community settings.
2. Explore assumptions, biases, and how the way you look at a situation impacts your interaction with diverse community members.
3. Explain a critical dialogic model.

19 questions

REFLECTION: I WANT TO HELP DISADVANTAGED KIDS IN POVERTY-STRICKEN NEIGHBORHOODS

Most traditional college students come to us with schooling experience as their only point of educational reference. If they are sitting in a college classroom, chances are that their schooling experiences worked for them. Once they begin to learn how the system worked for them in ways that it may not have worked for others, they begin to adapt a social justice orientation that propels them to want to help. This is a wonderful thing, but before engaging in service, students need to reflect on their reasons for helping.

Do you want to help because you understand that educational projects benefit some while it disadvantages others? What role, if any, do issues of race, ethnicity, class, and other factors play when it comes to access to services? How do you begin to explore these issues in a productive manner that will allow you to effectively work with community members?

Many of our students want to help but are unaware that "new racism" is an invisible system of dominion and power. Individuals may eschew being racist, but racism is built into knowledge production, institutional structures, and social relationships in very insidious ways (Fazakarley, 2009–2010; Fiske, 1993; Veloria, 2015). How do you begin to explore your assumptions and biases? How do you understand the various forms of knowledge(s) resulting from individual and collective experiences within and outside of mainstream political, economic, and social systems?

Please answer the following guiding questions before reading further. Reflect on your responses, as those pertain to who you are, what motivates you, and the reasons you want to help others!

Guiding Questions

Where did you grow up? What do you recall from your experiences?

_____

_____

_____

Did you or your family ever need help? Did anyone in your neighborhood? If so, what type of help?

_____

_____

_____

What do you recall from your neighborhood? What sticks out the most and why?

_____

_____

_____

What issue(s) impacted members from your community?

_____ ④

_____

_____

Who addressed those issues and how? Who had the authority or power to address them?

_____ ⑤

_____

_____

How did social class intersect with race, gender, and sexual orientation?

_____ ⑥

_____

_____

Armed with theories and equipped with newfound knowledge, you are ready for action, correct? Well, not so fast. Theories and knowledge will get you only so far. Action is foregrounded by authentic reflection, critical dialogue, and learning to see anew. It is out of this process that collective action emerges. Who are you and how do you see the world? Freire (1994) posits that those individuals who authentically commit themselves to the people must re-examine themselves constantly.

By now, you understand the relationship between the individual (you) and the multiple systems in which one lives. The reality is that you have been influenced by multiple forces that have shaped your understanding of yourself and others; hence, why **reflexivity** is essential before any action. This involves individual reflection of the self, internal and external processes, and representations of our social position and interaction, to critically examine powerful social structures and relations.

> **Authenticity requires self-awareness**
> **Self-awareness requires reflection**

The concept of **positionality** focuses on the idea that dimensions of our identity (e.g., gender, race, class, immigration status, sexual orientation) serve as markers of relational positions within specific social contexts rather than essential qualities of one's self (Alcoff, 1988). Social identities reflect the way individuals and groups internalize established social categories within their societies, such as their cultural (or ethnic) identities, gender identities, class identities, and so on. These social categories shape our ideas about who we think we are, how we want to be seen by others (as well as, how we see others), and the groups to which we belong.

Social identity theory began with work on social categorization (Tajfel, 1978). Later, Tajfel and Turner (1979) proposed that there are three mental processes involved in evaluating others as "us" or "them" (i.e., "in-group" and "out-group") in the following order, as shown in Figure 6.1.

Social Categorization	→	Social Identification	→	Social Comparison

FIGURE 6.1 Three Mental Processes

The first is **categorization**. As humans, it's natural for us to categorize objects to understand them further and later identify them. As early as elementary school we are taught to cut pictures and classify them as either food or clothing by coloring, cutting, and pasting in the appropriate boxes. Do you recall those ditto sheets? When you did this work, you learned specific things about each category, a useful exercise especially as we attempt to learn how to compare similarities versus differences. These exercises help us make sense of our world. We are socialized to categorize from an early age, which is why we use categories like fruits, vegetables, students, teachers, black, and white to categorize objects and people.

When we assign people to a category, we are making statements about them and where they belong. By the same token, we find out things about ourselves by how we categorize ourselves and how others categorize us. In a society, these categories carry meaning and significance and serve as markers of who we are and who we are not. Social categories inform things such as ways of acting and behaving and the norms of the groups we belong to and so forth. At any time, we can belong to many different groups, and these may change as we age, learn to see ourselves in a different light, or through the creation of new self-defined labels and categories.

This can be a complicated process given that we tend to adopt the identity(ties) of the group we have categorized ourselves or have been categorized by others as belonging to. For example, when you first entered college, you began to identify as a college student. You probably looked around and noticed the ways that other college students behaved. For example, not raising your hand to ask to go the restroom, coming to class with a drink in hand, or staying after class to talk to your professor. Essentially, you began to act in ways you noticed other college students behaved. This signals conformity of the norms of the group. No longer in high school, you began to take on the identity of college student along with the significance of this group membership. This refers to **identification**.

Reflect: The reality is that there is a large degree of emotional significance to any group identification. Sometimes we feel affinity and sometimes we feel dissonance, particularly if our membership in one group conflicts with our membership in another group. For instance, what if you were told repeatedly that you are not "college material," that students who look like you (belong to a particular category) do not make it to college? How would you feel sitting in a college classroom and feeling like you do not belong based on what you were told? Would your identity as a college student conflict with any other group identity you hold? Reflect on these questions.

_____

_____

_____

Self-esteem is also connected and maintained by our group memberships. Once we categorize ourselves or are categorized by others, we begin to identify with aspects of the group(s) and will find ourselves comparing ourselves to others.

Another important concept to consider is the concept of **"othering,"** which is central to sociological analyses of how majority and minority identities are constructed. This is because the representation of different groups within any given society is controlled by groups that have greater political power. To understand the notion of "the other," it is crucial that you explore the ways in which social identities and inequalities are constructed and reproduced. Identities are often thought as being natural or innate—something that we are born with—but sociologists highlight that this taken-for-granted view is not true. Do you agree? Just recap the process involved in evaluating others as "us," "them," or "other."

Reflect: How do you know what you know?

_____

_____

_____

How can individuals look at a phenomenon and arrive at different conclusions?

_____

_____

_____

How does our upbringing affect how we see the world? How does our social positioning impact what we see?

_____

_____

_____

LOOKING-GLASS SELF

Food for thought from Popular Social Science: _do you sometimes experience that the mere presence of other people leads to feelings of discomfort and tension? When not knowing exactly what other people think of you, it may lead to self-doubt and feelings of insecurity._ Per American sociologist Charles Horton Cooley (1864–1929), the degree of personal insecurity you display in social situations is determined by what you believe other people think of you. Cooley's concept of the looking-glass self, states that a person's self grows out of a person's social interactions with others. The view of ourselves comes from the contemplation of personal qualities and impressions of how others perceive us. How we view ourselves does not come from who we are, but rather from how we _believe_ others see us.

The main point is that people shape their self-concepts based on their understanding of how others perceive them. We form our self-image as the reflections of the response and evaluations of others in our environment. As children, we were treated in a variety of ways. If parents, relatives, and other important people look at a child as smart, they will tend to raise him or her with certain types of expectations. Thus, the child will eventually believe that he is a smart person. This is a process that continues when we grow up. For instance, if you believe that your closest friends look at you as a superhero, you are likely to project that self-image, regardless of whether this has anything to do with reality.

The concept of the looking-glass self represents the cornerstone of the sociological theory of socialization. The idea is that people in our close environment serve as the "mirrors" that reflect images of ourselves. Per Cooley, this process has three steps. First, we imagine how we _appear_ to another person. Sometimes this imagination is correct, but may also be wrong since it is merely based on our _assumptions_. Second, we imagine what _judgments_ people make of us based on our appearance. Third, we _imagine_ how the person feels about us, based on the judgments about us. The ultimate result is that we often change our behavior based on how we _feel_ people perceive us.

This is important to understand, as it affects the way we interact with others: what we see, how we position ourselves, the questions we ask, how we frame those questions, and our perspectives of situations. Thus, **standpoint** is another important concept to consider, given that our perspectives are shaped by our social identities as well as our social and political experiences. It becomes imperative that we reflect constantly on the types of biases we may bring into a situation. After all, our perceptions and reactions in any given situation may become the tools that another may use to construct their own sense of self. Not only do we see ourselves through the eyes we *think* others may see *us*, but social others see themselves by how they believe *we see them*.

> **Reflect:** Let's take the following example. You are appalled to learn that most of the children you work with at the community center live in an apartment complex that has lead paint contamination. Knowing that lead can have adverse neurological effects in children, you ponder: why have the families not opted to move out of the apartment complex? Why do they stay given the risks associated with lead poisoning? How are you viewing this issue? From which perspective? What external factors will you need to consider, if any? Reflect on these questions before reading further.

> The answer to these questions depends on your **positionality**—where you stand in relation to others as well as the power and social dynamics in the situation. You may believe that opting to live in a lead-contaminated apartment is morally wrong and shortsighted, but when the issue is placed and framed in a larger social context, you may begin to see how peoples' choices (or lack thereof) are based on their social positioning, which includes issues of knowledge, language, and power.

> How is the issue of lead contamination being framed? Who is framing it or for whom? Who is heard, and who may not be heard? When faced with limited options, is living in a lead-contaminated complex better than living in a shelter or on the streets? Do the children and families need saving, or do they need to save themselves? Who decides? Write your thoughts on these questions.

KNOWLEDGE, LANGUAGE, AND POWER

Addressing community problems requires innovative solutions from all, well-meaning stakeholders, but mostly from the people who are most affected. Despite this, people who are most affected are often not heard. Not because they do not have a voice, but rather because when it comes to language and power, you need to understand the place of language in society: that language is centrally involved in power, the struggle for power, and it is so involved through its ideological properties. At the core, language is a social practice that is determined by social structures (Fairclough, 2001).

Let's continue with the issue of lead contamination. This will require critical thinking. Thinking critically frees us from personal, environmental, and institutional forces that prevent us from seeing new directions (Habermas, 1979). Furthermore, once we become critical thinkers, we are no longer passive recipients of knowledge and products of socialization. Rather, through practicing thoughtful scrutiny and continuously asking questions, we become active participants and arrive at our own ideas and commitments. As you begin to ask questions, consider the following:

1. Identify and challenge your assumptions.
2. Be aware of place and time in our culture.
3. Search for alternative ways of thinking.
4. Develop reflective analysis.

Consider what you believe about families who continue to live in lead-contaminated apartments despite potential harmful effects.

> **Reflect:** How might you challenge the beliefs and assumptions that you hold? How does your personal experience thus far influence the beliefs and assumptions you hold about the conditions (and consequences) of where these families live? Could your family opt to move freely? If so, what does this say about the power and or privileges you may hold in a situation such as this one? Reflect on these questions before reading further.

_____

_____

_____

Now that you've had some time to think about your own position and assumptions about this situation, let's try to think about these issues from the perspective of the families themselves.

> **Reflect:** What do you know about the families of the children you work with? What are their concerns, their desires and options? What do you know about the community as a whole? What type of information do you have access to? And most important: where did you get that information? Was it from the community center? The media? Remember that the source of information matters—a lot. You may also need to think more broadly and ask yourself: What is happening socially and politically with respect to lead removal? Try to answer these questions before moving on.

_____

_____

_____

As you can see, the answers to some of these questions are not so easy to come by. The original gut reactions we have toward situations tend to be informed by our own experiences and result in biases in the way we have come to perceive the world, our values and our goals. What may seem like "common sense" to us may very well not be the case. From your perspective, it may be "common sense" for these families to move out of their houses because they are falling apart and they are dangerous for their children. Yet, it may be "common sense" for them to be able to keep a roof over the heads of their children instead of being homeless, regardless of the condition of the home. Deferring to common sense rarely leads to productivity. It isn't until we engage in critical thinking and questioning our own positionality and privilege that we can start to enact change.

SOCIALIZATION AND INEQUALITY

As we age, we become socialized into the ideology and thought processes in which we grow up. It thus becomes very difficult to question our own assumptions, or to even realize that we have any biases to begin with. *But what does that even mean?* you might ask. Let's say that growing up, your parents always instilled in you that hard work and dedication would get you a great job, that this was the country of opportunity, and that everyone who wanted to better themselves could do so if they just tried hard enough. Upon moving to college, you find yourself in a city with a large homeless population and your first thoughts upon seeing many of them with signs asking for money, food, or shelter are along the lines of *Why don't they just find a job? Why don't they ask for government aid? This is the land of opportunity; why don't they just try a little harder?* These questions may be "obvious" from your point of view, given what you grew up hearing. Yet, your experiences do not reflect those of the individual on the other side: the homeless person. You may also not be aware that while there may be jobs and government aid, these things both require applications—which ask that the individual provide a permanent address and a valid state ID. Some types of aid may require individuals to submit evidence of income (e.g., IRS documentation, W2s) to show that they are at or below the poverty line and eligible for services. For individuals who may be homeless, it may be next to impossible to provide all this documentation. Thus, no matter how hard they try, or how many opportunities there may be, they may simply not qualify for them. It is the social structures that prohibit their advancement, but it is our assumptions that ultimately contribute to the negative views that we have of the disadvantaged in society.

Research has shown us that inequality can take many forms, but it is important to remember the four most prominent themes across all types of inequality. Understanding these themes may help us become critical thinkers and recognize when and how inequalities may be taking place.

Themes of Inequality

1. Inequalities depend on our enforcing symbolic boundaries that position some people as more valuable than others. While this is problematic, it is commonplace in our society. We give voice and power to individuals which we deem credible; usually individuals who speak from a perspective we agree with or those who may hold some position of power in an area or within a group to which we belong (see Figure 6.2).

FIGURE 6.2   Being Invisible

2. We need not intend for our thoughts and actions to result in inequalities for them to do so. This one is a little tricky, because it forces us to question every situation we encounter. Inadvertently, we will say or do something that will not mesh well with the experiences of others. Own it! It is not required that we agree with everyone else's position, but it is important that we take a step back and listen to their experiences. This is something we don't do often, and we should strive to learn from one another as much as we can.

3. People who are unfairly disadvantaged may be able to change their own oppression. This, of course, does not come easily; it is a long and painful process. Yet, it is important for us to realize that individual action may very well turn into collective action. If we can do our part to help these marginalized communities, we should. Remember, while we may hold privilege in some social identity categories, we do not hold privilege in all of them. We are bound to be disadvantaged in some aspect of our social lives, and we need to work together to persevere as individuals and as a global community.

4. Oppressed individuals may inadvertently contribute to their own and others' marginalization. Unfortunately, society is a complex system of social structures and hierarchies, and individuals are forced to use every tool in their arsenal to attempt to stay afloat. Some populations may seek to adopt characteristics of the group in power to leverage what little power they can and distance themselves from members of their own disadvantaged group to deflect stigma. This type of identity work practice is what sociologists call **defensive othering**, and it has been observed in many situations (Schwalbe, Godwin, Holden, Schrock, & Thompson, 2000). Homeless men who refer to other homeless individuals as "lazy bums" (Snow & Anderson, 1987), women who join men in claiming that some of their female co-workers may be unattractive (Padavic, 1991), and even gay men who engage in behaviors that will highlight their masculinity while claiming that effeminate gay men are not "real men" (Peña-Talamantes, 2013): these are only a few examples of how individuals may seek to deflect stigma and consequently reproduce biases and stereotypes of the larger society, instead of being the agents that could potentially assist in deconstructing some of the ignorant viewpoints about the communities in general.

So, why is this important to know? Well, we live in a society that values the voice and position of some and not that of others. Most of the conclusions we come to stem primarily from the sources we are made believe to trust—regardless of whether these sources should be trustworthy to how they construct and back up their claims. The reality is that an encounter with any issue requires us to draw from our past experiences and perspectives to attempt to interpret the situation. This may entail contending with insufficient experiences, which requires gathering new information to help us make sense of the issue at hand. The key is to place our sense making within a broader context to allow us to generate new ideas and new questions along with new ways of asking them to build new knowledge (Wells, 2009).

DIFFERENT WAYS OF KNOWING

Belenky, Clinchy, Goldberger, and Tarule (1986) contend that there are **different ways of knowing** or various forms of knowledge(s). Clinchy (1990/1996) posits a form of knowing, as connected knowing. This entails a collaborative way of knowing that draws on personal experiences, reactions, and interactions. Connected knowing involves putting yourself into another's frame of reference to try to understand the issue at hand. Thus, connected knowers try to ally themselves to another's point of view to try to see things through that other person's eyes. Connected knowers try to empathize with the other person and to refrain from judgment. As such, connected knowers:

● Take everything at face value

● Try not to evaluate the other's perspectives

● Try to understand multiple perspectives

● Do not ask questions to ascertain whether they are right, but rather, to clarify your own assumptions and seek meaning

● Ask "what do you think" not for evaluative purposes or as a way of seeking evidence, but rather, for the exploration of the experiences that have led individuals to hold certain positions

● Probe for the stories behind an issue, and thus attend to narrative ways of understanding people's experiences.

(Clinchy, 1990/1996)

This type of knowing allows for "different ways of knowing" and understanding complex issues especially if you cannot relate from a personal perspective. Going back to our examples, if you have never had to contend with living with toxic elements, how can you possibly understand why people do what they do despite the dangerous side effects of living in such an environment? Similarly, if you have never experienced the struggle associated with being homeless, how might you be able to assume that the individuals affected are not trying to get out of their current situation? In addition, who are you getting your information from? Are you inadvertently reproducing deficit views of a population? These are very important questions to ask yourself and think about critically. They require self-reflection and true willingness to open yourself to different points of view and to give validity to the lived experiences of other individuals. Try to answer these questions before moving on.

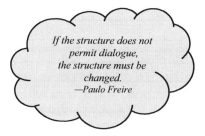

If the structure does not permit dialogue, the structure must be changed.
—Paulo Freire

_____

_____

_____

AUTHENTIC LISTENING REQUIRES HUMILITY

Have you ever had a problem and your friends and/or family offered solutions before you could fully explain yourself? If so, how did that experience make you feel? Did you feel fully heard, understood, respected? Often, well-meaning people offer solutions without fully understanding the issue at hand. When working with community members, well-intentioned activists do the same. Thus, approaching an issue with the understanding that you may not have all the answers and may, in fact, have questions, requires that you be humble, silent more often than not, and willing to listen with humility before engaging in meaningful dialogue.

Freire posits that any structure that does not permit dialogue must be changed. This is based on the notion that dialogue allows you to remain open to the other, to difference, and to the possibility of new understandings. It is the basis of any relationship which relates to how people interact with and treat one another (Shields, 2008). Take the example of the families that live in the lead-contaminated housing complex: how would you engage in dialogue with them about their situation? How will you change the structure when that may be changing beliefs and perceptions? If you view them as people who do not care about their children's health outcomes, for example, then you are not open to engaging in meaningful dialogue. Shields (2008) comments that permitting assumptions and prejudices to enter our psyche closes us to the individuals in front of us, which may prevent us from entering a dialogic relationship with them. Again, emphasizing the importance of understanding the self in relation to how we see the other and making sure we steer clear from the reproduction of inequality.

Therefore, critical reflexivity presupposes meaningful dialogue and is crucial for the development of critical awareness. **Conscientization** is the key process by which we develop a critical awareness of the world based on the concrete experiences of everyday life. This critical awareness refers to "learning to perceive social, political, and economic contradictions, and to take action against the oppressive elements of reality" (Freire, 1970, p. 17). Before acting, however, it is important you understand complex issues through various perspectives. This entails being open to communicating across lines of difference and expressing a willingness to engage in constructive dialogue even with contention.

Freire proposed a dialogical theory of action based on communication and cooperation as the necessary base not only for understanding the mediating role of sociohistorical, cultural, economic, and political relations, but also for the active work of changing them (Ragut & Osman, 2013). As you think about engaging in meaningful action, you need to think about the importance of engaging in meaningful dialogue. Building on the work of Freire, we offer an expanded dialogic model that connects the branches of knowledge and knowing found in both "connected knowing" and "conscientization" and roots them in cultural, economic, historical, and political contexts.

MOVING TOWARD CRITICAL DIALOGIC SYNERGY

To generate new ways of engaging in meaningful dialogic interaction, we reconceptualized the dialogic model put forth by Freire and taken up by others such as Souto-Manning (2010) that focuses on cyclical relationship of generating themes, problem posing, codifying themes, offering promising solutions, and agency and action.

In this organic reconceptualization, the cultural roots express the customary beliefs, social norms, values, and material traits of a group of people. They also represent issues of cultural differences and even stereotypes that emerge in any society. This is because culture is fluid, in flux, and changes depending on historical contexts and power dynamics that are embedded in hierarchical structures.

When language is viewed as a practice determined by social structures, we can see how actual discourse is determined by socially constituted orders of discourse, which are sets of conventions associated with social interactions. These are ideologically shaped by power relations in social institutions and in society as whole (influential elements). These are entangled in any form of dialogic interactions, and together with the cultural roots form the basis for the ideology that stems from the complex interplay of one's own lived experiences and external social structures. Now with this foundational understanding, let's take each of the petals by revisiting the lead-contaminated housing complex.

Model of Critical Dialogic Synergy

Veloria and Peña-Talamantes | Copyright © 2015

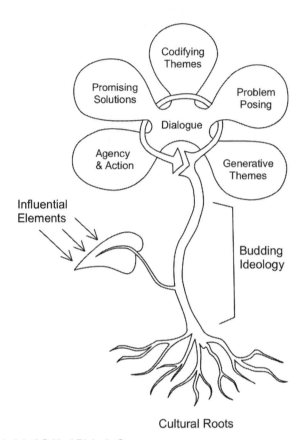

FIGURE 6.3   Model of Critical Dialogic Synergy

If your goal is to explore the issue with the hope of engaging in meaningful dialogue before action, you would need to consider the budding ideologies around the issue by collectively *generating themes* (see Figure 6.3): what are they? Who is generating them? Who has more power in society to advance them? This needs to emerge in cooperation with the families of the children living in the apartment complex. How are they dialogically making sense of their situation?

Next, *problem pose*. How can you place the generated themes in a broader social context? Who is responsible for the clean-up? What's the role of environmental protection agencies? What happens if residents complain? What happens if they stay or if they do not? Is everyone willing to take on the collective action? The answer to these questions needs to come from the community. They are the most affected and should live with consequences of any form of (in)action. The reality is that a strategy may need to emerge in terms of which issues will be attended to first. This may be done by *codifying the prevailing themes* and exploring pros and cons of moving forward to the point that everyone is aware of the costs and benefits of *promising solutions*. It is only then that a collective decision can be made regarding the route the community will choose to take to address the issues at hand.

By engaging in this process through critical dialogue, we ensure that the voices of those most affected are heard and incorporated in the implementation of possible solutions. Unfortunately, most of the time, decision making is reserved for those people with power who do not understand the experiences of the affected individuals. Consequently, individuals in the affected community feel invisible and retreat; they give up because they feel that true change cannot occur. It is thus imperative that we realize that the most transformative change can come from the collective voice of the people who are directly affected by an issue. When people feel that they are heard, they become empowered to be their own agents of social and cultural change.

CONCLUDING THOUGHTS

Now you're ready—or are you? Let's revisit. Those who commit to working alongside communities also need to commit to the ongoing need to be reflexive about one's social identity(ties) and what one brings to any interaction, but particularly interactions across difference. You will need to continuously revisit your positionality by being mindful that certain social categories and identities carry power that can potentially reproduce inequality. The reality is that the work for reflection is never done. For those who commit to effecting change in communities, the process is ongoing.

The model of critical dialogic synergy purposefully builds on the notion of "authentic praxis" that is foundational in Freire's work. This entails an approach to learning, from self and others, that involves reflection, agency, and action. The reconceptualized model considers cultural histories, prevailing ideologies, and influential elements, which can change and may be unforeseen—for example, a natural disaster or the outcome of an election. Influential elements include attention, resources, and priorities that impact how individuals and communities respond and what actions they decide to take. To help, you will need to listen attentively and authentically to various stakeholders with varying points of view. What matters most, however, is that you're thoughtful, reflective, and willing to engage in critical dialogue before any kind of action that entails the act of helping and serving alongside others.

Reflect: Why do you think reflexivity is important? Is it a one-time or an ongoing process?

_____

_____

_____

Why must you continuously revisit your positionality? How is it that who you are and how you view the world impact your interactions with others?

_____

_____

_____

How do social identities connect to issues of knowledge and power? Can you cite an example?

_____

_____

_____

Why is critical dialogue necessary for collective action? What other factors does The Model of Critical Dialogic Synergy account for?

_____

_____

_____

RESOURCES

Family and Youth Services : www.ncfy.com/pdy
Freire Project: www.freireproject.org
Popular Social Science: wwwpopularsocialscience.com
Project Approach: www.projectapproach.org/
Story of Stuff Project: www.storyofstuff.com
Understanding Race: www.understandingrace.org/

REFERENCES

Alcoff, L. (1988). Cultural feminism v. post-structuralism: The identity crisis in feminist theory. *Signs*, 3(13), 405–436.

Belenky, M. F., Clinchy, B. M., Goldberger, N. R., & Tarule, J. M. (1986). *Women's ways of knowing: The development of self, voice, and mind*. New York: Basic Books.

Clinchy, B. M. (1990/1996). Connected and separate knowing: Toward a marriage of two minds. In N. R. Goldberger, J. M. Tarule, B. M. Clinchy, & M. F. Belenky (Eds.), *Knowledge, difference, and power* (pp. 205–247). New York: Basic Books.

Fairclough, N. (2001). *Language and power* (2nd ed.). London: Longman.

Fazakarley J. (2009-2010). "Racisms "Old" and "New" at Handsworth, 1985." *University of Sussex Journal of Contemporary History* 13. Retrieved from www.sussex.ac.uk/webteam/gateway/file.php?name=13-fazakarley-april2010-2&site=15

Fiske, S. T. (1993). Controlling other people: the impact of power on stereotyping. *American Psychology*, 48(6), 621–628.

Freire, P. (1970). *Education for critical consciousness*. New York: Continuum.

Freire, P. (1994). *Pedagogy of hope*. New York: Continuum.

Habermas, J. (1979). *Communication and the evolution of society*. Toronto: Beacon Press.

Padavic, I. (1991). The re-creation of gender in a male workplace. *Symbolic Interaction*, 14, 279–294.

Peña-Talamantes, A. E. (2013). "Defining machismo no es siempre lo mismo": Latino sexual minorities' machoflexible identities in higher education. *Culture, Society and Masculinity*, 5, 166–178.

Ragut, E. J., & Osman, A. A. (2013). Reflections on Paulo Freire and classroom relevance. *American International Journal of Social Science*, 2(2), 23–28.

Schwalbe, M., Godwin, S., Holden, D., Schrock, D., & Thompson, S. (2000). Generic processes in the reproduction of inequality: An interactionist analysis. *Social Forces*, 79, 419–452.

Shields, C. M. (2008). Leveling the playing field in racialized contexts: Leaders speaking out about difficult issues. Paper presented at the biennial conference of the Commonwealth Council for Educational Administration and Management, Durban, South Africa.

Snow, D., & Anderson, L. (1987). Identity work among the homeless: The verbal construction and avowal of personal identities. *American Journal of Sociology, 92,* 1336–1371.

Souto-Manning, M. (2010). *Freire, teaching, and learning: Culture circles across contexts.* New York: Peter Lang.

Tajfel, H. (1978). The achievement of group differentiation. In H. Tajfel (Ed.), *Differentiation between groups: Studies in the social psychology of intergroup relations* (pp. 77–100). London: Academic Press.

Tajfel, H., & Turner, J. C. (1979). An integrative theory of intergroup conflict. In W. G. Austin & S. Worchel (Eds.), *The social psychology of intergroup relations* (pp. 33–47). Monterey, CA: Brooks/ Cole.

Veloria, C. (2015). Maybe this is because of society? Disrupting and engaging discourses of race in the context of a service-learning project. *Humanity & Society, 39*(2), 1–21.

Wells, G. (2009). *New perspectives on language and education series: The meaning makers: Learning to talk and talking to learn* (2nd ed.). Bristol, England: Multilingual Matters. http://www.popularsocialscience. com/2013/05/27/the-looking-glass-self-how-our-self-image-is-shaped-by-society/

CHAPTER 7
BECOMING CULTURALLY SENSITIVE

Felicia P. Wiltz

AIMS OF CHAPTER

1. Understand role of social institutions in shaping our ideas about those who differ from us.
2. Define cultural sensitivity and outline steps toward more cultural sensitivity.
3. Understand role of social institutions in shaping life circumstances of those we serve.

REFLECTION: AM I CULTURALLY INSENSITIVE? WHERE DO MY BIASES COME FROM?

Many courses I teach address issues of social inequalities, particularly pertaining to race, gender, social class and poverty, citizenship and immigration, family status, sexual orientation, and others. At the start of the semester, I initiate a discussion about the preconceived ideas we have about these topics and about the populations we will cover. As a strategy to unpack the influences of socialization we experience in our lives, I introduce "Uncle Bob." Uncle Bob, although a fictional character who does not represent any one gender, race, age group, and so forth, is a real representation of a person, person(s), or social institution who very often shares their opinions on various social topics. His or her opinions are very biased, sexist, racist, homophobic, and so forth and not based on empirical facts. The high level of confidence with which he or she speaks influences our own ideas and attitudes toward those different from us. As I introduce Uncle Bob to the class, I explain that we all have an Uncle Bob in our lives. He or she might be a family member—a parent, a sibling, or other relative. He or she might be a friend or peer. Uncle Bob could represent a public figure, a television show, or a YouTube channel we subscribe to. In fact, from time to time, we ourselves may be "Uncle Bob"!

As we learn more about others, we begin to realize that the opinions of Uncle Bob are not quite accurate and drive his or her biases rather than facts. At this point, most students nod their heads and picture who this person, persons, or thing in their lives might be. Do you know an Uncle Bob in your life? How has Uncle Bob shaped your ideas and attitudes toward those who are different? How can we unpack the role Uncle Bob plays in our own socialization, and how can we insure we do not become Uncle Bob? Why is this important to consider as we serve within the community?

IMPACT OF SOCIALIZATION

Socialization is the process through which we learn to become members of society and various groups within society. Our cultural beliefs, values, and norms play a large part in who we are and in the transmission of these ideas across generations. Socialization is a lifelong process that begins at birth and continues throughout the life cycle. Some argue socialization may begin before birth. Imagine you have been invited to a baby shower. One of the first questions asked of the expected parents is "Do you know if it is a boy or a girl?" If they share this knowledge with you, you will likely proceed to purchase a gift that fits some notion of gender appropriateness within society.

You continue to be socialized even today. Consider your role as a student. When you began college, you likely attended numerous orientations. Your academic department may have invited you to meet the professors and other students. On these occasions, you likely learned about curriculum, your responsibilities as a member of the department and college, the norms of behavior for students, the beliefs of the college, and institutional values. As a member of the institution, you were instructed on how to conduct yourself as a member and how to succeed. As a current student, you are being socialized to become a professional in your career field of interest. Consider some ways that college plays a role in your socialization to become a professional.

AGENTS OF SOCIALIZATION

The process of socialization is accomplished through agents of socialization, with many agents playing a role in your socialization throughout your life. Figure 7.1 illustrates a few of these agents.

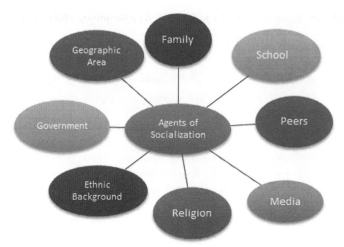

FIGURE 7.1 Agents of Socialization

Various agents impact you differently depending on where you are in the life cycle. Let's look at a few of these agents.

Family is the first and primary agent of socialization. When children are first born, those who care for them represent the first contact with society and the culture. It is in this context that we form our earliest values and beliefs. We learn about various social roles within society, including our gender roles. As children, what we first learned, shaped by this primary agent, influences how we began to think about ourselves and others. Unfortunately, this can include biases and prejudices.

School serves the purpose of teaching us academics. It also plays a strong role in teaching the norms and values of society. One example is understanding your role as a student. For instance, when you entered your classroom on the first day of the semester, where did you sit? Did you sit in the professor's chair at the head of the classroom? Did you sit facing the back of the room? Why do you suppose you sat where you did? Early in your primary education, you were taught your role as a student, including where to sit and how to behave in a classroom setting. School also socializes us on values such as individualism and meritocracy.

Peer pressure—the pressure to do what our peer group does—includes conforming to the norms and values of peers. While not the primary agent of socialization, peers strongly influence how we view ourselves and others.

Media including television, music, and social media are more influential than the past, considering advances in media technology that give us access to information and people not available before. How strong the impact of newer technology on socialization is yet to be determined, but it is likely powerful.

These agents of socialization, along with others, serve as powerful influencers on how we think about and view others. Fortunately, our strongest traits include the ability to learn. Take heart. We can become more culturally sensitive, debunking biases and prejudices learned through various agents encountered throughout life. We may even better understand how and why "Uncle Bob" became "Uncle Bob."

Reflect: *Uncle Bob*

Describe your "Uncle Bob's" role in your socialization.

_____

_____

_____

What other agents of socialization impacted your ways of viewing yourself or others?

_____

_____

_____

In what ways have you been an Uncle Bob?

_____

_____

_____

CULTURAL SELF-AWARENESS

Before we learn about others we may encounter in our communities, we need to spend more time learning about ourselves. In learning about ourselves, we open the door to understanding and learning about others. For example, Arrendondo and Glauner (1992) identified the dimensions of personal identity model to help us reflect on identity factors that influence our view of the world and how we interact with others. According to this model, We "*are all cultural beings affected differently by [our] dimensions of personal identity and contextual factors including historical events, sociopolitical enablers and barriers and economics*" (Fouad & Arredondo, 2007, p. 16). Figure 7.2 illustrates the model.

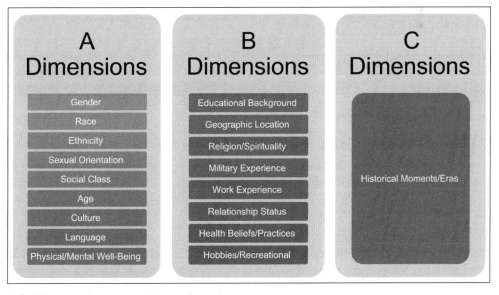

FIGURE 7.2   Dimensions of Personal Identity

Source: Arrendondo and Glauner (1992)

A Dimensions represent ascribed statuses within our society. Ascribed statuses are those we gained with little to no effort. These highly identifiable dimensions help us understand how stereotypes shape our worldview.

B Dimensions represent achieved statuses of our identity often gained with little primarily from our own efforts. Less visually identifiable, it can be more difficult to explore how these stereotypes shape our worldview.

C Dimensions represent historical moments/eras experienced in a life span. These moments/eras impact a historical cohort of people in such a way as to shape the person's worldview. For example, in 2001, I tried to explain the relevance the historical moments/eras in our lives to a group of students. I asked the class to identify any historical moments/eras that shaped their lives. Many had trouble answering this question up until September 10, 2001. Our next class met on September 12, and while we discussed the attacks on September 11, one student sadly stated, *"I think we have our historical moment."*

PRIVILEGE

I was once part of a group participating in a diversity train-the-trainer program and during our first training, we watched a short video about being in the dominant group vs. being in the minority group. After the video, our facilitators asked to reflect on when we have ever felt part of the dominant group and when we have felt part of the minority. As an African American female, it was quite easy for me to think of instances in which I felt a minority. On the other hand, it was difficult for me to think of any instance in which I truly felt that I was part of a dominant group.

As I struggled with this, the facilitators asked for each participant to share their thoughts. I had a sense of panic that I was unprepared to share, but was relieved that the facilitators started on the other side of the room. Perhaps I can think of something before it was my turn. I listened with interest to each person describe their experiences, but I truly had an "aha" moment when Sharon (name changed) spoke. Sharon is a lesbian who was raising two children with her partner (at the time, [LGBTQ] marriage was not legal yet). She described the difficulties she experienced as a lesbian mother. The stares. The rude comments and treatment. She shared her anxieties every time their children had a new teacher. Would this teacher accept them? And if not, how would that affect their children? I remember this moment as if it were yesterday. It were as if a light bulb went on over my head . . . Oh my goodness, I'm heterosexual! Immediately, my mind was flooded with all the privileges I never noticed I had. I could walk down the street holding hands with my husband, without fear that our love would attract some hateful response. I could kiss him in public or even more than that and the response we'd get would be more like, "Ahhh, they're still in love after all those years" or "Get a room." Not once have I felt unsafe because of my love for my husband. Not once have I wondered if our love would be a detriment to our children. I then began to think about how privilege is something that is rather invisible to those who hold the privilege. I don't have to think about my heterosexuality because it is the norm.

Recognizing and acknowledging our own privileges can be difficult. Our privileges are often very hard to see. Why do you think that is? Well, for starters, we often don't wish to think we obtained something not earned. One of our most important values in the United States is the notion of meritocracy. You know meritocracy. I'm sure you've heard the saying, "if you work hard, you will succeed" or that so-and-so "pulled himself or herself up by their bootstraps." **Meritocracy** is the notion that your success is an exclusive result of your hard work. It essentially ignores all other ways success is gained. Now there is no doubt that hard work can lead to success, but we must also acknowledge the various hidden privileges and advantages some have over others. We must also acknowledge that many work very hard and still do not succeed.

Privilege is a product of the society in which we are a part. While we are not always conscious of our privilege, it can affect how we think about others and their circumstances. For example, having class or racial privileges can make it difficult to understand the struggles of those in poverty or those in racial and ethnic minority groups and the social structures that adversely affect their life chances. It can also make it difficult to see that the lack of this privilege for others can have devastating consequences.

Privileges can also blind us to the biases we develop over the course of our lives. We all have biases. They are part of being members of societies that themselves uphold certain biases. Throughout our lives, we have absorbed biased ways of thinking and acting through our various agents of socialization—our families, peers, the media. In some cases, our biased views have become normalized within the context of our biased society or community. Our biases can be the basis for establishing stereotypes about those who are different from us. Stereotypes are oversimplified, generalized beliefs about a group of people that do not allow for the acknowledgment of individuals and individual circumstances. We must acknowledge both the privileges we have for each of our dimensions of personal identity and seek to understand the effect it has had on the formation of our biases.

Reflect: As you consider your "A" dimensions of personal identity, what privileges can you identify?

_____

_____

_____

How can acknowledging your privileges help you understand the impact of a lack of privilege on others?

_____

_____

_____

Why do we need to recognize our own biases and stereotypes to be effective helpers?

_____

_____

_____

THE DIVERSE COMMUNITIES WE SERVE

Poverty

We are constantly bombarded with rhetoric and stereotypes about the poor from many different sources, both privately and publicly. It is important to recognize the dangerous influence these and other stereotypes and our own biases have on our attitudes and thus our work with the poor. It affects how we view and treat them as well as our ability to advocate for them.

We must recognize the biases and assumptions we have about those in poverty, some of which are deeply rooted. Everyone has biases, and to deny this is to ignore the dangers that will impede our effectiveness in service. We must also question our biases and assumptions, remembering that individuals are multidimensional, with a unique set of circumstances, not a stereotype. In addition, we must seek to continue to learn more about the populations with whom we work and serve.

We must recognize the structural challenges facing those in poverty. It is these challenges that make it difficult for individuals and families to escape poverty. While there are certainly individual challenges each person must contend with, the structural challenges are deeply rooted in our society, are beyond their control, and work against efforts to get out of and stay out of poverty.

Poverty is the state of being in which individuals and families live below cost of living thresholds and cannot provide for many of their basic needs without help. To define poverty, the US Census Bureau uses a set of income levels (dollar amounts) that vary by family size and composition. If a family's total income falls below this amount (the Poverty Threshold), they are considered in poverty (US Department of Labor, 2015). The 2014 Poverty Threshold was a mere $23,850 for a family of four and $19,790 for a family of three. The *Poverty Threshold* (or poverty line) is calculated by multiplying the cost of food in 1963 by three (3), in today's prices and updated for inflation annually. Food costs have certainly increased since 1963 (see Table 7.1 for examples); however, food costs have not climbed as much as other, more costly family expenses (see Table 7.2 for examples).

TABLE 7.1   Comparison of Various Food Item Costs: 1960s and 2014 (average price per pound)

Various Food Items	Cost in 1960s	Cost in 2014
Cheese	.39	5.58
Butter	.67	3.50
Potatoes	.04	0.69
Pork Chops	.59	4.17
Bacon	.79	6.07
Eggs, dozen	.49	1.98
Sugar	.38	0.60
Ground Beef	.45	4.01
Whole Chicken	.29	1.57
Apples	.49	1.40
Grapes	.14	2.13
Lettuce, iceberg	.25	1.11

Source: US Department of Labor and Bureau of Labor Statistics (2015) and The People History (2015)

TABLE 7.2   Comparison of Various Expenses

	1960	2014
Average Cost of a New Automobile	$2,600	$31,252
Median Sale Price of a New Home	$12,700	$302,000
Median Monthly Gross Rent	$350	$905
Average Annual Cost of Health Care (paid by workers)	$147	$4,565

Source: US Census Bureau (2015); The Henry J. Kaiser Family Foundation (2015); USAToday.com (2015); Justfacts.com (2015)

Since the increases in other cost of living items are not considered in the calculation of the poverty threshold, there are many families who are thus not *considered* poor but who are certainly unable to meet their basic needs.

Poverty can be relative or absolute. The Organisation for Economic Co-operation and Development measures global poverty and defines relative poverty by considering the average cost of living in a local community. They, along with other developed nations, use this definition to measure poverty rates. Absolute poverty is defined as living below a fixed dollar amount needed to provide one's family a level of basic survival. The United States uses an absolute standard to measure poverty, which acknowledges only the struggles of those that fall below this level.

Poverty affects people from all backgrounds and communities—some more than others. According to the 2014 US Census Bureau, 46.7 million people live in poverty (US Census Bureau, 2015), representing an official poverty rate of 14.8%. Poverty rates differ by groups, but there are two groups who experienced an increase in poverty between 2013 and 2014: people with a bachelor's degree or more; and married-couple families (DeNavas-Walt & Proctor, 2015). One of the fastest growing groups in poverty today is the working poor. Poor working adults work on average 2,500 hours per year, which means they are working more than one job (Waldron, Roberts, & Reamer, 2004). In addition, many of the poor work low-wage, dead end jobs that do not offer the type of upward mobility to allow them to leave poverty behind for good. The lack of good job opportunities in poorer communities are the result of a combination of things such as deindustrialization, or the shifting of our economy from manufacturing based to information based. Before this shift, which occurred in the 1970s and 1980s, these communities had more employment opportunities even for those without a college degree. These jobs were stable, with prospects to move up within the company. One only needs to drive through urban or rural communities to see the remnants of buildings that once housed these companies standing as stark reminders of what was once.

Barbara Ehrenreich, best-selling author of *Bait and Switch: The (Futile) Pursuit of the American Dream* and *Nickel and Dimed: On (Not) Getting By in America*, investigated the lives of the working poor by working alongside them, uncovering the hidden and brutal reality of their lives. In response to the notion that only a small percentage of people work more than one job, she states:

> *Well if it's only a small percentage of people who work two jobs, I must have met all of them then, because it was just so common among the people I worked alongside. A lot of people can't afford to work just 40 hours a week. They have to work, say, sixty, even eighty hours a week.*
>
> (Ross, 2002)

Poverty affects some groups at higher rates than others. The US Census Bureau (2015) reported 42% of those in poverty are white compared with 23% black, 28% Hispanic/Latino, and 5% Asian. However, proportionately, the poverty rates by race and ethnicity are 10.1% for white, 26% for black, 23.6% for Hispanic/Latino, and 12% for Asian. Because of these disproportionate rates, many of the community members you will work with may be members of racial and ethnic minorities. An important part of becoming culturally sensitive is learning to work with these populations.

Race and Ethnicity

Race and ethnicity are two dimensions of personal identity that play a central role in the United States, since its early beginnings. You will often serve in diverse communities and often with people who are racially and/or ethnically different from you. It is important for you to understand the role of racial and ethnic identity within our society and how individuals and communities have been and continue to be impacted. As mentioned in our discussion of poverty, we must recognize our own preconceived notions about race and ethnicity. We must shed light on our own biases and prejudices and seek to understand how our privileges might hinder our ability to effectively work with and advocate for the communities we serve. Read the following reflection and critically reflect before reading further.

Race has been defined in many different, often inaccurate, ways. It has been based on mistaken notions of a genetic superiority of the white race and inferiority of racial categories that are different. The formation of these categories has its origins in physical differences, such as skin color, and in the erroneous conceptions that one race can be superior to another. While the United States is vastly diverse, our difficult and contentious history of racial categorization and placing values on these categories directly affect the life chances and experiences of members of each racial category. This failure to address historic racism continues to impact laws and policies and how we view groups who are different.

Reflection

You are serving in a nonprofit community agency working with at-risk youth of color, conducting group activities and discussions on various topics such as staying in school, working, and family and other relationships. One of the youths, Shawn, does not fully participate and often seems agitated. During one discussion, you ask the group if they'd completed a small assignment to think about their future career aspirations. Shawn abruptly speaks up to say, "Why are we doing this? What difference does it make? Nobody cares about black people! My cousin did all this, he can't get a job and the cops are always hassling him. We don't stand a chance."

Melia emigrated from a Central American country with her family when she was very young. You have been working with her to identify colleges she might consider applying to. She is a senior in high school and is a very bright student, and you want her to explore all options. She confides in you that she does not plan to go to college because she is undocumented. She has already witnessed her parents being arrested, detained, and deported, and she is currently raising her younger brother with the help of other relatives. In this current climate, she cannot afford to risk being deported.

Reflect: How would you handle these situations? How do you validate Shawn and Melia's experiences while also encouraging and supporting them? How do your background and experiences either help or hinder your ability to work effectively with Shawn and Melia?

_____

_____

_____

Race has been used by those in power (the dominant group) to maintain that power. It has been used as a justification for the genocide and removal of Native peoples from their land; for the forced migration, enslavement, and continued subjugation of African peoples; for the history of restrictionist immigration policies, including the Chinese Exclusion Act of 1882, the first legislation targeting a specific ethnic group, which was later expanded to include immigrants from all Asia Pacific countries; and even for the discrimination and maltreatment of certain European and Eastern European immigrants, until they were afforded the opportunity to "become white." Today, we still see it used as justification for anti-Mexican and anti-Muslim rhetoric and policies.

There are some who want to believe we are in a post-racial society, one in which "we don't see color" and "everyone has the same opportunities." Many saw the election and re-election of Barack Obama, the nation's first black president, as proof that our racial troubles are behind us. Nothing could be further from the truth. One needs only to look at the persistent racial inequalities and injustices within our society to see that our nation's legacy of white supremacy, racism, and discrimination are very much ingrained and has not magically gone away. In your work, you must acknowledge the impact of racial inequalities and injustices on the communities and individuals you serve and work with them to find solutions to the challenges they face.

Ethnicity is another important "A" dimension of personal identity. It is a part of a person's membership in a group or groups that are set apart because of specific cultural practices, beliefs, languages, nationality, and so forth. It is a broad term that encompasses subcategories such as race. While not all ethnic groups are considered or treated as minority groups, there certainly are ethnic groups who have experienced discrimination as minority groups. As with race, we must acknowledge the ways in which the ethnic groups we work with have been affected, both historically and contemporarily. We must also understand that, just as each ethnic group is different from other ethnic or racial groups, their experiences in the United States may also be very different. In other words, all minorities are not the same. Take the time to learn about the community and individuals you will work with. Explore how past and present discrimination, policies, and ideologies might affect them.

It is also important to understand that within ethnic or racial groups, there are subgroups with vastly different experiences in this country. For example, an African American whose ancestors were slaves and then sharecroppers in this country have different experiences and perspectives from a Haitian immigrant who came to this country more recently. Early Cuban refugees left Cuba with wealth and resources and have had different experiences from poorer Cuban refugees who came later. A physician from China who immigrated to this country will differ from a laborer who emigrated from the very same country. These are only a few examples. Each person you work with is multifaceted, having many different dimensions to their identity. Each community, while perhaps sharing some similarities with others, also has unique experiences and challenges. Practice viewing each person and each community without comparing them to others or judging their experiences.

The process of becoming culturally sensitive is a lifelong process. Each of us begins this process in different places based on our backgrounds and past experiences. It can sometimes be a difficult experience as you shed some of your beliefs and preconceived notions about those who are different from you. However, your effectiveness in service learning and in helping professions depends on your journey toward being culturally sensitive. Included in this process is the importance of learning about and understanding yourself and accepting the challenges of change. Enjoy the process and the growth it will bring.

Reflect: *What concerns do you have about your ability to effectively work with people and communities different from you, particularly in terms of class, race, and ethnicity?*

_____

_____

_____

Think about individuals or communities with whom you currently work. How are they different from you? What will you do to increase your cultural sensitivity?

_____

_____

_____

REFERENCES

Arrendondo, P., & Glauner, T. (1992). *Personal dimensions of identity model*. Boston, MA: Empowerment Workshops.

DeNavas-Walt, C., & Proctor, B. D. (2015). *Income & Poverty in the United States: 2014*. Current Population Reports. Economic and Statistics Administration. Washington, DC: US Census Bureau. Retrieved September 22, 2015, from www.census.gov/content/dam/census/library/publications/2015/demo/p.60-252.pdf

Fouad, N. A., & Arredondo, P. (2007). *Becoming culturally oriented: Practical advice for psychologists and educators*. Washington, DC: American Psychological Association.

Henry J. Kaiser Family Foundation. (2015). Health Costs. Retrieved from www.kff.org/health-costs/.

Justfacts.com. (2015). Retrieved from www.justfacts.com/ healthcare.asp

Ross, R. (Director). (2002). *Wage slaves: Not getting by in America*. North Hollywood, CA: Termite Art Productions.

The People History. (2015). 1960s Food and Groceries Prices. Retrieved from www.thepeoplehistory.com/60sfood.htm/

US Census Bureau. (2015). Poverty Data. Retrieved August 19, 2015, from www.census.gov/hhes/www/poverty/data/

US Department of Labor and Bureau of Labor Statistics. (2015). Average Retail Food and Energy Prices, US and Midwest Region. Retrieved September 15, 2015, from www.bls.gov/regions/mid-atlantic/data/AverageRetailFoodMidwest_Table.htm

USAToday.com. 2015. "Average Used Car Price Hits Record High in 2014". Retrieved September 22, 2015 (http://www.usatoday.com/story/money/cars/2015/02/18/record-used-car-prices-in-2014/23637775/)

Waldron, T., Roberts, B., & Reamer, A. (2004). Working Hard, Falling Short: America's Working Families and the Pursuit of Economic Security: A National Report by the Working Poor Families Project. Retrieved September 15, 2015, from www.workingpoorfamilies.org/pdfs/Working_Hard.pdf

CHAPTER 8
DECONSTRUCTING GENDER AND SEXUAL IDENTITY

Christina Athineos and Kathryn Kozak

AIMS OF CHAPTER

1. Understand the gendered structure of society and how it contributes to oppression.
2. Explore theory and activism that attempt to subvert patriarchy and promote equality.
3. Engage with tools and skills that help build compassion and reduce oppression.

REFLECTION: "THINGS ARE SO MUCH BETTER THAN THEY USED TO BE." YES, AND . . .

Whenever someone tries to tell us that things are better than they used to be, it can be hard not to burst out with a litany of ways that things have stayed the same—or how they aren't good enough yet. As graduate student women, we are both sensitive to the fact that women faculty have more difficulty achieving tenure, that they are less likely to be in director or chair positons, and that as more women enter a profession, salaries go down. Sometimes it's too easy to get stuck on the "Yes, AND . . . "

In this chapter, we want to focus on both pieces. Things are so much better than they used to be—marriage equality legislation in the United States marks a milestone in the national conversation on LGBT+ rights, and a woman has run as a major party candidate for president of the United States.

Yes, AND . . . hurdles still exist based on gender and sexuality. We hope to validate the experiences of readers struggling with oppression based on their gender identity, gender expression, biological sex, or sexual identity. We also hope to educate helpers as to how they can acknowledge the role of patriarchal and heteronormative oppression in the everyday lives of those around them.

You may or may not identify as a feminist, but we certainly do! You might have heard the phrase, "If you believe that women are equal to men, then you are a feminist." But contemporary feminism is a little more complicated than that. In this chapter, we will address some common myths about patriarchy and explore how biological sex, gender identity, and sexual orientation can be sources of oppression. Then, we will discuss how feminism and LGBT+ movements address patriarchy. We provide tools to help you work effectively with people affected by patriarchal oppression as well as tools to better understand and undermine this system.

Reflect: So, what is patriarchy, anyway? Does patriarchy still exist in the United States?

_____

_____

_____

We live in a *patriarchal* society—one where men are automatically given certain power and privileges over women or nonbinary individuals. We also describe our society as *heteronormative*, meaning that the "norm" or baseline is to identify and behave as heterosexual. Despite numerous civil rights movements that have fought for "equal rights" for women, we remain entrenched in patriarchy due to both structural and cultural factors.

Men, cisgender, and heterosexual-identifying people typically *benefit* from the system. For example, men are typically regarded as strong leaders for exhibiting qualities such as decisiveness and aggression, whereas women are regarded as abrasive or bossy for the same behaviors. As another example, women who marry a man traditionally take his last name, and if they have children, the child gets the man's family name.

Women, transgender, and non-heterosexual-identifying people are often *harmed* by the system, even though some people in these groups don't notice oppression in their day-to-day lives. Examples of this oppression include high levels of violence, domestic abuse, and homicide against individuals in these groups (World Health Organization, 2013); there's also inequality in the workplace that might take the form of wage gaps, difficulty securing tenure/promotion, and poorer performance reviews.

Sometimes patriarchal oppression is a little less obvious. For instance, there are only two gender options in the English language: he and she, man and woman. People who do not identify as men or women are often misgendered or face resistance against using alternative pronouns, such as *ze* or *they*. Check out Box 8.1 for another example of how patriarchal rhetoric has been ingrained into much of the world's belief systems.

Over the past century, social activism has given rise to new legislature and legal protections to secure civil rights for women and LGBT+ individuals. Despite activist gains, pervasive issues such as rape culture, discrimination, and violence remain serious challenges.

Box 8.1 Religion, Patriarchy, and Gender

In designing this chapter, multiple people raised the question of how religion plays a role in maintaining patriarchal systems.

Patriarchal images and masculine language are often used in religious texts. For example, in most Christian religions, God is typically depicted as male. Additionally, many religious leadership positions are exclusively reserved for men.

For individuals who don't identify as religious, it may be tempting to exclude yourself from this dialogue, but consider this: in 2016, Pope Francis was named the fifth most powerful person in the world by *Forbes* magazine (Ewalt, 2016). Furthermore, America has never had a president who did not identify as Christian. What might it mean for women that so much of the most commonly practiced religion in our country is written from a male-dominant perspective?

—Radford Ruether (n.d.)

In your work, you will likely encounter individuals who have faced serious oppression related to their gender or sexuality and there's a good chance that you won't know about the challenges they face (but more on that later!). Feminism and the LGBT+ movement address this oppression.

COMMONALITIES BETWEEN COMMUNITY PSYCHOLOGY AND FEMINISM

Feminist psychology has critiqued traditional psychology's individuation and pathologization of women's collective distress (Astbury, 1996; Caplan, 1995; Caplan, 1985; Kaplan, 1983), asserting that traditional psychology has no right to state what women are like without including women in the study of the female psyche. Community and critical psychology has similarly critiqued traditional psychology's systematic decontextualization of issues, focusing on individual treatment targets as opposed to considering a public realm for intervention. Both community psychology and feminist psychology emphasize the importance of context in understanding behavior.

Considering context can mean many things, including conducting research in naturalistic settings, working with family and community systems instead of individuals, and looking for sociopolitical, as opposed to intrapsychic, explanations for presenting problems. This also means diversifying the voice that speaks on behalf of all psychologists to ensure that women and men are given equal opportunities to be heard. Similarly, women do not all share one voice, and it is critical to actively seek out the voices of women from all walks of life when considering the female perspective.

Both community and feminist psychologists encourage the use of ecological models to promote a holistic understanding of the interrelatedness of all human experiences. These models aid in understanding structural inequalities and power differentials as causes of personal distress, but must incorporate social justice considerations if they are to create interventions that will lead to social change.

When considering the ways in which community-based organizations as well as local and national governments work with community members to support the strengths of that community and address individual and collective needs, it is important to consider power and partnership.

Power

Power differentials can either constrain or expand the choices available to individuals in a range of social contexts. For example, gendered power inequalities increase the risk of a woman experiencing violence within a relationship and decrease her power to escape it. Therefore, power and empowerment are central concepts in feminist analyses. The phrase "personal is political" is often seen in feminist theory, sociology, and community psychology, referring to our need to always acknowledge our relative power and privilege in everything we do.

Partnership

Partnership implies equality; however, this relationship is often compromised, as researchers may see themselves as separate from the community they are meant to work with. Rather, partnerships should be thought of as occurring at multiple levels, in a variety of combinations that rarely involve equal power. By being aware of these power differences, psychologists can actively work to minimize these differentials to create relationships that more effectively respect groups with less direct access to power while simultaneously accessing the resources available to more privileged groups.

Confused?

Reading about these concepts can be a little confusing if you're only considering them in the abstract. That's why we've included some personal stories to make connections between the content and our lived experiences and serve as a jumping-off point for you to reflect and apply these ideas to your own life. Check out the personal reflection to learn more about how power may be playing a role in how we define and identify *feminists*.

Reflect: How do you define feminism? Do you consider yourself a feminist?

One day, I (CA) asked my mother, "Are you a feminist?" expecting a simple, "Yes, duh!" or some equally encouraging response. But instead I was answered with a curt "No." "What?!" I hollered back, "How can you say that?"

She answered with what I thought would only come from members of a much older generation, "I don't think that women should be better than men." How could my own mother, who raised me to be a self-sufficient and powerful woman, be telling me that she wasn't a feminist? How could she be so misguided in not knowing what this term meant?

Years later, the misperceptions have changed so that instead of being associated with "bra burners" and "lesbians," feminists are now labeled "social justice warriors," "overly sensitive," and "whiney liberals." It seems that despite all the advancements women have made, little has changed in the way society views feminists. We're still just "man-hating bitches." Where did these misconceptions come from? Why were they created and spread? Who are the ones keeping these false definitions alive?

> ### The Feminist Agenda
>
> "The feminist agenda is not about equal rights for women. It is about a socialist, anti-family political movement that encourages women to leave their husbands, kill their children, practice witchcraft, destroy capitalism, and become lesbians."
>
> —Television evangelist
> Pat Robertson (1992)

FEMINISM—DECONSTRUCTING THIS "DIRTY WORD"

Today, feminism has come to be associated with so many false definitions that many people, men and women alike, prefer not to identify as feminists. The smear campaign against feminism has led to many commonly held, widespread misperceptions:

Feminists Hate Men

Feminists don't hate men, and they don't think women are better than men. Feminists hate the patriarchy and believe that men and women are better than the patriarchy allows us to be. Feminism is about opposing sexism, which oppresses all genders. Giving women equal right to political, social, and economic justice does not take away these rights from men, nor would feminists want it to!

Feminism Is Only About Helping Women

Feminism did start out with the goal of gaining women rights, and it still holds that goal, but it has come to be much more inclusive than that. Feminism is for people of all genders, not just women. Feminism focuses on changing the systems that oppress women, men, trans, and nonbinary people. Further into this chapter we'll discuss the third wave of feminism and the movement's attempt to become more *intersectional*.

Men Can't Be Feminists

Yes, they can! Anyone who believes in ending sexism can identify as a feminist. And, news flash—feminism helps men, too! Feminism is all about freeing people from oppressive gender norms and that includes the patriarchal views of masculinity that force stereotypes on men. We'll talk more about how feminism helps men in a little bit.

Feminists Don't Do Anything but Complain

Feminists have fought for women to have the right to vote, to get an education, to work outside the home, to hold political office, to have greater control over their health and child-bearing. Feminists are still hard at work trying to decrease the wage gap, gain greater reproductive rights, decrease the number of rapes and sexual assaults, and so much more.

Feminists Are Just Angry Women Who Can't Take a Joke

Just because feminists don't enjoy jokes made at the expense of a group of people based on their gender, does not mean that they don't have a sense of humor. Feminists just aren't fans of comments aimed at demeaning other people or encouraging oppressive stereotypes.

Feminists Are All Lesbians and Bra Burners Who Don't Shave Their Armpits

Some feminists are lesbians. Some are straight. Some are bi. Some are trans, cisgender, nonbinary—the list goes on! Some are even men. Some shave; some don't. Some wear army pants, and others pink dresses. Who cares? There is no one image that captures all feminists, and feminism is not defined or confined by any of these stereotypes. In fact, feminists actively fight against these very stereotypes that tell people what they can and can't do based on their gender.

So, let's clarify this once and for all: *feminism* is none of these myths. *Feminism* is the belief that all genders should have the right to political, social, and economic equality. Feminists are simply the individuals who hold this belief.

FEMINISM FOR THE BOYS

Even after reading about the misperceptions of feminism, you may still be thinking that feminism is all about women's issues, women's equality, femininity, and so forth. But, feminism isn't just for women. Even though women are oppressed in many ways that men are not, traditional gender roles oppress us all—men included.

Reflect: Stop and think for a minute about the lessons life has taught you: what does it mean to be a "real man"?

_____

_____

_____

In Table 8.1, you'll find some examples of how patriarchal stereotypes oppress both men and women. Notice if any of these ideas popped up into your response to the previous reflection question, then take a moment to fill in your own ideas.

If you're struggling to come up with ideas, check out some more suggestions in the table at the end of the chapter. Although these are not concrete rules across the board, these unspoken expectations

TABLE 8.1 Body, Sex, Personality, Interests, and Work Stereotypes

	Women	Men
Body Stereotypes	• Skinny • • •	• Muscular • • •
Sex Stereotypes	• Virginity is sacred • • •	• Dominant • • •
Emotional/Personality Stereotypes	• Sweet • • •	• Tough • • •
Stereotypic Interests/Hobbies	• Dancing • • •	• Video games • • •
Work Stereotypes	• Nursing • • •	• Police officer • • •

underlie American society. Feminism helps men by focusing on changing the gender roles and sexual norms that limit our possibilities for how to act, think, and feel. Feminism allows individuals of all genders to freely pursue life outside of rigid, traditional understandings of femininity and masculinity.

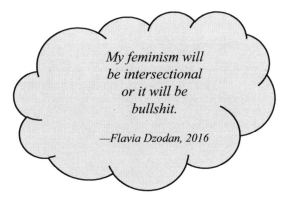

My feminism will be intersectional or it will be bullshit.

—*Flavia Dzodan, 2016*

While women and *nonbinary* individuals (those who don't identify as either male or female) have been speaking about the damaging effects of gender norms for years, it's only recently that men have started to share their experiences of oppression under these expectations. More people should be encouraged to start this conversation and spread the reality that feminism isn't just a women's rights issue; it's a human rights issue.

THINK YOU HAVE THE HANDLE ON FEMINISM? HOW ABOUT *WHITE FEMINISM*?

As we discussed earlier, feminism is the belief in equal rights for individuals of all genders. However, the feminist movement is currently at a crossroads, where many believe this more basic, traditional view of feminism to be outdated. The idea of *white feminism* has emerged as a "one-size-fits-all" version of feminism with middle class, white women as the norm, whereas the experiences of women of color and other marginalized groups are often ignored.

Women of color, trans women, immigrant women, differently abled women . . . there are many women who can't simply choose to not deal with the -isms and phobias that many white women can ignore. While some definitional variations exist, we define white feminism as a set of beliefs that allows for the exclusion of issues that specifically affect women with less privilege. This, of course, includes a racial component, with the focus on white wants and needs, in disregard of those of color. But it's also about more than just race. White feminism ignores women who don't fit the white, middle class, English-speaking, able-bodied, straight, cisgendered agenda. It's a "one-size-fits-all" feminism, where a few of the most privileged women have falsely assumed that their experiences of marginalization and oppression as women are universal, and in doing so, have inadvertently silenced the voices of others.

White feminists may be unaware of the privilege they have, as their focus more easily turns toward the ways in which they themselves are marginalized or oppressed. When white feminists are unaware of their privilege and assume that their experiences of marginalization and oppression as women are universal, they silence the voices of others, including women of color,

FIGURE 8.1 History of Feminism

differently abled, immigrant, and transgender women. By centering the feminist movement only on one group of women, the individuals who already have the most privilege and visibility end up with all of the power.

To be an inclusive social justice movement, feminism needs to incorporate an intersectional framework that recognizes the multiple aspects of identity that enrich the lives and experiences of *all* women and that compound and complicate oppressions and marginalizations.

Intersectionality refers to overlapping, or "intersecting," elements of our identity, such as race and gender. Recognizing the need for intersectionality and the compounding experience of marginalization and oppression of women of color can help us enrich the lives and experiences of *all* people to fight for social justice for everyone.

DEBUNKING THE MYTHS AROUND INTERSECTIONAL FEMINISM

Why is admitting to the existence of white feminism so scary? Throughout my experience, I've (CA) heard many reasons listed for why "white feminism" is a myth and intersectionality is either unnecessary or damaging. So, let's take a moment to address some of these thoughts and explain why they are misguided:

FIGURE 8.2   Feminists of Yesteryear

"Intersectionality Is Just Going to Further Divide the Feminist Movement."

Some people argue that including the calls for intersectionality within the feminist movement encourages division and undermines the unity of all races, classes, sexualities, and so forth from being unified simply as *women*. But when feminism focuses only on the oppression we all share, it neglects women and nonbinary individuals who face other forms of marginalization as well. In other words, even though all women are faced with sexism, not all women face racialized sexism, classist-sexism, trans misogyny, and so forth. We're always stronger together, but that doesn't mean we must erase the parts that make us unique to unite.

"We Don't Need Intersectionality."

Some don't understand why there is a need for intersectionality and mistakenly assume that their concerns map onto the needs and concerns of others. The goal of feminism is to challenge causes of injustice so that we may move toward gender equality. What some people have failed to realize is that these causes of inequality are not the same for all women. Many face different forces of oppression (racism, classism, etc.) which intersect with not only one another, but also with sexism. Intersectionality recognizes these aspects of identity that compound oppression outside of sex alone

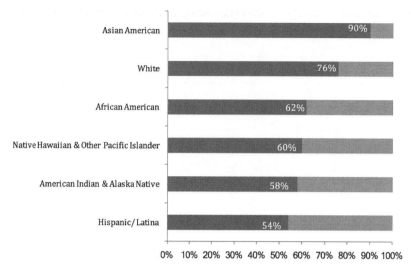

FIGURE 8.3 Women's Median Annual Earnings as a Percentage of White Men's Earnings

Source: AAUW, 2016

(Dzoden, 2011). Without intersectionality, only the problems affecting those with the most privilege are addressed, and the concerns of those with compounded areas of marginalization continue to be ignored. For a more contemporary example, consider the wage gap. Did you think to yourself, women earn about $0.76 for every $1 white men earn? Well, you'd be correct if you were referring only to white women. By comparison, African American women earn just $0.62 and Latina women earn only $0.54 (see Figure 8.3 for a complete breakdown).

"White, Privileged Women Shouldn't Be Involved in Intersectional Efforts. They Don't Have Personal Experience With This Type of Oppression and Therefore Shouldn't Speak to It."

It's extremely important for white women to talk about the issue of intersectionality in feminism. Other women already get it; it's white women who need to get on board. Intersectional movements need white women to be speaking out about these issues for a few main reasons:

● First, it's white women who already have some power. So, if the hope is to get others on board with intersectional feminism, this message is going to be most well-received coming from white women.

● Second, white women are part of the problem perpetuating white feminism. They need to own that if they're going to change the system in ways that will allow power to be shared equally.

● Third, and finally, white women need to face their discomfort with not being experts in every area of oppression and start speaking out anyway. It's impossible to be an expert on racism, ableism, sexual orientation, and so forth if you don't live it. So, if white women continue waiting until they know more about these experiences, they'll never speak up and join the fight.

Reflect: Before reading further, take a moment to reflect on your own experiences with feminism and answer these questions: how can you, personally, create spaces that will promote marginalized voices? Be sure to consider your own intersecting identities and how this may affect your decisions to engage in different ways.

_____

_____

_____

What can women with privilege do to shift the balance of power and foster equity?

_____

_____

_____

What can men do to shift the balance of power and foster equity?

_____

_____

_____

As members of the feminist movement ourselves, we currently struggle with these same questions. After years of contemplation, we've come up with three simple ways to go beyond just intellectualizing intersectionality and move toward practicing it. All you need to remember is that as proponents of social justice, this is our JOB.

Journal. Throughout this chapter and the rest of this book, you've been given spaces to stop and think about what you've been reading and how you can take it one step further. Don't shrug off this opportunity and leave those spaces blank! Take a moment to reflect and jot down what you come up with. Self-reflection is one of the first steps to recognizing your own privilege and the power that comes along with it. Understanding your own identities not only allows you to notice the oppression of others but also makes it easier to act against inequality and bias. Writing down your thoughts forces you to make your beliefs more concrete than merely thinking about them alone. So, please, don't leave this book looking pristine—highlight important passages, note questions you still have, and put down your ideas. Go back to earlier chapters and self-reflect; you will increase your understanding and consciousness dramatically.

Open your understanding of what feminism is meant to tackle so that it can include not just sexism, but also the things that compound this oppression and make inequality even more complex. Other great writers talk about doing this same thing by calling for us all to "decenter our perspectives" (Uwujaren & Utt, 2015). It's easy to keep feminism focused on the oppressions of those with the most power. But if we expand our understanding of feminism so that we avoid centering the movement on ourselves and those of the most privilege, we begin to create spaces for other individuals to speak about their experiences. This allows us to learn about ways in which our feminism can become more inclusive to perform truly transformational work.

Be uncomfortable. Thinking about your own feminism and moving toward intersectionality isn't going to be easy, and it certainly isn't going to be comfortable. Acknowledging our own privilege and how that impacts and oppresses others is a challenging, uncomfortable process. Be open to exploring these feelings. It's this discomfort that should inspire us to change.

TRY IT OUT!

To get started, why don't you try dipping your toes in the discomfort by testing your own implicit biases? Project Implicit, created by Harvard University, has many activities you can engage with to test your implicit biases, or attitudes, about things like gender, race, age, sexuality, and much more. These demonstrations might help you to become more aware of biases you didn't know you had, so consider this a first step in educating yourself! A link to these tests can be found at the end of the chapter under Resources.

Reflection

Several years ago, I (KK) was in a program of about eight students from the United States studying in Eastern Europe. One of us had a "What's your pronoun?" button on her bag. It sparked a discussion amongst the group about pronouns and misgendering, and she mentioned that she likes to introduce pronouns when she leads groups or meetings to open space for people who might otherwise be misgendered, or have others refer to them using pronouns that don't match with their identity. We all felt progressive and liberal, as asking pronouns was a relatively new practice. The conversation itself felt subversive, like we were doing something useful and important by discussing pronouns.

Several months later, another person in the group quietly mentioned to me that despite that whole conversation, no one asked their pronouns. This person prefers they/their/theirs but had been misgendered for weeks because despite the initial conversation, no one bothered to put it into practice. Myself included. That interaction has stuck with me and changed the way I approach conversations about oppression. Talking about tools and practices isn't enough. We must act in our everyday lives to make space for LGBT+-identifying people, because we're the ones with the voice to start the conversation—and continue it.

GENDER STUDIES AND THE LGBTQ+ MOVEMENT IN THE UNITED STATES

As a queer woman, I (KK) have found myself deeply invested in issues related to gender and sexuality. This moves beyond issues of legal equality, permeating through the justice system and even everyday interactions with those around us.

First, what are we even talking about? LGBTQIA isn't just "alphabet soup," but a meaningful acronym intended to be inclusive of *nonheteronormative* identities, or identities other than "straight" or "heterosexual" (see Box 8.2).

- L = Lesbian, or people who identify as women who are attracted to other people who identify as women.

- G = Gay, or people who identify as men who are attracted to other people who identify as

Box 8.2 Forgetting the Box

Humans love to put things into categories— and we love when things "fit neatly!" But life is messy, and many things don't fit neatly into a box. *(And, yes, we appreciate the irony of talking about boxes in a box!)*

Some people feel as though their identity doesn't "fit" with traditional labels. For example, many people don't identify as "men" or "women," but in English, we use gendered pronouns to refer to people. Instead of "he" or "she," some people prefer "they," whereas others use nontraditional pronouns such as "ze."

"Misgendering" is essentially trying to put people into the wrong box by using a pronoun other than what the person prefers. It can be accidental, or it can be a deliberate move to invalidate an identity.

What would life be like if we didn't use labels or try to fit identity into a box?

men. *Gay* is sometimes used as a catchall for any person attracted to others of the same sex or gender.

- B = Bisexual, or people who are attracted to two different genders (traditionally, men and women).

- T = Trans, or people whose gender identity does not match their sex as assigned at birth. This group includes people who identify within the gender binary, that is, as a man or woman, as well as people who do not identify as being a man or woman.

- Q = Queer (or, sometimes, *questioning*). Queer is "reclaimed," or a word whose original meaning is derogatory or pejorative, but has been taken back by the community in an act of empowerment. *Queer* is often used as a catchall for anyone who does not identify as **cisgender** or heterosexual.

- I = Intersex, or people who have the physical characteristics of both males and females.

- A = Asexual, or people who do not experience sexual attraction as it is traditionally understood in Western culture.

In this chapter, we use LGBT+ as an umbrella intended to include all nonheteronormative identities, even beyond those represented by the letters *L, G, B, T, Q, I,* and *A*. However, identities and experiences within the LGBT+ umbrella are diverse. Check out Box 8.3 to learn more about microaggressions and power within the LGBT+ community.

Box 8.3 Micro Aggression Can Come From Anywhere

LGBT+ people aren't "immune" to homophobia, transphobia, misogyny, or other forms of bigotry and oppression. I (KK) have found myself "grilled" on my sexuality by other self-identifying members of the LGBT+ community. I came out to a friend who identified at the time as cis and gay. The word I used to describe myself at the time was *bisexual*, and the friend unleashed a whirlwind of personal and intellectual questions. "I just want to understand," he said. He concluded the conversation by saying "I don't know, I just personally don't think it's possible to like men and women equally, I feel like one must be more just sex." I was stunned, confused, and hurt. I found myself wondering, did I just fail an entire sexuality because I didn't fit in with his ideas?

That was the first micro aggression I experienced based on my sexuality, but it increased my awareness of micro aggressions I've committed against others. Identifying as queer doesn't mean I'm more accepting, or that I don't contribute to oppression. It's just given me more firsthand experience with oppression myself and has helped me shape how I want to treat others—based on how I want to be treated.

Reflect: The word *gay* used to be a catchall term for anyone who wasn't straight, but many people prefer *queer* or *LGBT*. Why do you think that might be?

_____

_____

_____

The queer, or LGBT+, movement in the United States has recently been traced back to the Stonewall riots. "Gayness" isn't a new thing—homosexual behaviors have been recorded all the way back to the Ancient Greeks—but identifying as a gay person is relatively new (Halperin, 1993). LGBT+ communities thrived in urban centers, such as San Francisco, as people sought refuge from harassment and discrimination throughout the United States. The idea of the "gay community" emerged as LGBT-identifying people found a sense of unity and fellowship that extended beyond physical neighborhoods (Weston, 1998).

However, the HIV/AIDS crisis of the 1980s and 1990s brought a resurgence of homophobia and changed the landscape of gay culture. Even today, gay and bisexual men account for 67% of all HIV diagnoses in the United States, with African American gay and bisexual men disproportionately affected (CDC, 2016). Activist organizations such as ACT UP were formed to combat the fear, misinformation, and violence against gay and bisexual men but more importantly advocated for medical research and resources to curb the epidemic (Bersani, 1987; Takemoto, 2003). Because LGBT+ people needed to organize politically to ensure their safety, political activism has lain at the heart of the LGBT+ movement. The overlaps between LGBT+ issues and women's issues has led to similarities in the language and conceptual tools used. For example, sex and gender are central to both feminism and many LGBT+ movements.

Reflect: In what ways are issues of LGBT+ identity personal to you or someone you know? In what way are these issues political?

AREN'T SEX AND GENDER THE SAME THING?

Traditionally, "sex" in the English language referred to both physiology and social roles. It was assumed that the two would "match up," with social roles dictated by your biological and physical makeup. The word *gender* has been used to tease apart the aspects of our identity that revolve around society's norms and expectations.

Today, we typically use *sex* to talk only about physiology. We use the phrase *sex assigned at birth* to acknowledge that some people identify differently from how doctors and parents labeled them at birth. "Sex" isn't as simple as we might think—there's no "official list" of what makes a male a male or a female a female.

We use *gender identity* to talk about how people think about themselves and *gender expression* to talk about how people communicate their gender to others. It's not as easy as man or woman!

BREAKING THE BINARY

Binary refers to a system that has two categories, or choices. We see binaries everywhere, because they can help simplify our understanding of the world.

The *gender binary* is the idea that there are two fixed genders. You can be a man, or a woman, but not both and not neither. Gender and sexuality in Western culture have traditionally been expressed using binaries, like gay or straight.

Reflect: What are some situations or categories where you have seen a binary or have been forced to describe yourself using a limited number of choices? Did you fit within one of the "boxes"? What was it like to describe yourself with only a few choices?

_____

_____

_____

So, going back to gender: some people don't think of themselves as men, but they don't think of themselves as women, either. Common words people may use are *nonbinary*, *agender*, *genderqueer*, or "*neutrois*." But while they might wear clothing and jewelry that are typically associated with, for example, women, this doesn't mean they "identify" as women!

This goes for sexual identity, too. Traditionally, in Western culture there was "straight" and "gay." We recognize now that it's not that simple. You might be bisexual, or "bi," and be attracted to people of two genders. Or you might be asexual, sometimes referred to as "ace," and not experience sexual attraction.

The important thing is that only *you* know how you identify! A person might "look like" a woman, but that might not be how they identify. A person might be in a relationship with someone of the opposite gender, but that doesn't mean that they are "straight." We'll talk about navigating others' identities later, in the etiquette section.

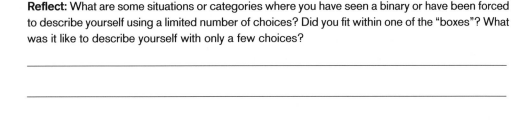

Gay Best Friend

Another common issue lies in the trope of the "gay best friend."

Think of characters from *Will and Grace* or *Mean Girls*.

While straight or cis people may feel like they're showing support for their friends' identities, it can be demeaning: calling someone a "gay best friend" reduces your friendship to their sexuality.

Being an Ally or Partner

If you do not identify as LGBT+, then you might work to be an ally or partner to the LGBT+ community. Traditionally, a "straight" person who "supports" LGBT people was considered an *ally*. Think: Genders and Sexuality Alliance, which was founded in 1998 to support students who wanted to organize clubs in support of LGBT+ issues (GSA, 2017).

However, the term *ally* has been heavily criticized as a way for people with straight privilege to pat themselves on the back without putting in the work to support LGBT+ issues. For example, a straight person might insert themselves into an LGBT+-safe space by calling themselves an ally, without taking the time to understand and help.

Instead, people who want to help are encouraged to use the word *ally* as a *verb*. An ally isn't something you *are*, but something you *do*. A good ally listens and learns but understands and respects boundaries.

Etiquette

It can be nerve-wracking or intimidating talking to others about their gender or sexuality. You might be scared to hurt their feelings or offend them. You might worry that you yourself could be "outed" and face bias. There are some tangible ways that we can show our respect for others, to reduce stigma and facilitate healthy partnerships. These tips are relevant for anyone who wants to encourage healthy relationships with others, regardless of how you identify.

Respect the Closet

You should never "out" someone or disclose information about their gender or sexual identity to others. Coming out as nonheteronormative is a personal choice, and it isn't your job to tell anyone else. I (KK) have a friend who identifies as a lesbian, is married to another woman, and who posts on Facebook about LGBT+ issues and her relationship with her wife. But that doesn't mean that everyone in the world knows that she's a lesbian. Maybe she isn't out to her boss or co-workers, and isn't friends with them on Facebook. You never know—and so you should let people disclose their identity on their own terms.

Respect Safe Spaces

While there's plenty of controversy over what a safe space is—and whether one can even exist—it's always important to be mindful of the space you are in. Are your comments or body language putting others at ease, or making them uncomfortable? When visiting an LGBT+ space such as a gay bar, be mindful of why you're there and how your presence might affect others there.

It's Your Job to Educate Yourself!

Don't rely on others, particularly LGBT+-identifying people, to educate you. Do the work yourself to seek out answers to questions you might have or clear up misconceptions. It can be tempting to ask lots of questions out of curiosity, or to try and inform yourself. But this can overstep boundaries. Plenty of vlogs, blogs, and articles are out there if you want to learn more (and you can find them in the Resources section of this chapter). Think: would you ask this question of a straight person?

Be Calm, Cool, and Compassionate

What do you do if someone comes out to you? Maybe they mention a same-sex partner, or maybe they tell you that they identify as asexual. It might take you by surprise, or you might have "known all along," and these are totally normal reactions. The best thing to do is to validate: "Thank you for sharing that with me!" Avoid phrases like "Oh, we all know!" or "Really? But you seem so normal" that might come across as disappointed or confused.

The bottom line is to be open and respectful. You don't need to know everything there is to know about LGBT+ issues to be a good partner or ally. Understand that LGBT+ people face more discrimination and more violence than their heterosexual and cisgender peers. And understand that these issues are compounded for people of color.

Reflect: Now, let's think about some ways that we can be strong partners to LGBT+ people in our community. How can you show your support for LGBT+ people, even if you don't know how they identify?

_____

_____

_____

You're working with someone who introduced themselves as they/them/theirs, but the site supervisor constantly misgenders them using he/him/his. What are some things you could do?

_____

_____

_____

As part of a research project, you are helping develop a survey to see whether demographic factors such as age, gender identity, and sexual orientation affect access to resources. What are some ways you could structure the questions to be inclusive to all identities?

_____

_____

_____

TYING IT ALL TOGETHER AND PUTTING IT INTO ACTION

There are three main things for helpers to focus on: educate yourself, educate others, and know when and how to disengage. It's crucial to gain an understanding of the world around you without encroaching on others' personal boundaries. We also must use our privilege and our voice for those who may not be understood or heard. But just as it's important to engage with others, sometimes we need to know how and when to prioritize our own mental health and physical safety.

COMMITMENT TO EDUCATION

Educate yourself. This can take many forms, such as compassionately listening to others share their experiences, looking up articles or video clips related issues, or joining new groups that expose you to new ideas or perspectives. The important point here is that it's _your_ job!

Be cautious when exploring patriarchal oppression not to ask overly personal questions out of curiosity. Friends and acquaintances aren't case studies—they're people with complex thoughts, feelings, and experiences. Don't ask a question you wouldn't ask anyone else. If someone comes out to you as bisexual, for example, don't expect them to explain bisexuality to you, and don't ask them about who they've slept with or who they're dating.

USING YOUR VOICE

We have opportunities to use our voice every day. As we've discussed elsewhere in this book, we fight oppression by calling out inappropriate or biased behavior. If your friend refers to their date as "my latest conquest," or if your classmate blurts out that they find homosexuality "morally repugnant," you can make a big difference by gently but firmly stopping and redirecting:

- _"Hey, that's not okay—please don't objectify women like that."_
- _"Excuse me, but that kind of language is really harmful."_

Reflect: Think of some other ways you could gently—and safely—stop and redirect inappropriate words or behavior.

_____

_____

_____

This can be challenging—and it doesn't always work right away. You might face pushback from someone who feels threatened or embarrassed. We have found that compassion and patience go a long way, even if it takes years of calling out sexism, misogyny, homophobia, transphobia, and other forms of oppression. But using your voice also happens when you engage in productive conversations with others, or when you advocate for yourself or others within an institution. See Box 8.4 to learn how one woman's voice ignited a movement that united over four million people.

Box 8.4 Anyone Can Organize: Women's March on Washington, DC

On January 21, 2017, the first day of Donald Trump's presidency, millions of people protested to protect legislation and policies regarding women's rights. People from across the world marched in solidarity to demonstrate that women's rights are human rights, regardless of race, ethnicity, immigration status, religion, sexual identity, gender expression, economic status, age, or ability.

With 673 marches taking place in all 50 states and 81 countries across the globe, this cause united over 4 million people, making it the largest march in American history. What started with one woman sharing her idea on social media grew into a movement striving to defend a myriad of social justice concerns, including immigration, health care, LGBT+ rights, racial inequality, religious freedom, Native American rights, and the environment. So, if you've ever thought that one person can't make a difference, just remember these activists. As Maryum Ali, eldest daughter of Muhammad Ali, stated at the march, _"Don't get frustrated, get involved. Don't complain, organize."_

CARING FOR YOURSELF

Patriarchy is a powerful thing. Everything in society, from our language to our institutions, is set up to preserve patriarchy. Sometimes fighting patriarchy can be exhausting, or even outright dangerous. Think back to the student reflections about safety and putting your oxygen mask on first. It's important to know when to step back, take a break, and reorganize. Finding like-minded people who support your ideas is a great way to regroup and regain strength and motivation. Check out the resources listed at the end of this chapter for more information about places you can find community and information about some of the topics we discussed in this chapter.

Example Table for Gender Stereotypes*

	Women	Men
Body Stereotypes	● Should be skinny but have curvy hips, large breasts, round butt ● Focus on being attractive ● No body hair ● No stretch marks ● No cellulite	● Need to be muscular ● Should be strong ● Well endowed ● Able to grow a beard ● Tall ● Deep voice
Sex Stereotypes	● Virginity is sacred ● "You're a slut" ● "You're a prude" ● "You're a tease" ● Showing too much skin or attire is too repressed	● Judged for being a virgin ● "You should be able to get sex whenever you want it" ● "You must be gay" ● Dominant
Emotional/Personality Stereotypes	● Soft ● Caring ● Sweet ● Innocent ● "She's crazy!" ● Emotional	● "Toughen up" ● "Men don't cry" ● "Stop acting like a girl" ● Aggressive ● Confident ● Rational/logical
Stereotypic Interests/ Hobbies	● Sewing ● Dancing ● Cooking ● Gardening ● Gossiping	● Video games ● Sports ● Drinking ● Women ● Cars, motorcycles, and trucks
Work Stereotypes	● Responsible for taking care of the children and the home ● Careers in nursing, teaching, secretary, hospitality, care-giving	● Need to be the breadwinners of the household ● Careers in business, finance, construction, science, engineering, fire, and police ● CEOs

*Remember, this is not an extensive list and is meant only to spark ideas

RESOURCES

For more information about HIV/AIDS: www.cdc.gov/hiv/statistics/overview/ataglance.html

For articles, videos, and information related to feminism and feminist causes: www.everydayfeminism. com

To get connected and stay informed about issues affecting women on college campuses: www. hercampus.com/

For a video clip of Katie Couric's interview with Carmen Carrera and Laverne Cox on respecting the privacy of transgender individuals: www.youtube.com/watch?v=sMH8FH7O9xA

For an article that explores how Katie Couric models ways to learn from past mistakes: www. thedailybeast.com/articles/2017/02/05/i-think-i-made-a-mistake-katie-couric-on-her-transgender-evolution.html

To test your own biases at Project Implicit: https://implicit.harvard.edu/implicit/takeatest.html

For a quick comic that illustrates intersectional feminism: www.upworthy.com/what-is-feminism-really-this-comic-sums-it-up-well

For resources and support for trans and queer youth: https://gsanetwork.org/
For a blog that provides space for queer and trans people of color: www.bgdblog.org/

REFERENCES

AAUW. (2016). *The truth about the gender pay gap (Spring 2017)*. Washington, DC: Author.

Astbury, J. (1996). *Crazy for you: The making of women's madness*. Melbourne: Oxford University Press.

Bersani, L. (1987). Is the Rectum a Grave? *AIDS: Cultural Analysis/Cultural Activism, 43*, 197–222.

Caplan, P. J. (1985). *The myth of women's masochism*. New York, NY: New American Library.

Caplan, P. J. (1995). *They say you're crazy: How the world's most powerful psychiatrists decide who's normal*. Jackson, MI: De Capo.

CDC. (2016, December 2). HIV in the United States: At A Glance. Retrieved from www.cdc.gov/hiv/statistics/overview/ataglance.html

Dzoden, F. (2011, October 10). My feminism will be intersectional or it will be bullshit. *Tiger Beatdown*. Retrieved from http://tigerbeatdown.com/2011/10/10/my-feminism-will-be-intersectional-or-it-will-be-bullshit/

Ewalt, D. M. (2016, December 14). The world's most powerful people 2016. *Forbes*. Retrieved from www.forbes.com/sites/davidewalt/2016/12/14/the-worlds-most-powerful-people-2016/?ss=powerful-people#11185e411b4c

GSA. (2017). History and accomplishments. *GSA Network*. Retrieved from https://gsanetwork.org/about-us/history (Accessed on February 26, 2017).

Halperin, D. M. (1993). Is there a history of sexuality? In H. Abelove, M. A. Barale, & D. M. Halperin (Eds.), *The Lesbian and gay studies reader* (pp. 416–431). New York: Routledge.

Kaplan, M. (1983). A woman's view of DSM-III. *American Psychologist, 38*(7), 786–792. doi:10.1037/0003-066X.38.7.786.

Radford Ruether, R. (n.d.). Feminist critique and re-visioning of God-language. *Theological Trends*. Retrieved from www.theway.org.uk/back/27Ruether.pdf (Accessed on February 26, 2017).

Robertson, P. (1992, August 26). Robertson letter attacks feminists. *The New York Times*. Retrieved from www.nytimes.com/1992/08/26/us/robertson-letter-attacks-feminists.html

Takemoto, T. (2003). The Melancholia of AIDS: Interview with Douglas Crimp. *Art Journal, 62*(4), 80.

Uwujaren, J., & Utt, J. (2015, January 11). Why our feminism must be intersectional (And three ways to practice it). *Everyday Feminism*. Retrieved from http://everydayfeminism.com/2015/01/why-our-feminism-must-be-intersectional/

Weston, K. (1998). *Long slow burn: Sexuality and social science*. New York: Routledge.

Women's March. (2017). The campaign. Retrieved from www.womensmarch.com

World Health Organization. (2013). *Global and regional estimates of violence against women: Prevalence and health effects of intimate partner violence and non-partner sexual violence*. Geneva, Switzerland: World Health Organization.

CHAPTER 9
NAVIGATING EDUCATIONAL SYSTEMS

Carol Sharicz, Shaina Hastings, and Debra A. Harkins

AIMS OF CHAPTER

1. Understand power dynamics within educational systems.
2. Examine the underlying dynamic of educational inequality.
3. Explore how to make systemic changes in our communities and schools.

REFLECTION: PAYING ATTENTION

The sign said, "Homeless and Struggling." That message tugged at my heart.

I (CS) walked past thinking about him and then immediately turned around to ask him if I could hear his story. I was also intrigued that he was sitting on the ground reading a book. He told me he is 27 years old, came from an old, industrial town in Central Massachusetts and has an Associate Degree in Culinary Arts from a well-known university. His mom died in 2009 and he has been suffering from depression ever since, which prevents him from finding work. We talked for 10 minutes and I asked his name; I wanted to use his name and for him not to remain nameless. His name is Dan, a very articulate young man. When I thanked him for his time, for which I paid him, he said he just wanted to "break out of this cycle." Those final words of Dan capture the essence of this chapter and perhaps, even, this book.

There is one overriding, provocative, disturbing theme that will anchor the discussion in this entire chapter. There is a growing trend in the United States that is creating class-based educational segregation (Putnam, 2015). This class-based system emanates from the growing wealth gap as shown in Figure 9.1, which illustrates that the share of adults living in middle-income households is in steady decline, and share in lower- and upper-income households is rising.

REFLECTION: NEW SCHOOL

I (SH) grew up living in an affordable housing complex in the Greater Boston Area. As a young white girl, when I thought about race I thought about my best friend, my neighbors, and my babysitter who lived in the apartment upstairs. At the time, I recognized that racism existed, but to me it felt like a distant memory, something that was taught in history lessons.

At the young age of 10, I moved about 30 minutes north of the city. Imagine the contrast between affordable housing to an apartment in a quaint, upper middle class, suburban neighborhood. Picture a typical old New England style town, with a perfectly tiny roundabout plopped right in the center. I vividly remember the first day of class. The stark contrast was shocking to me. The first thing I noticed was that there were only white students in my classroom . . . that was when I first realized that racism was not as distant of a memory as I originally thought.

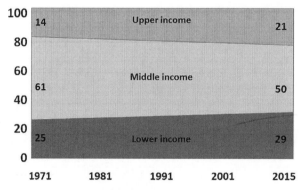

FIGURE 9.1   Percentage of Adults in Each Income Tier

Note: Adults are assigned to income tiers based on their size-adjusted household income in the calendar year prior to the survey year.

Source: Pew Research Center Analysis of the Current Population Survey, Annual Social and Economic Supplements

Reflect: Before we describe what happens in our school systems and what we need to do about it, reflect on your school experience.

What was your personal experience in the schools you attended (e.g., preschool, elementary, middle school, or high school)? Was your experience positive, negative, or something in between?

_____

_____

_____

Reflect on how your personal experience might have been different from students different from you (e.g., gender, class, race, disability)?

_____

_____

_____

This chapter focuses on what we can do on a practical, systemic basis to help to make changes in our communities and schools. You may be asking why schools are the focal point for this chapter and not some other institution. That would be a good and fair question to ask. Education is our passion; we believe in the power of education to change lives. More importantly on a larger level, education has been, and still has the potential to be, a significant equalizer.

There are several key resources listed at the end of this chapter. Among them is Robert Putnam's (2015) book, *Our Kids: The American Dream in Crisis*, which does a great job of documenting with solid research and personal stories the crisis affecting our children and the nation. We will illustrate through a causal loop the challenges we face and then proceed to focus on what we can **do** to make transformational changes. The aim of this chapter is practical and focused on the mesosystem first introduced in Chapter 1; that is, that school and communities provide a key leverage point in making change in educational injustice. Figure 9.2 illustrates the top level dynamic that forms the systemic basis of the class-based system. This dynamic is a synthesis of the data and research provided in Putnam's (2015) book.

Researchers demonstrate how perceived discrimination in the school system negatively impacts students' education. For example, Steaton and Douglass (2014) found that 97% of their students

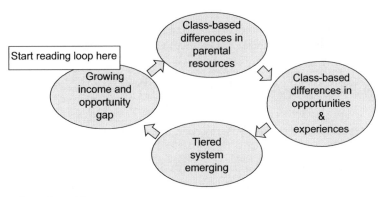

FIGURE 9.2   Class-Based System

experienced at least one discriminatory event in a 14-day period. Per English, Lambert, and Ialongo (2014), these events lead to higher depression rates, which in turn lead to negative impacts on education.

Reflect: Before we delve deeper into this complex issue, reflect on what you think is the relationship between race, class, and education.

Because of a long history of inequality and lack of opportunity, minorities often live in poverty. This history includes slavery, which ended only 151 years ago, and then *lawful* segregation, which ended only about 60 years ago. This is just a snippet to give perspective of how recently these crimes were committed. Since the United States has a long and shameful history regarding race, which still runs deep in the roots of our nation today, segregation is still implemented through redlining and white flight.

> Since there is a lack of race integration in our school systems, how do you think students (of any race) are impacted?

The term *redlining* is coined from an old government home owner loan practice when specific neighborhoods, particularly black, would be outlined in red. People from these neighborhoods would be denied loans for mortgages. That is now technically an illegal practice; yet, ongoing lawsuits allege that banks continue to refuse to give mortgage loans to residents in certain neighborhoods today. Retail redlining also happens through gentrification; when trendy shops open and bring in wealthier people, it has a negative impact on residents. Rent prices start to increase, and eventually it pushes the previous residents out of the neighborhood (Lerman & McKernan, 2007). Controlling rent prices and denying mortgage loans keep specific groups of people in selective zones.

White flight is also an issue that creates self-segregation. This happens when white residents start moving after a certain percentage of minorities move into a previously predominant white town. The only way to fix this trend is education about diversity and the importance of integration between races.

Let's use Boston as an example of segregation in the school system. The Boston Redevelopment Authority found that the poorest areas in Boston consist of three major minority groups: African American, Latin American, and Asian American populations. Dorchester represents the highest levels of people in poverty in Boston, and the 2010 census found that 43% African American, 22% white, 17% Latin American, 9% Asian, and a small percentage of other populations reside there. In turn, schools that are in impoverished cities are left behind. Figure 9.3 demonstrates the average amount of money spent per pupil and the percentage of African American and Hispanic students that reside there.

EDUCATION AND RACISM: KEY FINDINGS

- On an institutional level, school systems are failing minority students. There is a huge disadvantage being a minority student from a low-income neighborhood.

- Because of inequalities in class and race, young students are subjected to a lapse in power in the school system. With high levels of segregation in the school system, there is a major impact on students' education. For example, researchers find that stronger feelings of racial discrimination are associated with an increase in depression among adolescents (English et al., 2014), which

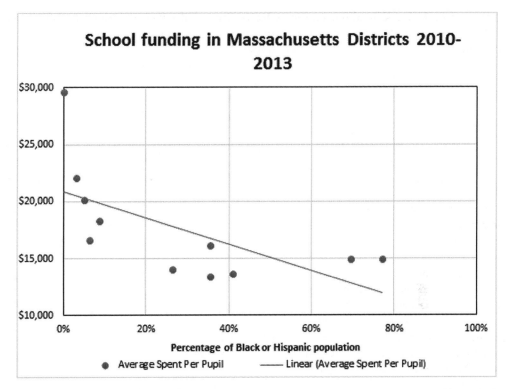

FIGURE 9.3   School Funding in Massachusetts

has a negative impact on education (Quiroga et al., 2013). It is crucial to acknowledge the negative impact on students' success rates and aspirations due to racial discrimination. It is important to evaluate the negative implications that discrimination has on academic success.

- Students as young as middle-school age suffered from racist acts that impacted their behavior and academic performance.

- Depression has a serious impact on academic achievement. Although it has been shown that depression adversely impacts academic achievement, previous research that examines the reasons that depression interferes with school are not well known (Quiroga et al., 2013). One reason for the drop-out rates of children with depression could be their belief that they are not competent at school.

- With evidence of discrimination and segregation affecting students' academic well-being, what is there to do? Steaton and Douglass (2014) found that the more integrated a school system is, the more it allows for students to feel less daily discrimination.

Reflect: So, what can be done about this race- and class-based injustice in our school systems? Reflect here on possible solutions to this social injustice before reading further.

_____

_____

_____

There are potential action plans that may be implemented to decrease the negative impact that discrimination and class have on students' education. An example of this would be turning schools into community hubs. A community hub creates a space for a conglomerate of public services. Haig (2014) wrote about the use of the community hub approach. This approach uses a school as a resource for the community. There is potential for schools to host resources for students and their families. Using that space outside of school hours potentially positively impacts the community that in turn would have a positive impact on the students within that community. For example, if a community has a specific need, such as preventing teenage pregnancy, there could be a resource for students to learn about safe sex and contraception. Another example could be mental health and family services. If a student or family member is struggling with mental health disorders, having a facility easily accessible should in theory have a positive impact on the community. This in turn would have a positive impact on students' education. Happy students = more productive and successful students.

Another important action plan would be furthering integration in US school systems. Gerrymandering can be defined as the manipulation of town lines to benefit a specific group or party. Educational gerrymandering can create either a lack of diversity or can be used to create greater diversity within the school system (Siegel-Hawley, 2013). Currently, gerrymandering seems to be causing the former. This is problematic, because as Steaton and Douglass (2014) point out, a more diverse school environment allows for less perceived discrimination. When there are perceived discriminatory acts, a student is less likely to be negatively impacted by the act when schools are more diverse. Look up a map of your nearest cities school lines. What do you see? Are the lines oddly shaped? Typically, district lines don't seem to have much of a rhyme or reason. If the district lines were reshaped to create higher diversity in race and socioeconomic status (SES) there would be better outcomes for minority and low SES students.

Reflect: How can we as a nation survive economically, culturally, and spiritually, with such a growing disparity? What will it take to change this trend?

_____

_____

_____

What kinds of changes do we need to make to help alleviate this gap?

_____

_____

_____

Now that we have discussed the prevalence of segregation present today, let's discuss how this impacts the classroom. It is clear on an institutional level that school systems are failing minority students. English et al. (2014) found that 97% of African American students in the study perceived at least one discriminatory event in a 14-day period. An overwhelming majority of African American students experienced an event that negatively impacted their educational and developmental health. Students as young as middle-school age suffered from racist acts that impacted their behavior and academic performance. Students who are discriminated against are known to have higher rates of depression (English et al., 2014). Higher rates of depression also create a negative impact on education such as poor grades and lack of participation (Quiroga, Janosz, Bisset, & Morin, 2013).

Depression has a serious impact on academic achievement (Quiroga et al., 2013). Quiroga et al. (2013) argue that one reason for the drop-out rates of children with depression could be related to the child's belief that they are not competent. Students with this mind-set are likely to create a self-fulfilling prophecy, which becomes a major issue for them. If a child consistently hears the message that they cannot succeed, it is more likely than not that the student would not try to reach their goal because of the belief and fear of failure. With evidence of discrimination and segregation affecting students' academic well-being, what is there to do? Steaton and Douglass (2014) found that the more integrated a school system is, the less likely students are discriminated against.

Reflect: What is within our control?

_____

_____

_____

The dynamic discussed previously is indeed systemic, which means it is something fundamental to the current school system. Fortunately, systemic shifts can happen, but they are not easy or fast. One significant practice that can be undertaken on any level—the personal, relational, or collective (all explored in other chapters)—is to engage in the process of developing a vision of an ideal school.

Reflect: What would a socially just and ideal school look like?

_____

_____

_____

The following is an action plan to help you move toward that ideal vision, followed by other practices that can be implemented to make change.

ACTION PLAN AND IMPLICATIONS FOR COMMUNITY SCHOOLS AND RESOURCES

Desegregation is the most important step that needs to be taken. There is no clear-cut action plan for desegregation. Although outright segregation is not technically legal, it still happens. Lack of investigation into illegal redlining allows the practice to happen along with gerrymandering. It is important to pay attention to local laws and policies and to become educated on issues that impact the community. Asking law makers serious questions about school segregation and spreading the word makes a difference.

White flight is another problem that impacts the ability to desegregate schools. This arises out of racial bias and can be changed through spreading the message and educating people about racial inequality. This takes time and consistent activism.

While desegregation will take fighting for, advocating for **community schools** could have a positive impact on a struggling community. A community school is one that partners with other community resources outside of academia. A community school not only focuses on learning but also is a place where students and families can go for other services. These services allow for educators, administrators, organizations, and families to work together any day of the week at any time (Blank, Melaville, & Shah, 2003). Let's observe a family who is well off. Marty, who comes from an upper middle class family, is struggling in his biology class. His parents hire a tutor for him, and he is also provided with his own laptop and a new textbook. On the other hand, there is Caren, whose single mother is working overtime to support her daughter. She is struggling in the same biology class that Marty is in. Caren's mother cannot afford a tutor or a computer; Caren has only the resources she is given through her school.

> **Reflect:** What would you think about Caren and Marty if you saw only their grades? It would not be wrong to think one tried harder than the other based solely on a letter. This is a view that lacks context. It is important to recognize this issue when debating with others who may lack perspective.

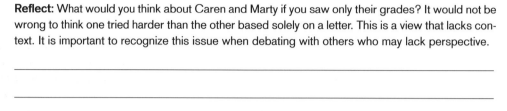

Having a school as a community resource would help give both Marty and Caren an equal opportunity to grow. It wouldn't harm Marty, and it would only help his classmate Caren. The hub allows students to have access to tutoring programs, after-school activities, health services (including mental health), and programs to help students with college and career preparation. Within community school programs, families can (and are encouraged to) help by planning, volunteering, and empowering students. The focus on community development is prevention oriented rather than crisis oriented (Dupper & Poertner, 1997).

An example of a community hub would be The Family Resource Center in Minneapolis. Parents were asked to take part of the council and were paid through grant money. Any parents who volunteered were given gift certificates. This technique served a critical role in giving parents a feeling of self-worth by recognizing and valuing their work. These parents encouraged their friends to get involved, and soon the whole school was participating (Dupper & Poertner, 1997). More information on the school is provided here: http://ecs.mpls.k12.mn.us/family_resource_center

THREAD is a program in Baltimore that connects high school students with volunteers who are going to be committed for the long term (see www.thread.org). Each high school student has a tutor and connections to the volunteers like a family member who will support not only their academic journey but also life goals. The resources include tutoring, college prep, help with health and legal services, and even risk management. Of the students who have been in THREAD for five years, 92% graduate high school, 90% are accepted to college, and 80% have completed a two- or four-year undergraduate program.

Parental involvement is imperative to the success of school community hubs, resulting in a more positive outlook in school and improved attendance. Issues to address include changing parent roles from "clients" to partners in this social service. There is a history of poor relations between parents and school staff in low-income neighborhoods. For example, low-income parents often stay away from their child's school because they feel they have nothing to offer academically and/or otherwise feel intimidated by teachers, administrators, and staff and consider them unapproachable and unreachable (Davies, 1984). Low-income parents cared just as much about their child's education as middle class parents; despite these findings, many school personnel blame parents for poor academic achievement (Dupper & Poertner, 1997).

Since there are implications of staff believing that parents are at fault for their child's poor academic achievement, there is a lack of understanding between the two. Since parents feel unwelcome in a school environment, it is unsurprising that they may avoid becoming involved in their child's education. If a parent feels inadequate, they will not feel they have the authority to make a change at their child's school, even if they feel it is underserving their children.

Allowing parents and school staff to work together in a hub provides a better relationship between the two. Having a better relationship between the staff and parents not only allows for a better community program but also helps the communication between parents, students, and staff to create a better school environment.

EXAMPLES OF DIFFERENT EDUCATIONAL MODELS

There are several educational models that have been populating the landscape in the United States and in New Zealand that will be highlighted here to address the inequities and also to provide children with an engaging educational experience. The authors do not profess any allegiance to or preference for any of these educational models. The criteria in selecting these educational models is to highlight their creative and unique philosophies, structure, and practices. The three educational models are community schools, charter schools, and Wildflower micro schools.

Community schools are those that partner with other community resources. Community schools not only focus on learning but also are places where students and families can go for other services. These services allow for educators, administrators, organizations, and families to work together on any day of the week at any time (Blank et al., 2003). Community schools can also make resources, such as computers, books, and tutors, available to any student.

The Institute for Educational Leadership (www.communityschools.org/)

> is a community school that is both a place and a set of partnerships between the school and other community resources. Its integrated focus on academics, health and social services, youth and community development, and community engagement leads to improved student learning, stronger families, and healthier communities. Community schools offer a personalized curriculum that emphasizes real-world learning and community problem solving. Schools become centers of the community and are open to everyone—all day, every day, evenings, and weekends.

There is also a community hub approach that was implemented in New Zealand (www.tony-wardedu.com/critical-design-praxis/a-community-hub). The architects of this community hub model see the community hub as an instrument for community development. Figure 9.4 shows the community hub model. It is both inclusive and holistic in its philosophy.

This community hub approach is using a school as a resource for the community, as discussed earlier. It is used for social resources and health-related resources. Using that space outside of school

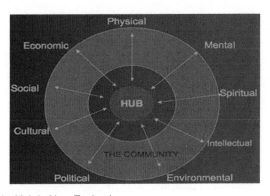

FIGURE 9.4 Community Hub in New Zealand

hours has a positive impact on the community, which in turn has a positive impact on the students within that community (Haig, 2014). This approach allows for a happier and healthier community, and in turn creates happier and healthier students. A positive affect is conducive to student's education.

Charter schools are schools that receive government funding but operate independently of the established public school system in which they are located and, in some cases, are privately owned (Wikipedia definition). Looking at the success of charter schools in Boston, Massachusetts, as just one example, the city's charter sector includes some of the best urban public schools in the country of any kind (Peyser, 2014). Over the past few years, several studies of charter school performance in Boston have been conducted by a variety of researchers using different methodologies. Regardless of the sponsoring organization or the research design, these studies all reach the same conclusion: Commonwealth charter schools in Boston are exceptionally high performing (Peyser, 2014). See Figure 9.5

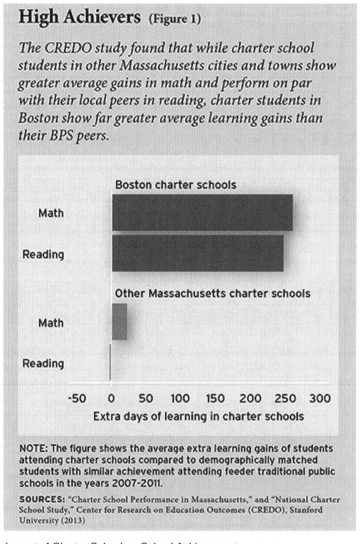

FIGURE 9.5   Impact of Charter School on School Achievement

for the average learning gains of students in charter schools in Boston compared with their Boston Public Schools counterparts.

Wildflower micro schools are private schools for low-income children and are being compared to the one-room schoolhouse from centuries ago. These schools are starting to sprout in many communities around the United States and in San Juan, Puerto Rico. These micro schools are small schools, having no more than 15 children. They are embedded in city neighborhoods that function as experimental spaces for data-gathering technology on children's behavior to better understand their needs and to test new materials for teaching modern-day concepts. Referred to as nodes in a network, the schools are unified by nine principles, such as an artist-in-residence in each school and an emphasis on parent education (Manzhos, 2017). A key goal is to create what Wildflower calls "ecosystems," which are clusters of multiple schools that are completely run by two Montessori-trained teachers in a single area, so that resources and expertise can be shared. Among Wildflower's funders are the Robert Wood Johnson Foundation, the Walton Family Foundation, and the Chan Zuckerberg Initiative (Manzhos, 2017). Some of the highlights of a micro school are as follows:

- Multiple ages learn together in a single classroom
- Teachers act more as guides than as lecturers
- A heavy emphasis on digital and project-based learning
- Education is highly personalized (Prothero, 2016).

OVERVIEW OF PRACTICES

The following are some key practices that are being recommended to start making educational changes. The practices listed here are fundamental. They address the deep, systemic level of change, as opposed to addressing just the symptoms of the problem.

1. Developing a vision of educational equity and justice
2. Creating school environments that are truly engaging for all students
3. Convening community dialogues with deep listening
4. Harnessing emerging trends such as entrepreneurship, collaborations, and networks
5. Leveraging the power of policy changes.

To elaborate on each one of these practices:

- *Developing a vision for educational equity and justice.* What is it that you want to create for educational justice? This vision can be on the three levels that we all inhabit . . . the personal level, in our relationships, and collectively. Know that developing a vision is not some lofty, "touchy-feely" idea. It is powerful; a vision provides that overarching guidance we all need to move forward (see short video in the Resources section on developing a shared vision presented by Peter Senge). See Figure 9.6.

- *Creating school environments that are truly engaging for all students.* Know that the emphasis here is not on the myriad educational practices and strategies and learning styles that can be addressed in any school or school system. Let us focus on those that can have insidious side effects. For example, when any school system focuses on "teaching to the standardized tests,"

FIGURE 9.6   Reading

researchers repeatedly demonstrate that, creativity takes a back seat in the classroom. Learning becomes more rote, boring, which can set up the dynamic of our kids losing interest and dropping out of school. In today's competitive, fast-paced, global environment, we need to find other ways to engage in learning where our students are presented with problems to solve, ideas to explore, and history to learn that takes on an engaging, deep involvement. Technology will continue to play a significant role in impacting learning in the future. *What ideas do you have to create a student-centered learning environment?*

_____

_____

_____

● *Convening community dialogues with deep listening.* Engaging in a dialogue is powerful in that this process taps into the deep wisdom and ideas and creativity that are within each individual person. Engaging in a dialogue is not the same as having a discussion where there are "sides" to an issue. A dialogue requires an open mind to really listen to another. When one has that open mind—even if one does not agree with the other—a thought spoken by one person can spark an idea or a new thought in the person listening. From there, new solutions may emerge. Every community has issues and challenges that are ripe for community dialogues and for really listening to each other (see Berg's TEDTalk on the *Power of Listening* in the Resources section). *How can we use the power of dialogue and listening to create ideal school environments?*

_____

_____

_____

● *Harnessing emerging trends such as entrepreneurship, collaborations, and networks.* Because our world is changing so quickly, and many people have become disillusioned with corporations, institutions, or school environments for different reasons, an emerging phenomenon is taking place . . . that of people relying on themselves to create new opportunities. These new opportunities, whether they are in starting businesses as entrepreneurs, nonprofits, or educational and community opportunities, are based on establishing new networks and collaborations. Inherent in these new networks and collaborations is the ability to meet new people, garner support for one's ideas, procure funding, and engage in networking to help the new idea grow and prosper. There is a self-reliance, confidence, and building of trust that is needed to develop such a network. There is a resilience that is needed and the fortitude to begin to go down this path. *What ideas do you have to use collaborations and networks to support educational justice?*

_____

_____

_____

● *Leveraging the power of policy changes.* The systemic shifts in inequality need to be addressed at the level of policy changes. There are groups and individuals who have the influence and power to begin to make these changes in equality. This is not a reference to any partisan politics because, fundamentally, this is a significant human, social issue that should transcend party politics *What types of policy changes can you foresee to ensure educational justice?*

> **Dream, Dream, Dream**
> **Dreams transform into thoughts**
> **And thoughts result in action**
> —Dr APJ Abdul Kalam (2002)

_____

_____

_____

These five leverage points for intervention and change delineated earlier inherently point to a fundamentally new shift in our individually and collectively developing different and new skills for ourselves, our schools, and our communities to begin to shrink the class divide that engulfs our nation. We need to start to do things differently to continue to prosper as a nation.

We would like to end this chapter with a small, yet empowering, story from the 2016 Washington State Teacher of the Year (see Box 9.1). His vision of education and his passion have a positive, long-lasting effect on his students. We should all be Nerd Farmers!

> ### Box 9.1 The "Nerd" Farmer
>
> Nate Bowling is the 2016 Washington State Teacher of the Year. "I joke about being a nerd farmer," Nate said. "I'm trying to cultivate a kind of scholarship in students, and a passion for learning. So, I bring passion to the classroom, and they see that and rise to the occasion." (Gates, B., 2016, Gates Notes blog). Nate teaches at Lincoln High School in Tacoma, Washington, about 30 miles south of Seattle. Half the students are African American or Hispanic and more than 70% are eligible for free or reduced-price lunch, which makes Lincoln a textbook example of what educators call the New Majority, reflecting the fact that more than half the students in American public schools today live in poverty.

Reflect: How do we begin to have a new, shared, vision that embraces all talents and aspirations?

_____

_____

_____

How difficult will it be to close the inequality gap? What will happen to us as a nation if we do not close this gap?

_____

_____

_____

How can our communities begin to have these kinds of dialogues on a widespread scale to make changes?

_____

_____

_____

RESOURCES

Berg, L. (2013). TEDTalk: The Power of Listening: An Ancient Practice for Our Future: www.youtube.com/watch?v=6iDMuB6NjNA

Boston Redevelopment Authority, Research Division, Poverty in Boston: www.bostonredevelopmentauthority.org/getattachment/01cef762-956d-4343-a49a-b41c280168ae/

Gates, B. (2016). A powerful conversation on schools, poverty, and race. *Gates Notes*. www.linkedin.com/pulse/powerful-conversation-schools-poverty-race-bill-gates?trk=eml-b2_content_ecosystem_digest-hero-22-null&midToken=AQFYazp71Hfoyw&fromEmail=fromEmail&ut=2_SW5ZJz_lITo1

Putnam, R. D. The Saguaro Seminar: Civic Engagement in America. Harvard Kennedy School of Government. Cambridge, MA 02138. www.hks.harvard.edu/centers/taubman/programs-research/saguaro

Reich, R. (2014). Why there's no outcry: http://robertreich.org/post/74519195381

Robinson, Sir Ken. (2010, October). TEDTalk: Changing Education Paradigms: www.ted.com/talks/ken_robinson_changing_education_paradigms

Senge, P. (2013). On Developing a Shared Vision: www.youtube.com/watch?v=vaw_xAaxZPo

THREAD. www.thread.org: A program in Baltimore that connects high school students with volunteers who are going to be committed for long term.

Ward, R. (2013). The Whakatane Community Hub. www.tonywardedu.com/critical-design-praxis/a-community-hub

REFERENCES

Blank, M. J., Melaville, A., & Shah, B. P. (2003). *Making the difference: Research and practice in community schools*. Washington, DC: Coalition for Community Schools, Institute for Educational Leadership.

Davies, L. (1984). *Pupil power: Deviance and gender in school*. London: Falmer.

Dupper, D. R., & Poertner, J. (1997). Public schools and the revitalization of impoverished communities: School-linked, family resource centers. *Social Work, 42*(5), 415–422.

English, D., Lambert, S. F., & Ialongo, N. S. (2014). Longitudinal associations between experienced racial discrimination and depressive symptoms in African American adolescence. *Developmental Psychology, 50*(4), 1190–1196.

Haig, T. (2014). Equipping schools to fight poverty: A community hub approach. *Educational Philosophy & Theory, 46*(9), 1018–1035.

Kalam, A.P.J.A. (2002). *Ignited minds: Unleashing the power within India*. London, UK: Penguin Books.

Lerman, R., & McKernan, S.-M. (2007, May). *Promoting neighborhood improvement while protecting low-income families*. Opportunity and Ownership Project. Washington, DC: The Urban Institute, pp. 1–4.

Manzhos, M. (2017, January 30). New approach to Montessori school's blooms: Wildflower "micro schools" spread across Massachusetts, country. *The Boston Globe*, B9–B10.

Peyser, J. (2014). Boston and the charter school cap. *Education Next*, 14–20.

Prothero, A. (2016, January 28). What is a micro school? And where can I find one? *Education Next Blog*. Retrieved from http://blogs.edweek.org/edweek/charterschoice/2016/01/what_is_a_micro_school_and_where_to_find_a_micro_school.html

Putnam, R. (2015). *Our kids: The American dream in crisis*. New York, NY: Simon & Schuster.

Quiroga, C. V., Janosz, M., Bisset, S., & Morin, A. S. (2013). Early adolescent depression symptoms and school dropout: Mediating processes involving self-reported academic competence and achievement. *Journal of Educational Psychology, 105*(2), 552–560.

Siegel-Hawley, G. (2013). Educational gerrymandering? Race and attendance boundaries in a demographically changing suburb [Abstract]. *Harvard Educational Review, 83*(4), 580–612. doi:10.17763/haer.83.4.k385375245677131.

Steaton, E. K., & Douglass, S. (2014). School diversity and racial discrimination among African-American adolescents. *Cultural Diversity and Ethnic Minority Psychology, 20*(2), 156–165.

What We Do. (n.d.). Retrieved April 27, 2016, from www.thread.org/what-we-do/#success

Wrigley, T. (2012). Poverty and education in an age of hypocrisy. *Education Review, 24*(2), 90–98.

CHAPTER 10
ADVOCATING FOR ENVIRONMENTAL JUSTICE

Patricia Hogan and David J. Jefferson

AIMS OF CHAPTER

1. Appreciate the complexity of environmental issues in urban areas.
2. Examine the origins of environmental justice and its contemporary importance.
3. Review environmental justice concerns relevant for community service.

REFLECTION: ARE SCIENTISTS AND ENGINEERS—AND THEIR EMPLOYERS—RESPONSIBLE TO THE COMMUNITY AT LARGE? ARE THEY RESPONSIBLE TO THE ENVIRONMENT?

I (PH) would argue yes. When I was one of the few women in my engineering school in the 1970s, I questioned both engineering faculty members and deans about the role of engineers in the broader society. As a female student, I was told two things: first, women who chose engineering as a career should not expect to marry and have children because the discipline is too demanding; second, that contemplating the broader implications of an engineering project was the work of politicians and regulators and not my concern as an engineer. My engineering career was to consist of performing the tasks I was assigned to do. Whether the project I was designing was welcomed or abhorred by the community in which it was to be undertaken was not my purview. However, this kind of thinking is inconsistent with both the definition and the ethics of engineering practice. Engineering is defined as the use of science and mathematics to make systems and products that are useful to people, and the first canon of the National Society of Professional Engineers Code of Ethics (NSPE, 2007) states that engineers shall "hold paramount the safety, health, and welfare of the public." So, in my worldview, engineering is a profession of service, and service learning is a natural fit for engineers.

THE 21ST CENTURY: WHAT'S GOING ON?

The 21st century is like no other. Humans have altered Earth's physical state and global planetary cycles to such an extent that some scientists argue that there is no longer any location on the planet that can be called a *natural* environment (Western, 2001). The time period in which we now live is designated the Anthropocene. The Anthropocene is a segment of the Holocene epoch (geological time period) in which human activity has become so extensive that its impacts are on the scale of geological processes (Steffen et al., 2011). Human activity has altered global carbon and nitrogen cycles, acidified and polluted the ocean, collapsed fisheries, deforested land, damaged soils needed for agriculture, and fractured ecosystems. We are now in the sixth mass extinction—an extinction that, like climate change, is laid at the feet of developed nations as their legacy to the next generations. Why is all of this happening?

One factor is the sheer number of people on the planet competing for resources. With the advent of the industrial revolution and its resulting technological advances, the ability to extract and transport resources has allowed human beings to flourish around the globe. The 2015 UN population projection is that 9.7 billion people will inhabit the planet in 2050, which represents an additional 3.6 billion people added to the planet since we hit the 6.1 billion mark in 2000 (UN DESA, 2015, July). In 2014, 54% of the global population lived in urban communities; the UN projects that by 2050, 66% of people will live in urban communities. However, these average values hide regional differences. For example, 82% of people in Northern America were reported to be living in urban communities in 2014 (UN DESA, 2015). The number of the largest urban communities—megacities with populations of 10 million or more—increased from 10 in 1990 to 28 in 2014, with projections of more than 41 to exist in 2030 (UN, 2014). Some aggregations of these megacities will spawn even larger urban conglomerates: hyper-cities of 20 to 40 million inhabitants and super-cities with populations greater than 40 million. Cities are major emitters of atmospheric gases, producing as much as 70% to 80% of their global carbon emissions.

In the megacities of today—and in the super-cities of tomorrow—there are both benefits and challenges from concentrating human populations in cities. Benefits include better use of land through compact development, more efficient movement of people via public transportation, and the effective allocation of green urban spaces. However, the challenges of urbanization are many and depend on whether urban growth occurs in the more mature cities of developed, industrialized nations or in rapidly changing emerging economies. Understanding how urbanization affects human health and the environment requires understanding cities' inputs and outputs.

CITIES ARE COMPLEX

Cities require large inputs of energy, water, and materials to function. Meanwhile, they can produce significant outputs of undesirable pollutants and environmental impacts. Given that most cities still rely on fossil fuel combustion for energy, they generate both primary air pollutants (directly emitted) and secondary air pollutants (produced in the air by reaction of primary pollutants), which most countries regulate. These air pollutants (e.g., sulfur oxides, nitrogen oxides, particulates, hydrocarbons, ozone) have deleterious human health and environmental effects. Depending on the location of a city, it may be plagued by temperature inversions that cause pollutants to be trapped in the city area (like Mexico City or Los Angeles) and particulates to be trapped in urban "dust domes." In addition to these air pollutants, combustion of any carbon-based fuel will result in the production of carbon dioxide, a potent greenhouse gas that impacts climate change and its effects. Disagreement exists at the global level over how to regulate carbon dioxide, so its release to the atmosphere continues.

Water must be brought to cities for domestic, business, and industrial use. The provision of clean water requires functioning water treatment plants and adequate distribution systems. Access to clean drinking water is considered a fundamental human right by the United Nations; however, poor communities, even in developed nations like the United States, must often fight for access. The Flint, Michigan, water crisis is an example of this dynamic. Once water has been used and becomes wastewater, the wastewater must be collected and treated before it can be released into receiving waterways without damaging them. Wastewater treatment is a common practice in developed nations but is less so in emerging economies, where water pollution is a serious problem. In some developing countries, rivers have been designated as "dead" because pollution has removed the dissolved oxygen in the water (necessary for aquatic life to thrive).

Solid wastes—all the garbage, trash, and hazardous materials—that are generated by individuals, businesses, and industries must also be collected and treated in some manner. Although solid waste minimization, recycling and reuse of materials, and energy recovery are stated goals for many communities and nations, the implementation of these practices is uneven. In emerging economies, solid waste is often collected in unsanitary open landfills. In developed countries, landfills are engineered to reduce emissions and odor, but they are still landfills. Incineration, with or without energy recovery, may cause air pollution problems if the pollution control systems are not correctly designed.

Cities also produce another form of pollution that is not an emitted material or a set of emitted materials: heat. Cities, because of their expanses of paved areas and concrete buildings, are typically several degrees hotter than the local natural environment. The increased average temperature of cities is called the heat island effect. Rain falling on cities becomes heated runoff that then travels to receiving waterways as a form of thermal pollution. This runoff may be untreated, in which case it is also a source of biological and chemical pollution.

All the complex urban infrastructure systems that control the inputs and outputs of goods and services must be managed. The issue of equitable distribution to all members of the urban community, including the most vulnerable (children, the poor, the disabled, and the elderly), is the purview of environmental justice initiatives.

WHAT IS ENVIRONMENTAL JUSTICE?

STUDENT QUERY TO PAT: *Environmental racism is a thing, right?*

PAT: *Yes, environmental racism is a thing: it is real, but hard to prove in the legal system. That is why we need environmental justice advocates and initiatives.*

There are many operational definitions of environmental justice (EJ). The US Environmental Protection Agency (USEPA, 2017) defines environmental justice in the following way:

Environmental justice is the fair treatment and meaningful involvement of all people regardless of race, color, national origin, or income, with respect to the development, implementation, and enforcement of environmental laws, regulations, and policies.

EPA has this goal for all communities and persons across this nation. It will be achieved when everyone enjoys:

- the same degree of protection from environmental and health hazards, and
- equal access to the decision-making process to have a healthy environment in which to live, learn, and work.

Robert Bullard, a leader in environmental justice since the 1970s, conceptualizes EJ as (Hoff, 2014):

Environmental justice embraces the principle that all people and communities are entitled to equal protection of our environmental laws. It means fair treatment, and it means all people—regardless of race, color or national origin—are involved when it comes to implementing and enforcing environmental laws, regulations and policies.

Regardless of the originating author or authority, the definitions share one core value: fair treatment and protection from environmental hazards, regardless of race, color, national origin, or income. The basic notion is that there is no human subgroup that may be acceptably exposed to dangerous and unhealthy environmental conditions.

Most nations measure success by economic parameters like gross national product (GNP). Such a paradigm values only those who are contributing to the economy through paid work. The unpaid work of women, children, and indigenous peoples is not considered. Marginalization from economic metrics means that effectively, these people do not exist, and as such, their voices are not heard. In a similar phenomenon, the ecosystem services that the natural environment provides—fresh water, air circulation, habitat provision—have not factored into economic equations through which countries measure success. Until recently, any damage done to the environment has not been included in business accounting methods either. However, due to impending physical resource limitations, accounting practices are evolving to include variables that monetize ecosystems and consider the environmental costs that may arise in the production of goods and services. Programs are increasingly valuing the three prongs of sustainable development—planet, profit, and people—but the application of these ideas remains uneven.

So, it is in this fragmented context that the work of bringing environmental justice to local communities must be performed. In many cases, negative environmental impacts are disproportionately applied to persons of lower socioeconomic status (SES) who have neither the money nor the organizational savvy to fight for the health and welfare of their families, neighborhoods, and communities. Persons of color, in both the United States and other countries, are often overrepresented in impoverished communities for historical reasons. Therefore, classism and racism may be intertwined with the unequal distribution of unhealthy environmental conditions. Thus, questions of responsibility arise: whose responsibility is it to ensure that the benefits and burdens of development are equally shared across economic strata and social and racial lines?

PERSONAL CHALLENGES IN ENVIRONMENTAL JUSTICE COMMUNITY SERVICE PROJECTS

Working with communities to help them address environmental justice issues means educating both yourself and your community partners about complex issues that cross multiple thinking boundaries: technical and scientific issues; governmental regulatory and compliance requirements; medical conditions and health effects; and community organization at multiple levels—neighborhood, city or town, and regional. Often communities impacted by negative environmental conditions are not well positioned to advocate for themselves because of economic or social status. To further complicate the work, EJ service-learning practitioners must work in a highly uncertain and rapidly changing global environmental and political landscape.

The experience of addressing environmental justice issues within the context of a service-learning project can be both exhilarating and challenging. Environmental problems are by nature multidisciplinary in both their scientific/technical nature and their social aspects. Gaining a thorough understanding of a community and the environmental issues that it faces requires a holistic thinking approach. At least two primary challenges characterize this experience:

- The need to build a solid scientific and regulatory understanding of the issues
- The need to maintain a strong and consistent sense of professionalism when faced with emotionally charged situations and delays or setbacks.

ENVIRONMENTAL JUSTICE CHALLENGES IN URBAN COMMUNITIES

The realization of environmental justice in urban communities hinges on the notion that all human beings the right to breathe, to be fed, to be sheltered, and to drink water without being harmed by these fundamental activities. However, many vulnerable populations, including those living in urban communities, have no alternative but to breathe polluted air, eat less nutritious food, live in substandard housing, attend under-resourced schools, and drink contaminated water. Growing up in a polluted environment impacts children both physically and mentally (Nocon, 1991). As they mature, these children often remain in such environments through adulthood, effectively passing environmental injustice to the next generation. Chronic health conditions—including obesity, diabetes, high blood pressure, asthma, heart disease, and early death—can become normalized. Furthermore, the mental health impacts—including anxiety and depression—of dealing with physical health issues can affect community members and their service providers alike.

It is sometimes argued that lack of personal agency, or individual choices cause the problems that low-income urban communities experience. Critics may suggest that the individuals who live in such communities should make better choices for their personal health and the well-being of the community. People who are both physically and mentally healthy, who live in healthful environments, and who enjoy adequate access to resources probably do make better personal choices than they would if subjected to environmental stressors. However, understanding and addressing environmental issues is a complex, multi-stakeholder process (see Box 10.1), and arguments that situate individual people and their personal choices as the loci of negative environmental health consequences ignore this complexity.

Box 10.1 Developing a Project Scope for Understanding a Local Environmental Issue

Where is the project located? (e.g., is this project bounded by a specific neighborhood or does the project involve an entire city or town?)

What is the primary environmental issue of concern? (e.g., is this primarily a water quality issue, an air toxins issue, a solid waste management issue?)

Are there secondary concerns related to the primary concern? (e.g., does a solid waste management issue also involve detrimental air emissions?)

How many people are affected? What is the demographic of affected persons?

Who is currently working on this issue(s)? List them and identify them by type.

- Government environmental entities (e.g., federal, state, local environmental agencies or offices)
- Other local government entities (e.g., board of health, conservation commission)
- Private companies or industries
- Schools and universities
- Legal entities
- Not-for-profit environmental groups
- Local citizens' groups.

Where are some sources of general background information for this issue? (Note: These are listed from easiest to read to most difficult for a non-scientist.)

- General background information sources (e.g., secondary and tertiary literature)
- Government publications on the topic (e.g., EPA, CDC, and NIOSH publications)
- Peer reviewed scientific literature.

Where are some sources of specific information for this local issue? (Note: There may be much documentation or little depending on how long the issue has existed and whether it has been documented adequately.)

- Local scientific studies (e.g., publicly available engineering reports, reports by local nonprofits, university studies)
- Documentation from public hearings and/or litigation
- Newspaper accounts.

In addition, this focus on the individual obscures the fact that many inhabitants of poor, urban neighborhoods possess neither the financial capital nor the organizational capacity to render their communities more environmentally friendly. Instead, such persons must rely on the collective efforts of neighborhood groups and NGOs to advocate for local, state, and federal actions to protect their communities. If the only source of groceries is a liquor store, the community's diet will be limited. If there are no green spaces located nearby and the outdoor air quality is poor, community members will stay inside and will not get adequate exercise. If the schools in the community are in a state of disrepair or have poor indoor air quality, the community's children will spend many days of the school year at home or in the hospital to treat symptoms of asthma or other illnesses. In contrast, if the community's built environment is redesigned and rebuilt, for instance incorporating controls on air pollution, green space and community food gardens, or environmentally friendly housing and schools, behaviors may be changed for the simple reason that change is now possible. The key here is that physical infrastructure—the built environment—can be modified to provide for better default options, so that individuals may make healthier decisions for themselves personally, and for the community.

In the following sections, we discuss the interaction between access to some key elements of the physical environment and community well-being while also underscoring the complexity of urban environmental challenges.

Access to Clean Air

There are two components to air quality: outdoor (also called ambient air quality) and indoor. Both may be deleterious to human health. Air pollutants in outdoor air can affect physical infrastructure, waterways, plants, and animals, including humans. When an urban community is located proximate to industrial facilities, solid waste landfills, or incinerators, or experiences high amounts of diesel-powered vehicle traffic, the resulting community air quality usually suffers. In the United States, many low-income urban communities—many of which are predominantly composed of people of color—are affected by poor ambient air quality. This lack of clean outdoor air can exacerbate many cardiac and respiratory conditions and illnesses. Indeed, asthma has become a focal point for environmental justice conversations and activism precisely because its prevalence has been correlated with poor air quality in a multitude of settings, including housing, transportation, and commercial/ industrial activities. Pollutants such as ozone (a chemical component of smog) and particulate matter (particles in the air that come from combustion exhaust, haze, or dust) can irritate the airways of even healthy persons and may trigger acute symptomatic episodes in asthmatic individuals. Serious asthma attacks can lead to hospitalization and even death.

For low-income people living in urban environments, exposure to poor air quality may not abate indoors. Living in substandard housing or attending poorly maintained schools may result in additional exposure to air contaminants, including mold. Indoor air quality can be improved to a certain extent through intensive cleaning, elimination of secondhand smoke, and control of allergens. However, as with outdoor air quality, these efforts are often possible only through coordinated efforts to mobilize community members and leverage resources, which often must be sourced from outside of the community.

The US Centers for Disease Control (CDC) maintains a database on asthma prevalence and demographics. According to 2015 CDC asthma surveillance data, asthma rates among blacks (10.3%) exceed that of either whites (7.8%) or Hispanics (6.6%) (CDC, 2015). Because of its prevalence in specific populations (e.g., African Americans and persons of lower economic status), asthma has become a "politicized illness experience" (Brown et al., 2003, p. 454). In 2010 CDC data, the inpatient discharges for blacks were 29.9 discharges per 10,000 compared with 8.7 discharges per 10,000 for whites, and in 2015 CDC data, the reported mortality rate for blacks was 23.9 deaths per million compared with 8.4 deaths per million for whites (CDC, 2010; CDC, 2015). The prevalence of asthma for black children (<18 years) was 1.8 times (13.4%) that of white children (7.4%) in 2015 (CDC, 2015). In another study, hospitalization data were used to find that the prevalence of asthma in children ages 5 to 12 in New York City was correlated with attending a school in a low-income neighborhood (Claudio, Stingone, & Godbold, 2006). Therefore, an environmental condition—poor air quality—can jeopardize the future of a community by impeding the healthy development of its children (Nocon, 1991). Environmental damage thus becomes intergenerational, and the incentive to actively pursuing environmental justice is salient.

Reflect: List all the ways that a school in a poor state of maintenance and repair could affect a child's health and interfere with his or her ability to learn. How is this infrastructure issue also an EJ issue?

_____

_____

_____

Access to Green Space

Access to green infrastructure (e.g., parks, community gardens, green roofs, and urban trees—and the biodiversity they support) has been demonstrated to positively impact human life in multiple ways. Such evidence should not surprise us, given that the modern urban world of impermeable concrete and steel constitutes a recent phenomenon in the history of humankind. Urban green spaces can provide diverse benefits. Parks offer opportunities for both physical exercise and mental relaxation. For instance, positive cardiovascular and mental health outcomes have been associated with access to green space (Richardson, Pearce, Mitchell, & Kingham, 2013). Meanwhile, the presence of well-functioning community gardens (e.g., those located in vacant lots or on rooftops) can yield community level benefits including providing opportunities for multigenerational social interaction, education about food and nutrition, development of horticultural skills, access to more nutritious and fresh food, and physical exercise.

However, there are many challenges associated with establishing or improving green spaces in urban communities, particularly where residents are predominantly of low socioeconomic status. For example, converting urban land (e.g., a vacant lot) into a community green space may be complicated by the following:

- The need to determine land ownership and obtain public access to the property for green space development
- The need to assess whether any environmental contamination has previously occurred, as well as whether any remediation of the land is necessary for green space development
- The possibility that gentrification could occur once the project has been completed.

Vacant lots that have remained unused for long periods of time exist in many urban communities. Negative associations may be tied to these properties when they are used for improper trash disposal or as spaces in which people with antisocial intent congregate. Vacant or abandoned urban properties may develop when former industrial cities face population decline. The exodus from an urban area of people who have the resources to relocate leaves the population generally poorer, and thus the city's tax revenue may be insufficient to upgrade degrading infrastructure (Schilling & Logan, 2008). In other cases, individuals who do not live in an urban community may own urban vacant lots. Absentee owners may keep these properties undeveloped and sell them for profit as land values in the city increase (Stanley, 2016). In either case, it is often impractical or impossible for the local community, without substantial multi-stakeholder help, to reclaim vacant or abandoned properties to create urban green spaces or other forms of locally held sustainable developments. In other instances, certain spaces in a community such as roadway dividing islands, easements near sidewalks, or similar areas are owned by the local government and therefore special permissions may be required for community members to develop these plots into urban green spaces. Finally, while potentially serving to empower local food movements, actions such as "guerilla gardening"[1] on urban properties can lead to fines or other forms of legal action.

Even where urban spaces are available to a given community for green space development, a subsidiary issue may arise. What is the actual condition of the land? Low-income communities may be in relatively less desirable portions of cities. If the area in which the potential green space is located has functioned as an industrial area, the possibility of soil contamination is a real concern. Urban lands that have been contaminated by prior use are called *brownfields*. This term distinguishes these areas from undeveloped land outside of the city, for example agricultural lands, known as *greenfields*. In general, it is considered environmentally preferable to remediate contaminated brownfields for use as urban green spaces than to build outside the city on greenfields, because the latter option would contribute to urban sprawl. Thus, the remediation and reuse of brownfields functions as a form of land recycling.

Although funding may be available for brownfield development, for instance in the United States through the EPA Brownfield Program, the process is difficult and complicated. The desired brownfield site must be initially accessed and a remediation plan must be developed. Remediation often involves removing large volumes of contaminated soil and replacing it with uncontaminated materials. Subsequently, post-remediation assessment is required to ensure that the site has been rendered suitable for use. For spaces that will be used as parks and/or food growing areas (e.g., permaculture; community gardening), properly remediating the land is fundamental to ensure that human health is not compromised. Young children are particularly susceptible to hazardous compounds in soils because of their low body weight and their tendency to ingest soil or plant materials.

A final challenge to urban green space creation is one that is infrequently considered at the outset of the development process: gentrification pressures. When poorer urban communities develop green spaces that enhance the livability of their neighborhoods, they also render their communities more attractive to developers and wealthier individuals. Thus, it has been argued that there exists a threshold of "greenness" beyond which poor communities risk being ousted to even more degraded parts of an urban community by the forces of gentrification and urban redevelopment (Curran & Hamilton, 2012; Wolch, Byrne, & Newell, 2014). When this occurs, the original members of the community are effectively priced out of their newly "greened" neighborhood. This unfortunate irony constitutes a significant environmental injustice.

Access to Nutritious Food

In recent years, scholars who study EJ issues have called for broadening the conceptualization of EJ to incorporate a range of issues that in the past had received scant attention from activists and advocates. Among these is the concept of food justice, which may be understood as a movement to transform our relationship with food, its production, transportation, and consumption (Schlosberg, 2013). Although the intersection between food justice and environmental justice has recently garnered increased attention, the issue of equitable access to nutritious food has been central to the phenomenon of urbanization for decades in many countries, including the United States.

For instance, efforts to simultaneously address economic, health, and food concerns led many American cities to establish public markets in the early 20th century. These spaces enabled new immigrants to more easily assimilate and provided employment opportunities (Morales, 2011). Subsequently, the exponential increase in urban poverty during the Great Depression inspired the creation of local food provision measures, including soup kitchens, as well as federal subsidy initiatives, such as the Food Stamp program.

More recently, efforts such as the establishment of community gardens and the development of community food systems have been undertaken in various cities across the United States as attempts to realize food justice. Increasingly, programs have been designed to explicitly address the enmeshment of issues of race and class in the food system. Scholars and advocates alike have recognized that low-income communities and communities of color are frequently absent from the narratives woven by the food movements which seek to re-localize food production in wealthy countries. Indeed, these communities may in fact be disproportionately harmed by the contemporary food system (Alkon & Agyeman, 2011).

For instance, numerous studies examining neighborhood disparities in access to affordable and nutritious food have found that low-income urban neighborhoods in developed countries—including the United States, Canada, the United Kingdom, Australia, and New Zealand—tend to afford greater access to food sources that promote unhealthy eating, such as fast-food outlets and convenience stores (Hilmers, Hilmers, & Dave, 2012). While such venues may be more prevalent in poor neighborhoods, these communities frequently lack access to full-service supermarkets (Weinberg, 2000). Generally, supermarkets are less prevalent in lower income versus higher income neighborhoods (up to 30% fewer), predominantly black neighborhoods have fewer food outlets than white ones, food quality tends to be lowest in areas where poverty is highest, and urban supermarket prices are typically higher than those of suburban stores (Walker, Keane, & Burke, 2010).

Thus, urban "food deserts" arise with greater frequency in neighborhoods that are racially segregated, exacerbating public health issues such as obesity and type-II diabetes, which are more prevalent for immigrants, low-income populations, and communities of color (Candib, 2007). Such issues illustrate the association between food justice and community health—focusing on access to and consumption of healthy foods—as well as the linkage between food justice and environmental justice (Bernhardt, Wilking, Gottlieb, Emond, & Sargent, 2014). Essentially, the built environment in which we live significantly impacts the fulfillment or failure of social justice. The flight of supermarkets from urban core communities mirrors the process of deindustrialization and job loss in these same areas. Thus, just as cities may undertake efforts to remediate brownfields or create urban green spaces, policies should be enacted to ensure access to nutritious food in under-resourced communities.

Access to Clean Water

The provision of clean water suitable for drinking, cooking, and bathing is of such high importance to human survival, health, and vitality that the United Nations has defined access to water and sanitation as a fundamental human right and as "essential to the realization of all human rights."[2] In recent years, significant improvements to drinking water supplies have been made at the global level. According to the World Health Organization (WHO), as of 2015, 91% of the global population had access to "improved drinking-water sources."[3] Nevertheless, in poor, urban communities around the world—shantytowns, favelas, slums—such access is still not adequate, and people resort to using any water available, even from open sewers, to survive. Thus, notwithstanding supply improvements, in 2015, 1.8 billion people relied on drinking water sources contaminated with feces, 663 million used unimproved drinking water sources, and more than one half billion people per year die from diarrheal diseases contracted from contaminated drinking water.

Access to clean water is a political as well as an infrastructural issue. Delimiting access to water is a method through which to control large populations. There is no substitute for water; therefore, whoever controls water controls people. Water is key to all human activities, but much of our freshwater—approximately 70% of the water that is removed from surface and groundwater supplies—is used for irrigation to grow crops. Yet despite its tremendous importance, global shortfalls—up to 40% by 2030—are predicted for water availability if countries do not radically change how this precious resource is conserved and used (UN, 2015). Solutions may be found through innovative measures. For instance, in its 2017 World Water report, UN Water promoted the use of treated municipal wastewater (i.e., sewage) as a source of water and other resources (WWAP, 2017). "Toilet to tap" technologies are already in place in some countries. Although such interventions offer interesting solutions to water shortages, they also demonstrate that freshwater scarcity is real and will continue to increase in the future. Access to clean water and sanitation is therefore a fundamental environmental justice issue for the 21st century.

A common misperception is that access to clean water and sanitation are issues of concern only in developing countries. Yet the water supply and treatment problems that recently occurred in Flint, Michigan, in the United States—often referred to as the Flint Water Crisis—is a case study that demonstrates the importance of these issues in wealthy nations. This example illustrates that parties well beyond the local community can be impacted by environmental justice concerns and may be involved in efforts to resolve the problem. Multiple stakeholders played roles in the Flint Water Crisis, including the impacted community itself, the Flint city government, the Michigan state government, the Michigan Department of Health and Human Services, the state attorney general's office, the federal EPA, private attorneys, local religious leaders, environmental activists, out-of-state universities, physicians, the American Civil Liberties Union (ACLU), the local and national press, the US House of Representatives, federal courts, and ultimately the President of the United States.

The Flint Water Crisis case has been extensively covered elsewhere. However, a brief synopsis of the story may be useful to serve as an illustration of how EJ service-learning projects might be conceptualized in urban settings in the United States or other developed countries. Flint, Michigan, was the former home of the largest General Motors manufacturing plant in the United States, which in the past supported a large worker base. The downsizing of this facility in the 1980s exacerbated Flint's multimillion-dollar deficit. Subsequently, the state of Michigan took the city into receivership and reallocated resources from the water supply fund to cover budgetary shortfalls. This coincided with a shift in Flint's water supply from Lake Huron to the Flint River in 2014. The Flint River is notorious for its long history of industrial, landfill, and agricultural pollution.

Because the Flint River water had not been treated with an anticorrosive agent, lead from the water supply lines leached into the drinking water. Lead is a toxin that has no threshold for developmental effects in children.[4] This means that there is no safe dose or level of exposure for children, and even low doses can have subtle, and permanent effects. The EPA limit for lead in drinking water is 15 parts per billion (ppb). Yet researchers from Virginia Tech University analyzed lead samples from 252 Flint homes in 2015 and found that the drinking water in 40.1% of households had first draw sample levels over 5 ppm. Several homes exceeded 100 ppb, and one exceeded 1,000 ppb (Virginia Tech Research Team, 2015). The effects of drinking water with such concentrations of lead can range from minor illnesses such as upset stomach to graver injuries.

In addition, high levels of the by-products of disinfectants, which may be carcinogenic, as well as fecal coliform[5] were found in Flint's drinking water. Yet even after these research findings, debates over how to cover the cost of water treatment or whether to change the water supply source continued. Eventually, a local pediatrician demonstrated that blood lead levels in Flint children had doubled and, in some neighborhoods, tripled, following the shift water from the Flint River. These findings were confirmed by the Michigan Department of Health and Human Services (MDHHS), and subsequently the governor of Michigan acted to discontinue the use of water sourced from the Flint River.

In the aftermath of the crisis, felony charges were filed against several individuals who previously controlled the Flint water supply, and a civil class action lawsuit claiming $722 million in damages was filed against the EPA on behalf of 1,700 Flint residents. Ultimately, in March 2017, a federal judge approved a $97 million settlement requiring the state of Michigan to replace the water lines for approximately 18,000 Flint homes, and in April 2017, the US EPA awarded a $100 million grant to Michigan for Flint drinking water infrastructure upgrades (US EPA, 2017, March 17).

The Flint Water Crisis demonstrates that environmental injustices may occur at large scales even in wealthy, industrialized nations like the United States. Often, these issues disproportionately affect members of low-income urban communities and people of color. Indeed, 41% of Flint residents live in poverty, and 57% of residents are African American.[6] The events in Flint represent the culmination of a long history of economic, housing, and environmental disparities in the community.[7]

CONCLUSION

This chapter has sought to fulfill several objectives surrounding the pursuit of environmental justice in the context of community service. The overarching purpose of the discussion has been to help those involved with community service—including educators and students alike—to better reflect on how to address environmental justice challenges through applied educational initiatives. To accomplish this goal, we have explored the conceptualization of environmental justice with a focus on how EJ issues have manifested in urban communities in the United States. In addition, we have elucidated some of the key challenges associated with environmental justice work. Ultimately, we suggest that working toward environmental justice in the context of service-learning initiatives implicates a variety of forms of literacy—including scientific, legal, sociological, psychological, and political forms of knowledge. Our hope is that this chapter will have enabled the reader to begin to contemplate the incorporation of environmental justice concerns into service-learning initiatives from multiple perspectives.

EXERCISE FOR ENVIRONMENTAL JUSTICE SERVICE-LEARNING COURSES

Reflect: In urban communities, we regularly witness environmental injustices that are so common that they may have become essentially invisible to us. Think about your usual path in the city as you walk to your school, your home, or your subway stop: what environmental issues do you see? Trucks idling and emitting greenhouse gases and particles into the atmosphere? A vacant lot collecting trash and debris? Contaminated runoff from a rainstorm flowing into a storm drain? Plastic that could be recycled accumulating in a trash can?

Pick one issue that you see in which you feel personally invested:

_____

_____

_____

Think about who "owns" this problem. Does the issue occur on a public or private property? Is this a problem of the many (groups of people who collectively generate the environmental problem) or the few (an individual or a small group of polluters)?

_____

_____

_____

Think about who is "in charge" of the problem. Is it a public health concern, for example, a matter for a board of health or the department of public works? Is it a safety issue, for example, a matter for the police or fire department? Is it a land use problem, for example, a matter for a wildlife division, conservation commission, or an open space committee? Some combination of these?

_____

_____

_____

Think about the specific next step that you should take to obtain more information about the problem. What is the very first thing that you think you should do?

_____

_____

_____

NOTES

1 Guerrilla gardening essentially refers to the actions of planting and harvesting edible plants without the permission of the property owner.
2 UN Resolution 64/292 July 28, 2010.
3 WHO Drinking Water Fact Sheet. (November 2016) Available at www.who.int/mediacentre/factsheets/fs391/en/
4 Agency for Toxic Substances & Disease Registry of the United States Centers for Disease Control and Prevention (CDC). (2010) Case Studies in Environmental Medicine (CSEM) Lead Toxicity. WB 1105. Available at www.atsdr.cdc.gov/csem/lead/docs/lead.pdf
5 Fecal coliforms are bacteria that are present in the guts of warm-blooded animals; their presence indicates that water is contaminated with feces.
6 United States Census Bureau. (2015) QuickFacts: Flint city, Michigan. Available at www.census.gov/quickfacts/table/PST045216/2629000
7 The Michigan Civil Rights Commission has documented the systemic racism occurring in Flint from 1900 through the period of the Water Crisis. See Michigan Civil Rights Commission. (2017) The Flint Water Crisis: Systemic Racism Through the Lens of Flint. Available at www.michigan.gov/documents/mdcr/VFlintCrisisRep-F-Edited3-13-17_554317_7.pdf

REFERENCES

Alkon, A. H., & Agyeman, J. (2011). Introduction: The food movement as polyculture. In A. H. Alkon & J. Agyeman (Eds.), *Cultivating food justice: Race, class, and sustainability* (pp. 1–20). Cambridge, MA: MIT Press.

Bernhardt, A. M., Wilking, C., Gottlieb, M., Emond, J., & Sargent, J. D. (2014). Children's reaction to depictions of healthy foods in fast-food television advertisements. *JAMA Pediatrics, 168*(5), 422–426.

Brown, P., Mayer, B., Zaestoski, S., Luebke, T., Mandelbaum, J., & McCormick, S. (2003). The health politics of asthma: environmental justice and collective illness in the United States. *Social Science & Medicine, 57*(3), 453–464.

Candib, L. M. (2007). Obesity and diabetes in vulnerable populations: Reflection on proximal and distal causes. *Annals of Family Medicine, 5*(6), 547–556.

CDC. (2010). National Asthma Inpatient Discharges. Retrieved from www.cdc.gov/asthma/most_recent_data.htm

CDC. (2015). National Asthma Mortality. Retrieved from www.cdc.gov/asthma/most_recent_data.htm

Claudio, L., Stingone, J. A., & Godbold, J. (2006, May). Prevalence of childhood asthma in urban communities: The impacts of ethnicity and income. *Annals of Epidemiology, 16*(5), 332–340.

Curran, W., & Hamilton, T. (2012). Just green enough: Contesting environmental gentrification in Greenpoint, Brooklyn. *Local Environment, 9,* 1027–1042.

Hilmers, A., Hilmers, D. C., & Dave, J. (2012). Neighborhood disparities in access to healthy foods and their effects on environmental justice. *American Journal of Public Health, 102*(9),1644–1654.

Hoff, M. (2014, June 12). Robert Bullard: The father of environmental justice. *Ensia.* Retrieved from https://ensia.com/interviews/robert-bullard-the-father-of-environmental-justice/

Michigan Civil Rights Commission. (2017, February). The Flint Water Crisis: Systemic Racism through the Lens of Flint. Retrieved from www.michigan.gov/documents/mdcr/VFlintCrisisRep-F-Edited3-13-17_554317_7.pdf

Morales, A. (2011). Growing food *and* justice: Dismantling racism through sustainable food systems. In A. H. Alkon & J. Agyeman (Eds.), *Cultivating food justice: Race, class, and sustainability* (pp. 149–176). Cambridge, MA: MIT Press.

National Society of Professional Engineers. (2007, July). NSPE Code of Ethics. Retrieved from www.nspe.org/resources/ethics/code-ethics

Nocon, A. (1991, April). The social impact of asthma. *Family Practice, 8*(1), 37–41.

Richardson, E. A., Pearce, J., Mitchell, R., & Kingham, S. (2013). Role of physical activity in the relationship between urban green space and health. *Public Health, 127,* 318–324.

Schilling, J., & Logan, J. (2008). Greening the rust belt: A green infrastructure model for right sizing America's shrinking cities. *Journal of the American Planning Association, 74*(4), 451–466.

Schlosberg, D. (2013). Theorising environmental justice: The expanding sphere of a discourse. *Environmental Politics, 22*(1), 37–55.

Stanley, B. W. (2016). Leveraging public land development initiatives for private gain: The political economy of vacant land speculation in Phoenix, Arizona. *Urban Affairs Review, 52*(4), 559–590.

Steffen, W., Persson, A., Deutsch, L., Zalasiewicz, J., Williams, M., Richardson, K., Crumley, C., Crutzen, P., Folke, C., Gordon, L., Molina, M., Ramanathan, V., Rockström, J., Scheffer, M., Hans Schellnhuber, H. J., & Svedin, U. (2011). The Anthropocene: From global change to planetary stewardship. *Royal Swedish Academy of Sciences, 40,* 739–761.

Suitts, S. (2015). *A new majority research bulletin: Low income students now a majority in the nation's public schools.* Southern Education Foundation. Retrieved from www.southerneducation.org/getattachment/4ac62e27-5260-47a5-9d02-14896ec3a531/A-New-Majority-2015-Update-Low-Income-Students-Now.aspx

United Nations. (2014, July 10). World's Population Increasingly Urban with More Than Half Living in Urban Areas. Retrieved from www.un.org/en/development/desa/news/population/world-urbanization-prospects-2014.html

United Nations. (2015). World Water Development Report 2015. *UNESCO.* Retrieved from the UNESCO website http://unesdoc.unesco.org/images/0023/002318/231823E.pdf

United Nations Department of Economic and Social Affairs. (2015). World Urbanization Prospects: The 2014 Revision. (ST/ESA/SER.A/366). Retrieved from https://esa.un.org/unpd/wup/publications/files/wup2014-report.pdf

United Nations Department of Economic and Social Affairs. (2015, July 29). World Population Projected to Reach 9.7 Billion by 2050. Retrieved from the United Nations DESA website www.un.org/en/development/desa/news/population/2015-report.html

United States Census Bureau. (2015). QuickFacts Flint city, Michigan. Retrieved from US Census Bureau website www.census.gov/quickfacts/table/PST045216/2629000

United States Environmental Protection Agency. (2017). Environmental Justice. Retrieved form the Environmental Protection Agency website www.epa.gov/environmentaljustice

Virginia Tech Research Team. (2015). Our sampling of 252 homes demonstrates a high lead in water risk: Flint should be failing to meet the EPA lead and copper rule. Flint Water Study Updates. Retrieved from http://flintwaterstudy.org/2015/09/our-sampling-of-252-homes-demonstrates-a-high-lead-in-water-risk-flint-should-be-failing-to-meet-the-epa-lead-and-copper-rule/

Walker, R. E., Keane, C. R., & Burke, J. G. (2010). Disparities and access to healthy food in the United States: A review of food deserts literature. *Health & Place, 16*, 876–884.

Weinberg, Z. (2000). No place to shop: Food access lacking in the inner city. *Race, Poverty and the Environment, a PLACE at the TABLE: Food and Environmental Justice, 7*(2), 22–24.

Western, D. (2001). Human-modified ecosystems and future evolution. *Proceedings of the National Academy of Sciences, 98*(10), 5458–5465.

Wolch, J. R., Byrne, J., & Newell, J. P. (2014). Urban green space, public health, and environmental justice: The challenge of making cities "just green enough." *Landscape and Urban Planning, 125*, 234–244.

WWAP (United Nations World Water Assessment Programme). (2017). The United Nations World Water Development Report 2017. Wastewater: The Untapped Resource. Paris: UNESCO. Retrieved from UNESCO website http://unesdoc.unesco.org/images/0024/002471/247153e.pdf

PART III
ASSESSING CIVIC ENGAGEMENT

CHAPTER 11
EVALUATING IMPACT

Debra A. Harkins

AIMS OF CHAPTER

1. Assess if your community service impacted your personal and professional development.
2. Examine if your student engagement benefited the community agency.

Recall the purpose of college students' community service engagement is to develop socially responsible and more civically minded citizens. The Coalition for Civic Engagement and Leadership's (2005) definition of civic engagement includes the following:

acting upon a heightened sense of responsibility to one's communities . . . [that] encompasses the notions of global citizenship and interdependence. Through civic engagement, individuals are empowered as agents of positive social change for a more democratic world.

So, the mission of higher education is to provide students with the opportunity to recognize injustice and inequality, to obtain skills to speak and act on unchallenged hegemonic systems, and to have the cultural capacity to work with others to promote liberation and social justice. Multiple levels of learning occur during your higher education training including: traditional learning objectives of cognitive and critical thinking, communication, knowledge, and insight as well as broader learning objectives of diversity, inclusion, leadership, team building, activism, conflict resolution, and civic growth. This chapter will help you assess your professional development in these areas as well as the impact your service had on the community.

ASSESSING YOUR PROFESSIONAL DEVELOPMENT

By evaluating your own professional development in community service, you have an opportunity to reflect on what you have accomplished, what you still need to do to create long-term impact, and what you still need to learn. Let's take a moment to reflect on these questions before reading on.

Reflect: How have your values, skills, and career plans shifted? Did you achieve what you wanted to achieve?

_____

_____

_____

Many aspects of your professional development can be assessed in personal, cognitive, emotional, social, and moral domains. Researchers examining the relationship of service learning and cognitive development find community service often increases academic learning, grades, and GPA as well as critical thinking and problem-solving skills (Deeley, 2007; Lockeman & Pelco, 2013; Wang & Rodgers, 2006).

Similarly, when researchers examine the relationship of service learning and personal development, they find community service enhances many facets of a person's development including social identity, personal efficacy, and interpersonal skills (e.g., leadership, communication, and team work) as well as spiritual, moral, and civic growth. For example, a meta-analysis conducted by Celio, Dulak, and Dynmicki (2011) who analyzed 62 service-learning programs, found significant gains in student civic engagement, social skills, academic performance, and positive attitudes of self, school, and learning. Another meta-analysis by Yorio and Ye (2012) of 40 studies similarly found significant, positive associations between service learning and understanding of social issues, personal insight, and cognitive development. More recently, Moely and Ilustre (2016) found students self-reported an increase in their ability to thinking creatively, synthesize and organize their skills and experiences and make better judgments about others' arguments, all of which they attributed to their college-required public service participation. Clearly, community service is good for your personal and professional development.

In terms of your cognitive development, do you think your knowledge and problem-solving skills improved? Check out Perry's stages of intellectual development (Box 11.1) to consider where you were in your cognitive thinking before you started your community service and where you might be now.

Box 11.1: Perry's Stages of Intellectual Development

Stage 1: Dualistic knowledge—right and wrong answers often based on rules of authorities
Stage 2: Subjective knowledge—often have conflicting answers so usually trust inner voice as guide
Stage 3: Relativistic knowledge—often use contextual rules based on reasoning as guide
Stage 4: Committed knowledge—constructed based on integration of knowledge from others, personal, experience and critical reflection.

Source: Perry (1970)

Socially, community service can improve leadership; increase cultural and racial understanding; promote increased extracurricular service participation; and increase social responsibility, activism, citizenship, commitment to serve, and future civic involvement (Bringle & Clayton, 2012; Deeley, 2015; Mitchell, 2008; Moely & Ilustre, 2016). Impressive, right? Well, these gains happen to many, but not all, who take a service-oriented course. Let's explore more specifically the changes observed by people who take community service courses so you can determine whether change happened, or did not, for you. In a recent longitudinal study by Barbara Moely and Vincent Ilustre (2016) of more than 670 students at Tulane University in New Orleans, students were asked about their civic attitudes, knowledge, and skills; their public service interests; their career plans; and their civic interests in their first year of college, following two and four years of study. Outcomes of their public service were examined by exploring civic and cultural perspectives, leadership and social understanding, cognitive and academic shifts, and plans for future. For example, Moely and Ilustre asked, *Describe briefly the public service experience that was most beneficial to your academic, career, and personal development. What about this experience made it beneficial?*

Reflect: Try answering this question for yourself before reading further.

_____

_____

_____

Before reflecting on these findings, note that Tulane students are required to take a service-oriented course in their first two years of college and then a second course in their last two years of college.

Now, consider what many students reported to Moely and Ilustre (2016) regarding civic, social, and career changes that happened to them based on their community service (see Table 11.1):

TABLE 11.1 College Student Self-Reported Outcomes From Community Service

Civic and Cultural Perspectives	Leadership and Social	Plans for Self and Future
See problems in a broader more systemic way	Interact better with other students	Built knowledge and skills for future career
Stronger cultural, racial, religious, and political awareness	Better at leading and making decisions	Increased understanding of self
View service community differently	Increased opportunities to lead	Developed a code of values and ethics
Broader awareness of societal problems and current events	Developed better leadership skills	Developed my plans for higher education
More civic awareness and civic responsibility	Better at problem solving	Developed plans for career and life
Inspired to seek out civic engagement in future	Increased positive relationships with faculty	Inspired to get involved in politics

Source: Adapted from Moely and Ilustre (2016)

Reflect: Which of these changes happened to you? Have you noticed other changes not captured in Table 11.1?

_____

_____

_____

STUDENT VOICES

In the following section, you will hear from two former students, Dylan and Amanda, who completed a community service course and went on to do more community service at the local and international level. Dylan went on to work with a local nonprofit serving the homeless while Amanda traveled to Somaliland to help in a maternity hospital—a country with high maternal and infant mortality rates.

Dylan was interested in getting more involved with a local not-for-profit (NFP) serving the homeless, an organization she had worked with during the prior semester. She decided to help this NFP further by serving as a coordinator with a project in which they sought help—creating an exhibit of the history of this organization that was later presented for a week at the Massachusetts State House. Dylan coordinated the service-learning students and compiled the documents, photos, and stories from the NFP that helped to make the photo exhibit a success for the NFP and the students who participated. Here is Dylan describing her experience:

> Through my experience with service learning, I learned the true meaning of helping. It's safe to say that anyone who is attempting to help or serve a community is well intentioned, yet so often, their efforts are inconsequential or even counterproductive. Helping isn't about doing what you think is best for an individual or group; it's about doing what they need from you. So much of helping is about listening and acting accordingly. It's about extending the resources available to you to those who may not have the same access as you.

I began my service learning working for a nonprofit in Boston. I got to know the people there, and it quickly became clear to me the importance of our work. The people I got to know were just like anyone else in my life with families and pasts—not unlike my own family. Somewhere along the road, they were dealt a tough hand, and before they knew it, they were homeless or living in poverty. Their stories made me realize how similar the experience of life is for all of us. What happened to them could just as easily happen to any one of us.

It's one thing to theoretically learn about the struggles that others face; it's another to hear from the people who are struggling and see what that looks like for each individual person. Learning through service and interacting one-on-one with individuals changes your perception of the homeless and low-income experience. People constantly make assumptions and judgments about homeless individuals and how they live their lives, but the truth of the matter is, you just don't know what each person is up against that's led to their current situation. The encounters through service learning changes perceptions and misconceptions of people drastically.

After volunteering for a semester, I helped coordinate volunteers for the new Community Psychology class. Though coordinating volunteers wasn't my specialty, I put my understanding of "helping" into practice and served as needed. Through this experience, I learned the ins and outs of working for a nonprofit, which requires flexibility and a focus on the mission of the organization. I learned how to be a more effective leader by working with the strengths of individual team members.

The most incredible thing I witnessed while coordinating volunteers for the organization was watching a team of people from completely different backgrounds and interests come together to create something that benefited others. Together with the community partner, we put together an exhibit on the history of Spare Change News that was displayed at the Massachusetts State House. Each student brought their passions, interests, and strengths to the project, and what came from it was nothing short of extraordinary. Serving others brought people together in a way that I never witnessed in a classroom setting. Unified in a cause, each volunteer found a way they could contribute to a project that helped raise awareness about an important organization. What I learned is that we all have something we can contribute to the betterment of others' lives.

—Dylan Santos, Community Psychology, 2014

Reflect: How can you take your newfound knowledge and experience to continue to work with your current community partner? What about a new community partner?

_____

_____

_____

Now read about Amanda Ponce, a former student, who took a monthlong journey to Somaliland (not to be confused with Somalia), a small poor country in Africa. Amanda decided to raise funds to go to Somaliland after taking a Community Psychology course where she learned about homelessness and poverty through her community service and after reading Nicholas Kristof's book *Half the Sky: Turning Oppression Into Opportunity for Women Worldwide*, where she learned about Edna Adan, who opened a maternity hospital to help reduce the high maternal and mortality rate in Somaliland. Amanda learned all she could about Somaliland, about the hospital and its founder Edna and watched YouTube videos and TEDTalks about the country and this remarkable woman. She writes about the background of Somaliland:

There is no reliable country-wide census, but Somaliland is recognized to have the highest maternal and infant mortality rates in the world where 15%–20% of children under 5 pass away; where over 95% of Somali women have undergone FGM by elders in the community with no medical training; with immunization rates at less than 50%; with poor diets of rice, pasta, high sugar, low in meat, fish, and veggies; with limited clean water. Edna Adan started building the hospital in 1998 and opened it in 2002 with 60 beds. Since then, over 12,000 babies have been delivered at this hospital.

Amanda even contacted Edna Adan about getting more involved and was surprised when Edna wrote right back and said: *"Please come, help and here's a list of desperately needed hospital supplies to bring with you."* Amanda created a Crowdtilt fund for purchasing the supplies and her travel costs. Other students helped spread the word about what Amanda was doing and helped her raise the funds to go to Somaliland. You can read and learn more about Edna and her hospital by watching a TEDTalk and reading the book *Half the Sky.* Here is Amanda explaining to her friends and family, who were understandably concerned for her safety, how she became inspired to journey to Somaliland and why she felt she needed to go:

I know my decision to volunteer in Somaliland, Africa, this summer came as a shock to many of you. I've received countless emails asking me to explain my rationale, why I chose Somaliland, and why it was necessary for me to go now even given current travel warnings. To be honest, I can't say this is something I had planned on. Though I've always been passionate about gender inequality and infant health, I'm a psychology major and had originally planned on spending my summer filling out graduate school applications. After watching Half the Sky, a documentary about the oppression of women, I knew I wanted to do something. It's difficult to explain but, for the first time in my life, I felt a calling to something greater than myself. You see, for me this isn't really a choice, rather a responsibility to address the injustice that women are facing.

The Edna Adan University Hospital was one of the organizations featured in the documentary. I was immediately captivated by the goals, achievements, and dedication to women and infant health exhibited by Somaliland's former First Lady, Edna Adan. Her hospital, located in an African region that is notoriously known for gender inequality and women's health issues, is dedicated to training midwives, fighting the practice of female genital mutilation, combating infant mortality, and providing basic health care to women and children in the region. Volunteering with Edna in Somaliland seemed like the perfect response to Half the Sky's call to action. Before I knew it, I was exchanging e-mails with Edna and applying to volunteer for the summer.

Yes, I could volunteer somewhere closer to home or just fundraise for Edna's hospital, but I believe that my experience volunteering at the hospital will have a greater impact than a local experience or just a donation. Experiencing the oppression of women firsthand will test my boundaries, challenge my beliefs, force me out of my comfort zone, and provide a real-world context to my mission. I am confident that this experience is just the beginning of my journey, and I can't wait to see where it takes me. So, I'm sorry if this seems a bit impulsive or rash, but I've never been as sure of anything. I am so thankful that I've been given this opportunity and can't thank you all enough for supporting me.

When Amanda arrived in Somaliland, she was surprised to find herself working in the delivery rooms of the hospital helping the midwives and doctors deliver the babies. She learned firsthand the challenges of trying to deliver a baby in a community where the male doctors are not allowed to touch their female patients; where midwives engage in midwifery dressed in burkas; where 95% of women have experienced female genital mutilation, further exasperating deliveries, and where few hospital supplies and staff are available for needed maternal and infant care. Here is what Amanda said about her experience:

I learned how blessed we are to live in America; that we often think we know but we really don't know how others live, think, and feel; and that, sadly, not everyone wants to help. I learned that women in Somaliland do not own their own bodies. I learned that you must be patient, flexible, and open to new experiences and adapt to situations quickly and that open discussions can be difficult across different cultures. I learned the importance of networking, of researching communities we wish to serve, and that knowledge is power. I now feel a strong sense of responsibility, connected to world, and a desire to learn more; I realize that I live in a country that is thriving, and I want to be a part of improving lives for those that do not live in a thriving community.

Amanda believes we can all make a change if we just move out of our comfort zone and try. She suggests:

You make a change if you first find a cause you're passionate about, then connect with others and research how others made change and begin raising awareness on that issue through social media, word of mouth, or blogging.

Reflect: Think about Amanda's experience. How could you could get involved with a cause that stirs your passion and social justice heart?

_____

_____

_____

ASSESSING SERVICE-LEARNING IMPACT ON COMMUNITY

In a recent report (2011) entitled, "Measuring Impact of Civic Engagement: Tracking Outcomes on Health, Education and Economics," the Kellogg Foundation suggests examining the following activities to determine impact with your community service site:

- *Advocacy.* Did you engage in activities that contributed to community empowerment?
- *Public policy.* Did you engage in actions or practices that led or may lead to new regulations, ordinances, or laws to support community members?
- *Building partnership.* Did you engage in activities that supported and/or expanded partnerships with potential community stakeholders?
- *Service delivery.* Did you engage in activities that advocated and/or supported community mission?
- *Funding or building new services.* Did you engage in activities that helped fund and/or build new community programs or services?

Reflect: How would you answer each previous question regarding your community service?

_____

_____

_____

Let's examine what community partners typically say about the impact of service learning on their community work. In Stoecker and Tryon's (2009) classic book, *The Unheard Voices: Community Organizations and Service-Learning*, more than 100 community partners from Madison, Wisconsin, were interviewed regarding how they define, perceive, and evaluate service learning. Several themes emerged from these interviews regarding the success and challenges for community partners who engage in service learning including:

- Relationships and communication
- Challenge of short-term service learning
- Challenge of diversity
- Evaluation.

Community partners view communication as the heart of a university-community partnership. If the relationship and communication is strong between the community and university partner, especially faculty, service learning is likely to be more successful. In those cases where university members have little or no communication with the community partner, service-learning experiences suffer and community partners question the value of working with university students, faculty, and staff. Consider the strength, or lack thereof, of the relationship and communication between your community partner and yourself, faculty, and relevant university members.

A big challenge that the community partners identified in Stoecker and Tryon's study was short-term service learning. That is, a semester-long service learning of fewer than 20 hours is not very useful to a community site. For example, K–12 schools have a different academic calendar than college academic calendars. This can create challenges especially around holiday breaks and the end of semester when service-learning students disappear, yet school children are still in need of services. One solution is for service-learning students to work on project-based activities that are not time sensitive. Many community partners question how much orientation, training, and selection can happen with semester-long service learning. Consider how your service hours contributed to or inhibited community mission and vision.

While communication and management of short-term support relates to internal issues of service learning, the next challenge relates to broader issues of cultural context. Those from the university that "have" are typically white and middle-class, whereas those that are served are those that "have less" and are typically people of color and working class. Community partners in the previous study identified diversity issues as common and often not adequately addressed. If diversity issues exist within the service-learning experience, then consideration of diversity and possible training is needed to address issues of power, privilege, and oppression. Consider how diversity issues were handled within your community service experience.

Evaluating the service-learning experience for the student, faculty, and community involves asking many questions. Amy Mondloch (2009), one of the community partners identified in the previous study, identified the following questions as important for assessing and planning for successful service-learning experiences:

- Did the service-learning fit with the community's mission?
- Did the service-learning collaboration help the community move their community's mission forward?
- What resources are needed for service-learning to be most effective at the site?
- Are these resources available to sustain service-learning for future collaborations at the site?
- What expectations did the community have for service-learning at the site? Are these expectations compatible with faculty and student expectations?

How could you find the answer to some of these questions regarding your current community service work? If you gather this important information, how could you constructively and supportively provide this information to relevant stakeholders?

COMMUNITY PARTNER VOICES

When the executive director of *Spare Change News* was asked about the impact of service-learning work on her goals and vision for the organization, she responded:

> One activity that stands out is when we had service-learning students pull together a multi-media look back on the 24-year history of Spare Change that included video, still photographs, documents, and memorabilia. Our exhibit was sponsored by the Massachusetts Senate Minority Leader and was open to the public in the State House Great Hall during the first week of June. Students interviewed the homeless/housing insecure vendors of Spare Change. This project not only helped SCN develop an important political ally for Spare Change by working with the Senator's office but, the public learned and engaged in an educational exhibit that humanized the homeless and underscoring the humanity of each featured vendor.

When Amanda Bernasconi, director of *College Access* for Boston Urban youth was asked about the impact of service-learning students' work on her goals and vision, she responded:

> As the director of a college access program in an urban community part of my job is to build bridges between the institution and community. Integrating service-learning opportunities into my pre-college curriculum proves to be a valuable and enriching opportunity for not only the community and the students served but for the service learners themselves and the university. Service learning offers community agencies a unique opportunity to leverage resources otherwise in-accessible to them. As a community partner, I always assess the following:
>
> 1. Is the need real? Are the service learners being asked to complete tasks and assist with assignments that have merit and purpose? Ensuring that service learners have predetermined tasks aligned with measurable outcomes of value to the agency prove vital.
>
> 2. Is the partnership mutually beneficial? Do both the service learner and community partner feel as if their needs are being met? In the past, we brought in service learners without pre-established roles or evaluating their progress. Thus, their skill sets and/or interests misaligned with the partner, with low motivation, and less valuable experience for all stakeholders.
>
> 3. Are we effectively evaluating? Having the students integrate pre- and post-assessment and performing regular check-ins with the service learners and community members establishes a level of rapport and trust. It also ensures that the work being done remains on task.
>
> Examples of how my program successfully integrated service learning include:
>
> 1. After-school sessions program for tutoring and after school assistance
>
> 2. Mentoring program where service learners worked to develop a "First Year of College" mentor program, allowing for community members to ask questions, expand their network, and build valuable relationships to work on skill development and better prepared college candidate
>
> 3. One-day seminars with topics in financial literacy, career development, and beyond including workshops, roundtables, and speakers.

When Mary Williams, founder of *Homeless Education Research Network*, was asked about the impact of service-learning students' work on her goals and vision, she responded:

> *Before our partnership, we had multiple tutoring programs to provide students experiencing homelessness with the extra support they needed to foster a healthy learning environment. Originally, we created a program that sent tutors to 10 shelters to help Boston Public School students with their academic performance. With the service-learning students, we expanded the program services to students outside the reach of the previous program by creating a mentoring-tutoring relationship that provides homeless students with a tangible path to higher education. By exposing children to different cultures and ways of life, the college students helped us accomplish the goals of providing a stronger and healthier learning environment for students experiencing homelessness. The partnership has the potential to expose more students to mentoring services over a sustained period, which can greatly improve the likelihood of the success of all parties involved especially the students experiencing homelessness. Also, given that the relationship building (service learning) is embedded in mentors' curriculum-program of study, their volunteering is likely to result in a cost savings for us, as we do not have to obtain funding to pay for these services. This cost savings can be invested in the program to further expand this component of the program or provide additional services.*

Evaluating the impact of service learning is critical to current and future work for all stakeholders in this powerful learning experience.

RESOURCES

Kellogg Foundation's report "Measuring impact of civic engagement: Tracking outcomes on health, education and economics": www.campusengage.ie/sites/default/files/resources/Measuring%20Outcomes%20inCivic%20Enagement%2C%20Lefkovitz.pdf

Perry's stages of intellectual development: www.cse.buffalo.edu/~rapaport/perry.positions.html

REFERENCES

Bringle, R. G., & Clayton, P. H. (2012). Civic education through service-learning: What, how, and why? In I. McGrath, A. Lyons, & R. Munck (Eds.), *Higher education and civic engagement* (pp. 101–124). New York: Palgrave Macmillan.

Celio, C. I., Dulak, J., & Dynmicki, A. (2011). A meta-analysis of the impact of service-learning on students. *Journal of Experiential Education, 34*(2), 164–181.

Coalition for Civic Engagement and Leadership. (2005). Retrieved from https://provost.umd.edu/MS07/B_Appendices/CCEL.pdf

Deeley, S. J. (2007). *Critical perspectives on service-learning in higher education.* New York: Palgrave Macmillan.

Lockeman, K. S., & Pelco, L. E. (2013). The relationship between service-learning and degree completion. *Michigan Journal of Community Service Learning, 19,* 18–30.

Mitchell, T. D. (2008). Traditional vs. critical service-learning: Engaging the literature to differentiate two models. *Michigan Journal of Community Service-Learning, 14*(2), 50–65.

Moely, B. E., & Ilustre, V. (2016). Outcomes for students completing a university public service graduation requirement: Phase 3 of a longitudinal study. *Michigan Journal of Community Service Learning, 22*(2), 16–30.

Mondloch, A. S. (2009). One director's voice. In R. Stoecker & E. A. Tryon (Eds.), *The unheard voices: Community organizations and service-learning* (pp. 136–146). Philadelphia, PA: Temple University Press.

Perry, W. G., Jr. (1970). *Forms of intellectual and ethical development in the college years.* New York: Holt, Rinehart & Winston.

Stoecker, R., & Tryon, E. A. (Eds.). (2009). *The unheard voices: Community organizations and service-learning.* Philadelphia, PA: Temple University Press.

Wang, Y., & Rodgers, R. (2006). Impact of service-learning and social justice education on college students' cognitive development. *NASPA Journal, 43*(2), 316–337.

Yorio, P. L., & Ye, F. (2012). A meta-analysis on the effects of service-learning on the social, personal, and cognitive outcomes of learning. *Academy of Management Learning & Education, 11*(1), 9–27. http://dx.doi.org/10.5465/amle.2010.0072

CHAPTER 12
NOW WHAT?

Debra A. Harkins

AIMS OF CHAPTER

1. Reflect on the complexity of the helper role.
2. Learn career paths available to reduce oppression and promote well-being and liberation.
3. Explore road map for community activist helper.

JOYS AND CHALLENGES OF HELPING

Before exploring possible career paths available for engaging in community-based helping, let's reflect on your recent community service experience. What resonated most for you with your service work? What made you feel the most passion, the most alive, the best you? How does your best service experience connect with the social issues you see in your community or in the world? A great life journey includes doing what makes you your best you.

Reflect: Reflect on when and how your best you emerged during your service experience.

_____

_____

_____

Let's go a little deeper by exploring on what was most challenging or disturbing in your service work.

Reflect: What challenged or confirmed your views? What responsibility to change do you feel you have now? What do you still need to learn to create that change? And, how will you determine or assess if you've successfully made that change?

_____

_____

_____

A great way to bring your ideas together on who and what you want to do in the future is to create a mission statement for yourself. Start by trying to answer the following questions. You could do this with a partner or write in a journal or a big piece of paper. What do you stand for? What is your purpose? What action will you take that reflects what you and your life stand for?

Be aware this will likely take quite a while, and you may have to put it down for a while and revisit it in a few days. When you're ready, try to write a one-sentence mission statement of you. Once you feel your mission statement captures you and your goals, keep it close by. Revisit and adjust regularly—once a year would be great.

Reflect: What do you stand for? What is your purpose? What action will you take that reflects what you and your life stand for?

_____

_____

_____

Now that you've learned how complicated helping is, you might be wondering how you can avoid working in a job that contributes to oppression and, instead, find a job that promotes well-being and liberation. I wish I could tell you that task will be easy. Let's review why you need to keep your critical justice hat on as you consider your work in the future. You see, as Paul Kivel (2000) pointed out in his article "Social Service, or Social Change?" many helpers are from the managerial class, or buffer zone (see Figure 12.1).

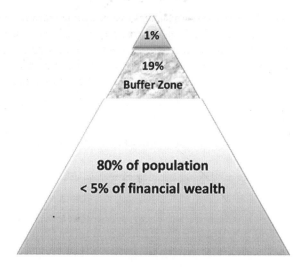

FIGURE 12.1 Economic Pyramid

Source: Adapted from Alberto Ledesma's economic pyramid illustration

What is the buffer zone? Well, to explain the buffer zone, you need to understand all the social classes in our social system. That is, you need to understand the difference between the 1% ruling class, 19% managerial buffer zone class, and the remaining 80% of the population.

The ruling class represents a very small but extremely powerful group of people in our society. As Kivel explains, the ruling class has not only vast sums of money but also wealth through stocks, bonds, and real estate. These powerful people are typically the heads of our large corporations; the owners of our largest banks; and the controllers of hotel, oil, pharmaceutical, medical, internet, and computers industries. They wield tremendous power through their executive positions in business and politics. They serve on boards of both profit and nonprofit organizations. And, the ruling class use their wealth to finance industries, politicians, and initiatives that benefit their interests and concerns. This includes funding politicians who support business over labor and serving on multi-policy groups at national and international levels.

Some of the most powerful policy-making groups in the world at the international level include Council on Foreign Relations, Bilderberg, The Trilateral Commission, and the Atlantic Council. Powerful national policy-making groups include The Brookings Institution, National Association of Manufacturers, RAND Corporation, and The Business Roundtable. Most of us know little about them, yet these policy-making groups create most of the national and international economic world policies. These groups direct money through individual contributions, PACs, and soft money to politicians who support their economic interests. Many of the ruling class sit on one or more of these policy-making groups. And, these policy groups are funded and supported by foundations that are run by the ruling class. Foundations are where the ruling class can keep their assets, avoid taxes, and retain control of their money. Some of the largest foundations include Rockefeller, Ford, Mellon and Carnegie Corporation, Bradley, Noble, Scaife, Richardson, Olin, and Koch family foundations. In 2000, the top 10 largest foundations controlled $101 billion of assets. In 2016, they controlled $121 billion of assets. In addition, foundations fund think-tanks where more research and policy development happens as well as promoting marketing policies including The Brookings Institution, American Enterprise Institute, The Heritage Foundation, Free Congress Foundation, Empower America, and the Center for Strategic and International Studies.

We rarely interact with the ruling class because they live in secluded communities; use private transportation; and go to private schools, clubs, and resorts. The ruling class tends to interact exclusively with other ruling class members and typically interacts with the managerial class only at work. The ruling class maintains and increases their wealth in ways directly connected to government policies as Kivel (2000/2012) explains. The following are created, managed, and funneled through the ruling class:

- **Corporate welfare for farm subsidies**, including reducing trade barriers via measures like NAFTA, GATT, and tax shelters
- **Privatization of natural public resources** and low-cost leases of mines, timber, water, sewers, and others
- **Tax exemptions** and lower taxes on overseas businesses
- **Military incursions** that protect international business holdings
- US-based companies **selling military armaments**, including the intelligence for making chemical, nuclear, and biological weapons to be sold to other countries
- **International debt** of less-developed countries to multinational banks
- **Domestic debt**, where the government borrows money from the wealthy and pays interest on the credit in bonds and loans, including housing, car, and student loans
- **Oil**, in that much of US policy involves the control of oil across the world
- **Drugs**, both legal (pharmaceutical) and illegal.

You might be thinking, *but what does that have to do with me and the buffer zone?* Well, a lot. You see, the 19% are the economic class that work for the ruling class—they are the managers of the economic system. These are people with less power than the ruling class but with training and expertise in technological, research, and practical skills to keep the current economic system functioning. The managerial class represents the *buffer zone* between the ruling class and the 80%. Most of us in higher education and those we teach are in or are being educated to be part of this managerial class. This includes doctors, lawyers, nurses, teachers, social workers, nonprofit staff, police, fire, security guards, and soldiers. As a helper of the underserved, you are part of this managerial buffer class. Let's describe the third and largest social group.

Those at the bottom of the economic ladder, approximately 80% of US citizens, represent the working force in our society who *produce* the goods and services for the ruling and middle class. They work in sweatshops; restaurants; small business; driving taxis, trucks, and delivering the mail; answering phones, filing, and organizing documents for organizations; doing the everyday things that keep our society functioning. Often those in this class struggle with daily living including violence and competition as well as food, health, and housing insecurity. This group benefits the most from uniting and organizing for better working and housing conditions (Kivel, 2000, 2012).

Consider America's founding father of the constitution and fourth president, James Madison's statement given at the Constitutional convention that *"The biggest conflict of all in our country was between those who had property and those who had none . . . [the role of government] ought to be so constituted as to protect the minority of the opulent against the majority."*

Reflect: In what ways is government's role continuing to protect the opulent against the majority?

_____

_____

_____

Unfortunately, the percentage of financial wealth ownership reveals even more economic inequality than when Kivel and Ledesma originally wrote in 2000. For example, in 2016, the owning or *ruling class* (with a very small number of *power elite*—400 people) own more than 42% of the financial wealth in the United States; while the *managerial class* (i.e., the *buffer zone*) own approximately 53% of the US financial wealth; and the remaining 80% of US citizens own less than 5% of the financial wealth of the country (see Washington Center for Equitable Growth, 2016). In 2000, 52 out of the 100 largest economies were corporations, not countries. In 2016, that number jumped to 69 out of 100. Citizens United, a ruling that allows corporations to fund political candidates, creates even more inequality between the ruling class and the rest of us by using their power and wealth to sway political elections. This threatens our very democracy, creating vast inequality and moving us ever closer to an oligarchy. The US economic pyramid provides a reminder that gaps in wealth inequality of this magnitude create health and safety injustice for the 80% of people at the bottom. Sadly, other countries are suffering similar or worse inequality related to global economic inequality directly connected to unfettered capitalism.

Let's return to the buffer zone class or managerial class as those people (and jobs) that keep the economic systems in place. This buffer zone involves three functions with certain jobs attached (Kivel, 2000):

1. Jobs involving *caring for the producing people* at the bottom of the pyramid. These are caretaking jobs like nurses, teachers, counselors, and case workers. These jobs are usually at the bottom of the buffer zone and typically performed by women.

2. Jobs that *keep people hoping* for something better. People in this middle level of the buffer zone often hand out benefits to others—these are managers and directors of programs and small businesses.

3. Jobs that *control the system and ensure that it stays in place*. These include police, fire, security guards, immigration officials, administrators, prison wardens, and soldiers. These jobs are usually at the top of the buffer zone and are typically performed by men.

Reflect: Where do you and your family fit in this economic system? Are you and your family in the ruling, managerial, or producing class? Who will you be in solidarity within this economic pyramid? How will you use your class position to create well-being and liberation for others?

_____

_____

_____

One purpose of exploring this economic system in detail is to help you understand that though you may wish to help, you must consider the ways in which professions and jobs you may have in the future keep this economic system in place. You need to think about how you may co-opt social change within and outside of the buffer zone. Most of the work to create social change will likely come from the 80% that are most oppressed by this system. Most social change arises from the bottom, including the Civil Rights Movement in the 1960s. Our role as helpers is not only to support and open space for such change, but also to be aware of how our own actions can oppress and make it difficult for the 80% to create needed change.

Reflect: Who will benefit from the work you decide to do? How will you ensure that you do not replicate or create more oppression?

_____

_____

_____

Exploring this economic pyramid also provides a reminder that wealth inequality gaps of this level create a lack of health and safety for the 80% of people at the bottom of this economic pyramid, fueling more discrimination, violence, pollution, and oppression.

CAREER PATHS AHEAD

Further education or training in community-focused service allows social justice-oriented helpers to work in education, health, disability, prison reform, restorative justice, trauma, peacebuilding, philanthropy, organizational development, community dialogue, NGOs, SMOs, government agencies, sustainability, food initiatives, micro lending, economic initiatives, environmental, social services, funding, and policy making. You could work at the local, state, national, or international level to address any of these issues.

Most community-focused graduate degrees are systems- and process-focused to address oppression, well-being, and liberation. Training involves developing your skills and knowledge in policy, evaluation, strategic planning, visioning, conflict resolution, communication, team building, emotional competency, group dynamics, leadership, inclusivity, and collaboration. Many opportunities await you to reduce oppression and promote well-being and liberation. You could do the following:

- Conduct action research to benefit communities in need
- Consult with NFPs, NGOs, and local community coalitions and groups
- Engage in strategic planning with NFPs, government agencies, and human service organizations
- Promote public policy initiatives that serve the needs of all people
- Teach and research ways to reduce oppression and promote well-being and liberation
- Develop, implement, and evaluate new programs
- Work directly with community-based organizations, advocating and empowering underrepresented groups.

Check out some examples of the settings, career paths, and job titles available to you in Table 12.1.

TABLE 12.1   Examples of Settings to Engage in Community Service Work

• Department of Public Health	• Educational settings	• Shelters that serve women, children, youth, veterans, or LGBTQ
• Community Public Health	• Housing and Urban Development	
• Department of Mental Health	• Environmental organizations	• Social policy institutes
• Community Mental Health	• Organizations working on immigration and refugee issues	• School boards
• Department of Education	• Organizations working on elder care issues	• Political office
		• Unions

TABLE 12.2   Possible Career Paths

● Teacher/professor	● Union leader	● Human resources manager
● Researcher	● Group facilitator	● Program evaluator
● Writer	● Prison reform advocate	● Program developer
● Public speaker	● Restorative justice trainer	● Program manager
● Consultant	● Social service advocate	● Health promotor
● Executive director	● Director at community service	● Unit manager
● Board member	agency	● Public policy analyst
● Worker of Department of	● Charitable foundation director	● Grant writer
Public Health	● Community council advisor	● Community developer
● Hospice worker	● Community mental health worker	● Team leader
● Grassroots organizer	● Trauma healer	

As you think about your career paths (see Table 12.2) and the settings you might find yourself in, ask yourself: where does the funding come from for these agencies, organizations, and businesses? How will you be able to help others if funding inevitably comes from the ruling class? In what ways will you ensure that your work will not separate you from the people you wish to serve? In what ways will you stand up to powerful forces when those interests do not align with those you wish to serve?

Kivel (2012) asks us to consider whether we will help as social service or social change agents. This is the question we started this field book journey with coming full circle to the meaning of helping for you. Of course, we do both kinds of helping but what will be your focus? Will you help people to "get ahead" in the current system or to get together to create systemic transformative change? Will you work toward nurturing, developing, and empowering leaders, solidarity, and commitment to ensure well-being and liberation for all? Note how different the goals are for each type of helping and how different your helping will depend on how you answer this question.

Reflect: Consider how helping will look from these two frames (i.e., social service or social change work) using your community service site or a possible career path as an example.

_____

_____

_____

We've covered a lot in this field book, and you've explored and reflected a lot on the theory and practice of civically minded helping. So, here are some final tips on some of the most important things to remember on your journey toward being a socially just helper in the future.

Six Steps on Your Journey as a Community Activist Helper

1. Critically assess if systems are liberating for all by looking behind the "curtains" of research, media, business, policy, and politics.

2. Delight in difference.

3. Maintain an open heart and mind.

4. Be a catalyst for well-being and social change.

5. Work in solidarity. Use your power to empower by giving voice to the silenced, oppressed, and forgotten.

6. Hold yourself and others accountable to work toward social justice.

Assessing social systems requires you to be vigilant regarding the who, what, why, and how of what is shared in research, through the media, in business, and through policy and politics. Learn who is behind the "curtain" of shared information. For example, who owns the media source, who funds the research, who supported the policy or bill, who is funding the politician. Do these "curtained" sources have a vested interest—or a conflict of interest—in the outcome of the research, media report, policy, or bill? Why is that information shared at a certain time and in a certain space? How are other sources presenting the same information? How is the information impacting the cultural narrative? This type of investigation requires much more work of you. It requires you to dig beyond the headlines of a story, research, or policy. You may find some sources more trustworthy than others. Figure out who you can trust by looking behind the curtain. And, every so often, go back and check to determine if a "curtained" source has infiltrated your trusted source.

Delighting in difference requires you to be on the lookout for the bizarre and the different and to try to hold off the immediate value-judgments we all make. Many of us pride ourselves on making quick judgments of people. When you avoid the judging, moralizing, and psychologizing of the other, you can begin to really get to know the other and learn to delight in what initially seems bizarre. *Maintaining an open mind and heart* requires that you suspend judgment and seek to learn intellectually, emotionally, and civically as much as you can from others.

Being a catalyst for well-being and social change requires you to work with the underserved, the oppressed, and the silenced. *Working in solidarity* means not working *on* or *for* but *with* the people, side by side, not in front or behind; using your power to empower and giving voice to others with little voice. Finally, *holding yourself and others accountable* to doing the work of social justice by being there. Beyond a commitment to showing up and helping, act on your commitments. Hold others to their commitments, whether it is friends, family, business, educators, religious organizations, or politicians.

Never doubt that a small group of thoughtful, committed citizens can change the world;

   indeed, it's the only thing that ever has.

—Margaret Mead

RESOURCES

Learn and Serve is a federal program to support young adults in service activities that increase academic learning and promote civic engagement and responsibility. www.nationalservice.gov/newsroom/marketing/fact-sheets/learn-and-serve-america

AmeriCorps is a federal program that places young adults into service activities that increase skills, earn money, enter the workplace, and increase civic awareness and responsibility. www.nationalservice.gov/programs/americorps

Peace Corps provides opportunities to serve abroad working with local leaders to create positive social change. www.peacecorps.gov/about/

City Year is a Boston-based program that places young adults into high-poverty communities to support and empower local communities. www.cityyear.org/what-we-do

Nonprofit or government agencies. Serve on a local nonprofit board or government agency committee. They are always looking for volunteers.

Research. Get involved in research at a university, hospital, or community agency. Researchers are always eager to work with young people.

Graduate school. Immerse yourself in graduate programs in any of the following: Community psychology, diversity and inclusion, public health, public policy, public service, criminal justice, law, restorative justice, education, public administration, higher education, nonprofit administration, or social services.

Mayer, J. (2016). *Dark money: The hidden history of the billionaires behind the rise of the radical right.* New York: Doubleday.

Zinn, H. (1995). *A people's history of the United States.* New York, USA: Harper Collins Publishers.

Washington Center for Equitable Growth is a research and grant writing organization that seeks to understand the structural issues impacting US economic inequality and growth. http://equitablegrowth.org/about/

REFERENCES

Kivel, P. (2000). Social service, or social change. Retrieved from www.PaulKivel.com

Kivel, P. (2012). *You call this a democracy? Who benefits, who pays and who really decides?* New York: Apex Press.

GLOSSARY

Accountability Obligation to finish on one's values and commitments.

Ameliorative intervention Purposeful interventions designed to alleviate results of living in unjust and prejudicial societies.

Anthropocene The current time period in which human activity has caused global changes in the physical environment and altered climate.

Axiology The relationship of researcher to participants.

Brownfield An urban site that has been previously used for commercial and industrial use and may need to be decontaminated before it can be redeveloped.

Capitalism An economic system in which the means of production are privately owned and operated for profit.

Categorization The process of grouping objects and people into categories to better understand and identify them.

Cisgender An individual whose biological sex assigned at birth aligns with their gender identity.

Collectivism A belief of the importance of groups and communities that shapes attitudes and behavior of citizens.

Community hub A resource that caters to the specific needs within a community.

Community psychology A sub-discipline of psychology that seeks to understand, work with, and actively engage with individuals from oppressed communities as they work, struggle, and resist oppression.

Community school Taking a community hub approach within the school system. Using a school as a source for not only students but also families.

Conscientization Developed by Brazilian educational theorist Paulo Freire, it focuses on the development of a critical consciousness, or one's ability to become open to the social and political contradictions we encounter, gaining a deeper understanding of the social processes behind these dilemmas, and acting against these elements.

Constructivism A method of study based on the paradigm that all knowledge is socially constructed.

Critical consciousness Becoming aware of psychological and sociopolitical factors that oppress people.

Critical dialogue A process of talking and reflecting to resolve community issues.

Critical praxis A process of becoming aware of one's and others' oppression.

Defensive othering A type of identity work strategy done by those seeking membership in a dominant group or by those seeking to deflect the stigma they experience as members of a subordinate group.

Ecology The study of the relationship between the environment and living things.

Educational segregation The separation of minority students and white students within the education system.

Empowerment Freedom, control, and choice to influence, also obtaining, producing, or enabling power, which can happen at many levels.

Environmental justice The principle that all people deserve equal access to decision making about environmental laws and fair treatment and equal protection under those laws.

Epistemology Study of the nature of how to know the real nature of reality.

Feminism The belief that all genders deserve political, social, and economic equality.

Feminist Someone who believes that individuals of all genders should be considered and treated equally.

Gerrymandering The manipulation of town lines to benefit a certain group of people of a political party.

Greenfield Land that has not previously been developed.

Green infrastructure Preserved and/or designed and engineered natural systems that use trees, vegetation, soils, and other natural elements to provide habitat, flood protection, or runoff treatment, or perform other ecosystem functions.

Heat island effect The phenomenon that built-up areas like urban communities are usually hotter than the surrounding rural communities by several degrees.

Heteronormative A society, culture, or system in which it is expected that individuals are sexually and romantically attracted to people of the opposite gender.

Individualism The belief of the importance and supremacy of individuals over groups or collectives.

Intersectionality The interconnected social identities, such as race and gender, that affect an individual and can lead to compounding areas of marginalization.

Interview A set of questions that usually lead to open-ended responses.

Liberation Freedom from oppressive and controlling situation and/or people, actively engage in seeking equal rights including social, political, and economic opportunities for a community.

Looking-glass self Notion that the self reflects the responses of others. More specifically, the self develops through a three-step process: (1) imagining one's appearance in the eyes of others; (2) imagining their judgment of that appearance; (3) internalizing their perspectives and developing a corresponding self-image and self-feeling.

Megacity A large city with a population of over 10 million people.

Meritocracy The notion that your success is an exclusive result of your hard work.

Nonbinary Describes any gender identity that is neither male nor female. Other terms meant to convey this same meaning are *agender*, *genderqueer*, and *neutrois*.

Nonheteronormative Referring to identities other than straight or heterosexual.

Ontology Study of the form and nature of reality or truth.

Othering The process whereby a dominant group defines into existence an inferior group. This process entails the invention of identity categories and ideas about what marks people as belonging to these various groups.

Patriarchy A sociopolitical and cultural system that perpetuates oppressive and limiting gender roles, sexism, transphobia, cissexism, and the gender binary.

Positionality The idea that dimensions of our identity (e.g., gender, race, class) are markers of relational positions within a social context rather than essential qualities of one's self.

Positivism A method of study based on the paradigm that objective truth can be sought by testing hypotheses using the experimental approach.

Post-positivism A method of study based on the paradigm that objective truth can only be approximated given that theories and values impact our study of knowledge.

Poverty The state of being in which individuals and families are living below a level of subsistence and cannot provide for many of their basic needs without help.

Privilege Advantages given or available to persons because of their membership in a group that has power within society.

Praxis The process of becoming aware of psychological and sociopolitical factors that oppress people.

Queer A reclaimed word used to describe identities and supporting movements that do not align with heteronormativity; that is, marginalized gender identities and expressions as well as marginalized sexual identities. *Queer* is also used as a subversive term to describe that which does not fit in with the norm, beyond simply describing gender and sexuality.

Redlining   The discriminatory obstruction of mortgage loans because of a current address.

Reflexivity   The process of allowing one's self to reflect on one's own actions, thoughts, and experiences. It further refers to the ability of an individual to make sense of their social position in the social order and become critical of the factors—both external and internal—that inform that position.

Socialization   The process through which we learn to become members and groups within society.

Social justice   A world where all people and communities have equal and equitable power to address their concerns.

Survey   A set of questions with clearly defined responses.

Transformative intervention   Intentional processes designed to alter the social conditions that lead to suffering and social injustice.

Transgender   An individual whose biological sex assigned at birth does not align with their gender identity; they may identify as another gender, or they may not identify with any gender. *Transgender* is an adjective, not a noun.

Vulnerable population   A group of people who may be economically disadvantaged, belong to racial and ethnic minorities, be very young or old, be homeless, or be ill.

Wealth   The abundance valuable resources or material possessions. The word *wealth* is derived from the old English *weal*, which is from an Indo-Europe word *stem*. An individual, community, region, or country that possesses an abundance of such possessions or resources is known as wealthy.

White flight   The migration of white citizens from one town to another after a certain percentage of minorities move in.

Wildflower micro schools   Small, Montessori-style schools that have alternative teaching styles, such as peer education.

APPENDIX
SUGGESTIONS AND THOUGHTS FROM FORMER STUDENTS

I used to be one of the many people that victim-blamed the less fortunate. One of the many that chose to remain comfortable in my own shoes, neglecting to accept any other reality from my assumptions. Service learning changed me though, and finally made me realize that I was part of the reason why the gap between the haves and the have-nots persists. It is really a life-changing experience, so I hope you can join me, and together let's make a change that is long overdue.

—Jee Ah Lee, Community Psychology, 2016

The attitude you have toward service is critical. Look to the mission and previous work done by the organization and let it inspire you. Most importantly, keep an open mind and don't forget that change starts locally, and it starts with people just like yourself.

—Christina Caso, Alternative Spring Break, 2014

Helping the people from the countryside in Suchitoto was an amazing experience because I was able to understand how they felt about the past civil war of the 1980s and help in the rebuilding of "La Concha Acustica."

—Yanitza Medina, Alternative Spring Break, 2008

I took a service-learning course at perhaps one of the most vulnerable times in my life—as a college freshman. It was during this course that I realized while we are all equal as human beings, our experiences—some our choice, but most are not—place us on the continuum of privilege of today's America. Unless we observe and respect these differences, we will get nowhere; at such a tumultuous time in the American political climate. This idea stuck with me throughout my service learning and I confidently state that service learning heavily influenced my career path today.

—Megan Caron, Freshmen Seminar, 2008

Service learning broadened my outlook and changed how I judge others. While working with my community, strangers stopped me at night on the street to say, "I want to be your friend." Others still asked for food only to throw it away later. While disconcerting at the time, I now understand each have a story. Working with the homeless taught me there is resiliency in the vulnerable even [if] I do not see it immediately.

—Thanh Huynh, Community Psychology, 2012

In 2016, I met homeless individuals who grew up in a hard-living environment, and some were mentally ill. Not everyone is going to be friendly or considerate; one must instinctively react in an appropriate manner on the spot. This can be one of the most challenging aspects of service learning while interacting with new people; however, a new social skill can be acquired from a unique situation. You can also learn from an individual who is willing to share their story. A stranger simply needs someone to listen, but make sure your safety is top priority.

—Pandora Baily-Gould, Community Psychology, 2016

I dreaded the community service work that I knew was ahead. Despite my skepticism, I started the semester with an open mind, and I am pleased to say that I ended the semester with an open heart. Not all people share the same goals and have the same needs. You cannot help someone by providing them with what you assume they lack. The key is to understand what it is that the person needs and work from there to help. I look back at my service-learning course as a time where I learned to be more accepting and present. I am a better person because of it.

—May Mishal, Community Psychology, 2013

As someone who has worked with a variety of marginalized communities in the past five years since my time in college, I can say that the reward in helping others lies partly in your own ability to embrace the discomfort and push yourself to fully understand the experience of others. I think the biggest lesson you will learn is that we are all more alike than we expect. I currently have a Masters in Social Work and have dedicated the beginning of my career to helping communities facing environmental justice issues. I can say with affirmation that the service-learning courses I took during college led me directly to this career.

—Ana Vargas, Community Psychology, 2012

First and foremost, service learning is about learning to be a caring individual. Seeking a deeper understanding of the role we play in society. Not many courses will offer you the chance to help, care for others, and consider the experiences of individuals that we help. I have always been a helper type as that was how I was raised, but this experience gave me a platform to assist and help make changes within my community and others. Through this process, I learned about the needs of other communities and saw similarities and differences that helped me broaden my understanding of the struggles so many other people face daily.

In college, we focus so much on bettering ourselves through grades and study that we forget that there is a world in need outside of our bubble. Through service learning, I changed my world perspective and learned to think about the communities that I was and am a part of and how I can be of help in any capacity possible. I realized that it wasn't just about helping others, it was about helping myself, about finding my place in that community and gaining a direct understanding that textbooks rarely offer. The stories that I heard and the experiences that I had were unparalleled to anything else I did in college. What I gained was the realization that I cannot control people to seek help when they need it, but rather I can offer help and be available to help when others need it whether on a personal or community level.

Coming into a service-learning course is something that requires a genuine self and ability to explore the deeper side of your humane self. This type of course can draw you in a way that is like no other course can do. You will have a genuine opportunity to see your course work effect real-life situations and real challenges in our world. This can also become an opportunity to be creative with how you can serve and help others. This is your opportunity to make an impact on the world we live in.

—Johnny Nguyen, Community Psychology, 2002

Many of my learning experiences have been while participating in service learning. To truly feel my sense of self, all aspects need to be interconnected, and the absence of any one burdens the feeling of self-fulfillment and balance. As an adult, I am continuously working on this lifestyle, as there is always room for improvement. I haven't always approached life in this way. In college, the goal was to achieve academic success, which hindered both my mental and physical health. One of the experiences that contributed to my holistic approach to life was the concept of service learning. Essentially, the goal was not solely to achieve academic success, but the ability to find ways to apply that to the community. To me, that was the spiritual aspect—the ability to bridge my mental self to something even bigger—applying myself and my skills to real-world issues, allowing me to get closer to understanding my civic duty.

—Justen Procter, Community Psychology, 2010

INDEX

Page numbers in bold represent glossary terms.